Kant and Mysticism

Contemporary Studies in Idealism

Series Editor:

Paolo Diego Bubbio, Western Sydney University

Editorial Board:

Mark V. Alznauer (Northwestern University), Francesco Berto (University of St. Andrews), Alfredo Ferrarin (University of Pisa), Elena Ficara (University of Paderborn and City University of New York), George di Giovanni (McGill University), Douglas Hedley (Cambridge University), Stephen Houlgate (University of Warwick), Wayne Hudson (Charles Sturt University), Luca Illetterati (University of Padua), David Kolb (Bates College), Simon Lumsden (UNSW), Douglas A. Moggach (University of Ottawa), Lydia Moland (Colby College), Maurizio Pagano (University of Eastern Piedmont), Paul Redding (University of Sydney), Julian Young (Wake Forest University)

The Contemporary Studies in Idealism series features cutting-edge scholarship in the field of classical German Idealism and its legacy. "Idealism" is considered both in a historical and in a theoretical sense. The series features projects that center upon Kant and the post-Kantian Idealists (including, but not limited to, early German romantic thinkers Fichte, Schelling, and Hegel) or upon other related forms of nineteenth-century philosophy—including those often considered to oppose Idealism, such as those of Kierkegaard and Nietzsche. The scholarship also seeks to critically assess the legacy of Idealism in the twentieth and twenty-first centuries. The series uses the resources of classical German Idealism to engage in contemporary debates in all subfields of philosophy.

Titles in the Series:

Kant and Mysticism: Critique as the Experience of Baring All in Reason's Light, by Stephen R. Palmquist

Kant and Mysticism

Critique as the Experience of Baring All in Reason's Light

Stephen R. Palmquist

LEXINGTON BOOKS
Lanham • Boulder • New York • London

Published by Lexington Books
An imprint of The Rowman & Littlefield Publishing Group, Inc.
4501 Forbes Boulevard, Suite 200, Lanham, Maryland 20706
www.rowman.com

6 Tinworth Street, London SE11 5AL

Copyright © 2019 by The Rowman & Littlefield Publishing Group, Inc.

All rights reserved. No part of this book may be reproduced in any form or by any electronic or mechanical means, including information storage and retrieval systems, without written permission from the publisher, except by a reviewer who may quote passages in a review.

British Library Cataloguing in Publication Information Available

Library of Congress Cataloging-in-Publication Data

Names: Palmquist, Stephen, author.
Title: Kant and mysticism : critique as the experience of baring all in reason's light / Stephen R. Palmquist.
Description: Lanham : Lexington Books, 2019. | Series: Contemporary studies in idealism | Includes bibliographical references and index.
Identifiers: LCCN 2019019945 (print) | ISBN 9781793604644 (cloth : alk. paper) | ISBN 9781793604668 (pbk : alk. paper)
Subjects: LCSH: Kant, Immanuel, 1724-1804. | Mysticism. | Critical theory. | Swedenborg, Emanuel, 1688-1772.
Classification: LCC B2799.M9 P35 2019 (print) | LCC B2799.M9 (ebook) | DDC 193--dc23
LC record available at https://lccn.loc.gov/2019019945
LC ebook record available at https://lccn.loc.gov/2019980114

To Natalya

Whose healing touch transmits the Light within

Table of Contents

List of Figures	ix
Preface	xi
Introduction: The Problem of Mystical Experience in Kant	1
I: Swedenborg's Influence on Kant's Critical Awakening	**9**
1 The Copernican Hypothesis as the Key to Kant's Awakening from Dogmatic Slumber	11
2 The Impact of Swedenborg's Mysticism on Kant's Metaphysical *Dreams*	17
3 Kant's Awakening: The Copernican Hypothesis as the Key to Critical Mysticism	31
4 Kant's Metaphysical Dream: A System of Critical Philosophy	43
II: Kant's Critical Philosophy as a Critique of Mysticism	**47**
5 Does Mystical Experience Always Prompt Delirium?	49
6 Kant's Critique of Delirious Mysticism	53
7 Immediate Experience of the Moral	63
8 Key Metaphors Guiding Kant's Critical Mysticism	77
III: The *Opus Postumum* as an Experiment in Critical Mysticism	**87**
9 Can the Original (Threefold) Synthesis Be Consciously *Experienced*?	89
10 The Categorical Imperative as the Voice of God	101
11 Matter's Living Force as Immediate Experience of the World	113

12 The Highest Purpose of Philosophy as Exhibiting the God–Man	121
Conclusion: Kantian Mysticism for the Twenty-First Century	135
Works Cited	149
Index	159
About the Author	167

List of Figures

Fig. 8.1	Four Basic Metaphors of Critical Mysticism.	83
Fig. 9.1	Kant's Distinction between Four Types of Being.	92
Fig. 9.2	The Original Synthesis of Ideas in Immediate Experience.	94
Fig. 12.1	The Unity of Transcendental Philosophy in *OP*.	122

Preface

Baring All in Reason's Light is the title I had originally planned for the book whose subtitle was to be *A Comprehensive Commentary on Kant's Religion within the Bounds of Bare Reason*. Shortly after the publisher of that book (Wiley, 2016) insisted on using the proposed subtitle as the full title, I met the General Editor of the present book series, Diego Bubbio, at a conference we were both attending in Macau. During our wide-ranging conversation, he asked whether I had any short books in the works, and I shared with him an idea I had been considering for some time: to extract passages from my book, *Kant's Critical Religion* (*KCR*), that related to mysticism, then revise and update them in the form of a self-standing monograph. My arguments defending what I call Kant's "Critical mysticism," I explained, might be more fully understood and appreciated—or more easily criticized—if they were not sandwiched between chapters that sketched Kant's theory of religion more broadly, as in *KCR*. Diego liked the idea, and the rest is now history.

What is now the subtitle of the present book is based on a metaphor that Kant introduces in his 1793/1794 book, *Die Religion innerhalb der Grenzen der bloßen Vernunft*. In "Does Kant Reduce Religion to Morality?," *Kant-Studien* 83:2 (1992), 129–48, which was revised and republished in 2000 as Chapter VI of *KCR*, I argued that the theory of religion that Kant defends in *Die Religion* revolves around the assumption that morality is the "bare body" of genuine religion, while the multifaceted historical traditions (i.e., the myths, rituals, and symbols) that are typically identified with religion actually serve to *clothe* this bare body; the latter provide forms that seek to accommodate the matter of religion (i.e., our moral nature) to the weaknesses we experience due to human embodiment. Kant repeatedly uses the term "*bloßen*" (which, like the English word "bare," can mean either "mere" or "naked") to refer to reason's attempt to strip away all non-essential forms of historical religion in order to bring their moral core into the light. Contrary to the common reading of Kant, as a philosopher whose focus on reason led him to *ignore* the role of experience (and so also, to interpret religion without giving proper attention to people's actual *religious experience*), I have argued that Kantian religion is first and foremost grounded on the most fundamental of all religious experiences, the experience of laying bare any and all pretentions of our preferred historical vehicle for religious faith to the unifying light of reason. Moreover, this experience, I argue in what follows, is the core feature of Kantian Critique.

The decision to include in this book's subtitle the phrase originally intended as the title of the *Commentary* is quite fortuitous, inasmuch as my claim that Kant presents us with the ingredients for a Critical mysticism relates first and foremost to the entire Critical philosophy, and only secondarily to his theory of religion. The present book therefore makes only occasional references to Kant's *Religion*; readers interested in a more detailed explanation of how Critical mysticism manifests itself in Kant's theory of religion should consult my *Commentary*. At the core of my argument here is the first *Critique*'s distinction between Kant's special concept of "experience," as intuited content that is *mediated* through a process of conscious conceptualization, and the notion of intuited content in its original or "immediate" (pre-conceptual) form. I discussed this distinction in detail in "Knowledge and Experience—An Examination of the Four Reflective 'Perspectives' in Kant's Critical Philosophy," *Kant-Studien* 78.2 (1987), 170–200, which later became the basis for Chapter IV of *Kant's System of Perspectives* (1993). In drafting the new Introduction and Conclusion for the present book, and so also throughout its main content, I adopted the convention of referring to the former, mediate experience simply as "experience" (just as Kant normally does) and the latter, pre-conceptual (or under-conceptualized) form of (immediate) experience as *encounter*. To guard against potential ambiguity, let me clarify here that I intend "encounter" in this sense to be a synonym of what I also sometimes call "immediate experience," while "experience" (when used without qualifications indicating otherwise) refers to *mediate* experience—i.e., to Kantian *Erfahrung*. My view, in other words, is that "immediate experience" is to "[mediate] experience" as "encounter" is to "experience." The former term in each pair refers to the elusive root of the latter, which refers in turn to the processed (mediate) form of knowledge-producing experience.

The ideas expressed in the twelve main chapters of this book, being the product of three decades of reflection, have been influenced and shaped by input from countless sources. Indeed, the number is so great that even to begin an attempt to identify them all would be futile. Instead, let me here acknowledge, with gratitude, the sources where earlier versions of various parts of this book have been previously published. Parts I and II have their earliest roots as a pair of journal articles: "Kant's Critique of Mysticism: (1) The Critical *Dreams*," *Philosophy & Theology* 3.4 (Summer 1989), 355–83; and "Kant's Critique of Mysticism: (2) The Critical Mysticism," *Philosophy & Theology* 4.1 (Fall 1989), 67–94. These were published with literally hundreds of errors introduced by the editors, largely as a result of their use of a (then new, but now—fortunately—outdated) computer program that automatically inserted all footnotes into the main text. The hopelessly muddled text that resulted was published in a rush, without first giving me (or, apparently, anyone else!) a chance to correct the proofs. Thoroughly revised versions of both papers subsequently appeared as Chapters II and X of *KCR*. The former also appeared in a newly revised form as "Kant's Criticism of Swedenborg: Parapsychology and the Origin of the Copernican Hypothesis," in Fiona Steinkamp (ed.), *Parapsychology, Philosophy and the Mind: Essays Honoring John Beloff* (Jefferson, NC: McFarland, 2002), 146–78. Portions of Part III originally appeared in an earlier version as *KCR*, Chapter XII. While readers of the aforementioned works would find many passages similar to passages in the twelve main chapters of the present book, they would not be able to find the arguments all brought together in one place, nor clarified and refined to the extent presented here, nor would they find that these former versions of this text are easily accessible, as *KCR* went out of print in 2007. Because Ashgate Publishing Company returned the copyright of *KCR* to me, following a decision to remove the book from their active book list, there is no danger of copyright violation in the case of any passages where portions of text may retain a form that is similar or even occasionally (for a sentence or two) identical to that in *KCR*.

I include references to my sources in the text wherever possible, directing the reader to the full details as listed in the Works Cited. I use abbreviations for all citations to works of Kant or to previous publications of my own. Sections A and B of the Works Cited explain these two types of abbreviations, respectively. References to these works use the abbreviation and (for Kant texts) the Academy Edition volume number, followed by the page (or sometimes section) number(s). Quotes from Kant's works use the Cambridge Edition translation, except for Kant's *Religion* (for which I use the translation presented in my *Commentary*); when I modify the Cambridge Edition, the abbreviation "alt." (for "altered") follows the page reference and I usually provide Kant's German in brackets at the point where a minor change occurs. References to works by other authors cite the author's surname plus the year of publication, followed (where relevant) by the page number(s). For all references, the first occurrence in every paragraph provides the full citation (as explained above), while subsequent consecutive citations of the same work in the same paragraph include only the page number(s), except that the volume number (followed by a period) is also included for any work (by Kant or others) that is published in more than one volume.

The research for this project was supported, in part, by several Faculty Research Grants provided by Hong Kong Baptist University and by a sabbatical leave in the Spring semester of 2016, for both of which I remain deeply grateful. Thanks, also, for the often helpful feedback from the many participants in academic events at which I have presented portions of this book's argument during the three-year period when I was waiting for it to appear in print. These include: presenting invited seminars for the English Department at the Chinese University of Hong Kong (April 2016) and for the Philosophy Departments at the University of Macau (December 2016) and the Chinese University of Hong Kong (September 2017); responding to an Author Meets Critics session organized by Helmut Wautischer and the Karl Jaspers Society of North America and held at the American Philosophical Association's Pacific Division Meeting (April 2017), in Seattle, Washington, at which four critics (Chris L. Firestone, Colin McQuillan, Ayon Maharaj, and Eric Nelson) offered extensive feedback; and presenting a paper for a panel sponsored by the Hong Kong Kant Society, held at the Eastern Division Meeting of the American Philosophical Association, in New York (January 2019). While the publication delays enabled me to respond to some of the feedback by making minor revisions in the text, much more work would be needed to respond in full to some of the excellent criticisms and suggestions given.

My sincere thanks to Jonathan Johnson and Simon Wong, for assisting in the onerous task of revising the Kant quotations in the (many) cases where *KCR* did not follow the Cambridge Edition translations (most of which did not yet exist when I first drafted this material), and to Brandon Love for proofreading the entire text of this book at the stage of the initial page proofs. Brandon not only suggested hundreds of minor changes and corrections that enhanced the overall clarity and consistency of the exposition, but he also drafted the Index. Lynn Liu assisted by inputting the edits to the final text, when I revised it one last time after signing a new contract with Lexington Books in early 2019. Most of all, thanks to Diego Bubbio for encouraging me to move forward with this project in 2015 and for diligently seeking a new publisher when the untimely passing of James Keith Davies in February of 2017 eventually led to the demise of Noesis Press, which had initially contracted to publish the book under the title *Baring All in Reason's Light: An Exposition and Defense of Kant's Critical Mysticism*. Thanks, finally, to Jana Hodges-Kluck at Lexington Books for catching the vision of this project and prompting me to come up with the present title.

Stephen R. Palmquist
Hong Kong
December 31, 2016; revised February 14, 2019

Introduction

The Problem of Mystical Experience in Kant

Imagine *being there* at the very instant, roughly 13.8 billion years ago (according to current scientific estimates), when light first emerged from the tiniest yet heaviest of all physical particles, exploding the particle into a lightning-fast expansion that initiated the space–time continuum that we call "the universe." Now imagine being present in and with every changing particle of that ever-expanding material as it shaped the galaxies, our solar system, the earth, and everything we cherish about life in a physical world. Then follow this expansion until it eventually leads, perhaps billions of years from now, to what many scientists believe will be the death of our universe as it collapses back into a singular particle of infinitely heavy matter. Of course, none of us is capable of actually observing this whole process of the creation, emergence, and destruction of spatio-temporal reality: trapped *within* the process itself, each of us can observe only its *parts*, as viewed from the specific perspectives we can adopt, given the standpoint where we find ourselves. Nevertheless, the mere thought of this ultimate wholeness has prompted mystics throughout human history to make extravagant claims, clothed in the language of whatever presuppositions were relevant to the person's culture, regarding the existence and nature of a spiritual reality that supposedly lies behind the physical universe.

In order to *experience* this absolute whole that we are obviously capable of thinking, we would need to have what Immanuel Kant famously called an "intellectual intuition" of "the thing in itself."[1] This type of intuition, he argued, would be possible only for God, who is presumably not bound by the space–time continuum;[2] we human beings can *conceive* of such an absolute whole, but we can have no concrete knowledge (i.e., no intellectual intuition) of it. Still, our ability to perform the foregoing thought–experiment has profound implications for the nature and limits of human reason, whose task is to lay bare the pretensions of human understanding by leading it to *encounter* the wholeness that it can never possess as an item of knowledge. For only when the mind's eye glimpses this idea of the wholeness of the universe does the corresponding wholeness of our own subjective being (what is traditionally called "the soul") come into view. (This is the core message of Kant's "Refutation of Idealism," which he added to the second edition of his monumental work, *Critique of Pure Reason*, in 1787.) Learning how to cope with the human experience of these three ubiquitous "ideas of reason"—the universe consisting of all space–time reality, the soul that thinks of itself as free from that universe, and the God who can presumably stand outside of the whole and perhaps even bring it into being—without allowing ourselves to be led astray by the false hopes they might generate is the central purpose of Kant's Critical philosophy.

In my 1993 book, *Kant's System of Perspectives* (*KSP*), I argued that an all-important "principle of perspective" operates at every level of Kant's Critical System, and that the apparent self-contradictions that interpreters often believe they have uncovered in Kant's texts can usually be resolved by taking into account the difference between the perspective Kant is adopting at different points in his text. Armed with the overarching assumption that, according to Kant, truth is (for us humans) inextricably bound up with one of several *perspectives* (i.e., with a question or set of fixed boundary conditions that defines how one must approach the subject matter under consideration), I offered a comprehensive reconstruction of the system advanced by the arguments in each of his three *Critiques*: each book adopts a discrete *standpoint* (of theoretical, practical, or judicial reasoning, respectively), and within each standpoint Kant's argument proceeds by considering the subject matter in terms of four distinct *perspectives* (the transcendental, logical, empirical, and hypothetical). While Kant's rather loose terminology tends to cloud the distinctions between these standpoints and perspectives, I demonstrated that he employs a set of terms as "perspectival equivalents" (i.e., words whose meaning is essentially synonymous with our contemporary use of "perspective"), and when these are recognized as highlighting technical terms, the systematic relationships between the various components of his System become more evident. I offer a longer summary of the contents of *KSP* in Chapter III of *Kant's Critical Religion* (*KCR*), which is Volume Two of a planned four volume series.[3]

One of the subordinate themes running through *KCR* was that Kant's whole philosophy can be understood as an attempt to revolutionize not only the branch of theoretical philosophy commonly known as *metaphysics* but also the branch of religious/spiritual practice commonly known as *mysticism*. Starting with a demonstration that Kant's serious consideration of Emanuel

Swedenborg's mystical thought was the primary impetus that led to Kant's Copernican Revolution (Chapter II), I argued that, although Kant's mature writings contain almost exclusively negative statements about mystical experience, they also imply a revolutionary *critique* of mysticism aimed at establishing a new way of understanding and practicing an authentically mystical way of life (Chapter X). I concluded *KCR* by offering a reading of Kant's *Opus Postumum (OP)*, whereby it aims to crown his philosophical System with a full-fledged explanation of what I call "Critical mysticism"[4] —a term Kant himself never uses. More recently I have demonstrated, in my *Comprehensive Commentary on Kant's Religion (CCKR)* that Kant's 1793 book, *Religion within the Bounds of Bare Reason (RBBR)*, has far more to say about the nature and purpose of religious experience than most readers have recognized. Although *CCKR* does not focus on Critical mysticism as such, I do argue therein that the four "General Comments" that come at the end of each of *RBBR*'s four "pieces" are where Kant most fully develops his Critical mysticism as an alternative to delusory forms of religious experience.

One of the key terms Kant employs in his discussion of religious/mystical experience, *Schwärmerei*,[5] calls for special attention here at the outset. Most Kant translations, and so also most of the secondary literature, has used "fanaticism" as this term's English equivalent—a practice I also followed in *KSP* and *KCR*. A major exception is that the Cambridge Edition of Kant's works typically renders it as "enthusiasm." In preparing a thoroughgoing revision of Werner Pluhar's translation of *RBBR*, while I was writing *CCKR*, I came to the realization that both of these options have serious flaws; the German term refers to a mental state that can be either highly excited or extremely depressed, not to any kind of "ism" and not merely to expressions of enthusiasm. While fans do sometimes exhibit such a mental state, "fanaticism" has various connotations that are not appropriate to *Schwärmerei*. I, therefore, adopted the new convention of translating *Schwärmerei* as "delirium," for reasons explained more fully in the Glossary to *CCKR* (520–21). I adopt this convention throughout the current work, inserting a form of "delirium" in place of whatever word appears in the translations I quote.

As I employ the term, "Critical mysticism" refers to a way of understanding the nature and possibility of our immediate experience of the world that acknowledges its "spiritual" aspect and yet remains consistent with the epistemological and moral restrictions placed on human life by Kant's Critical philosophy. Kant himself, I maintain, made this application, especially in *RBBR*, a profound though cryptic work that has the distinction of being the first book he wrote after finishing all three *Critiques*. He simply never explained this position explicitly or with a self-confessed acknowledgment that the metaphor that was central to his early book (1766), *Dreams of a Spirit-Seer, Elucidated by Dreams of Metaphysics (DSS)*, continued to lie at the center of his concerns for the rest of his life. In *DSS* Kant confessed that his own early metaphysics bore striking similarities to certain views defended by Emanuel Swedenborg in a work that offered accounts and interpretations of his own mystical experiences,[6] then presented a harsh criticism of the legitimacy of such a position—criticism that applied equally to the metaphysical theory and to the mystical experiences—and ended with a balanced call for a critique of reason's powers as the only way to correct the problems that he had unearthed. We shall examine the details of this early work in Part I.

Part II will then present an overview of the core features of Kant's mature Critical mysticism, portraying it as a vision of wholeness (or what Kant dubs "totality") that arises out of our immediate experience of the world and thereby gives rise to our moral calling[7] as human beings, as well as to our ability as human beings to appreciate beauty and natural purposiveness. In order for this vision to arise, we must choose to remain silent about the particular things we know (or might know) about the world and instead look at the world *overall* (*überhaupt*; typically translated, "in general"). Mystics often refer to their special mode of experience as requiring a person to transcend or lay aside the subject–object distinction out of which our ordinary knowledge of the world arises. Kant, undoubtedly aware of this common claim through his reading of Swedenborg, insists that it is never *actually* possible to suspend this distinction entirely *and* to come away with any concrete knowledge about what we have encountered. Nevertheless, he does not deny altogether the possibility of encountering the elusive thing in itself; rather, he insists only that, encountered or not, the thing in itself remains unknowable.[8]

That Kant was aware of the need to account for the mystic's experience of the world overall is suggested by the fact that, when referring to the thing in itself *as encountered* by the human subject (i.e., as no longer "in itself"), he employed the distinct term "transcendental object."[9] Depending on whether Kant uses *Objekt* or *Gegenstand*, this term refers either (a) to the bare fact (i.e., the presupposition) that an otherwise unknown something, which Kant calls the transcendental *Objekt*, must *impact* the *subject* of experience in order for us to have any knowledge of the external world, or (b) to the fact that, once we have obtained empirical knowledge, we must read an unknown something back into the contents of our knowledge in order to unify them through a transcendental *Gegenstand*. In either case, thinking about the implications of this (mystical, yet philosophically interesting) object-overall constitutes what Kant calls "transcendental reflection"—i.e., thinking about the conditions that are necessary in order for knowledge to arise in the subject and attempting to determine which human faculty (or capacity, *Vermögen*) is active in different situations. That this core feature of Kant's Critical philosophy shares the same name with a major post-Kantian approach to mystical experience (i.e., "transcendental meditation") is no accident; similarly, the American Transcendentalists were well aware of Kant's philosophy and thought of it as a suitable foundation for their mystical practice.[10]

Kant is rarely thought of as contributing any positive view of mysticism, primarily for two reasons: first, after completing *DSS* in 1766, his scholarly attention was preoccupied with the mammoth task of applying the insights arising out of his transcendental reflection to the task of solving the problems of metaphysics; and second, when he did refer in passing to mysticism, as mentioned above, he tended to pigeonhole the term as referring solely to the *mistaken*, "delirious" form of mystical experience that he believed Swedenborg exemplified (cf. Fischer 2017, §1). In what follows, we shall see that the true situation is considerably more complex than Kant himself presented it. In short, just as Kant's critique of reason's powers enabled him to demonstrate the shortcomings of both dogmatism and skepticism in favor of an approach to metaphysics that synthesizes both traditional approaches, so also it enabled him to demonstrate the shortcomings of two forms of delirium: that of the spiritually oriented person who joyously succumbs to the delusion of claiming *secret knowledge* based on alleged mystical experiences of God or of a hidden spiritual realm; and that of the anti-religious skeptic who depressingly rules out any form of mysticism from the start. Once we recognize that Kant's epistemology provides a framework on the basis of which we can understand how mystical experience actually operates and that his insistence on a *moral* solution to metaphysical problems provides the basis for a way of distinguishing false (delirious) approaches to mystical experience from genuine (Critically aware) ones, we can appreciate in a more balanced way the relevance of Kant's philosophy to all forms of mystical experience.

As already noted above, in order to conceive how knowledge can arise at all, we must assume that we (as "subjects" of knowledge) somehow *interact* with something that is not us (some "object"). All we know at this stage is that "something overall" functions as an unknown "x" that provides the material of what the human mind forms into concrete objects of cognition. Mystics attempt to *experience* this immediate clash of subject and object and even, for those most adept at the spiritual arts, to get *beyond* the subject–object distinction altogether in order to encounter the ultimate Oneness of all things. What Kant's mature epistemology teaches us is that *all* human experience comes in the form of either *sensible intuition* (as shaped by space and time) or *intelligible conception* (as shaped by a special set of twelve categories, the most notable of which is the law of the necessary connection between *cause and effect*). Empirical cognition arises whenever these two are synthesized in a way that enables them to cooperate. But when intuitions arise that have no corresponding concept, or when we form concepts that cannot be instantiated through any given intuition, strange things happen. Discerning the implications of these strange encounters is the topic of Kant's third *Critique*, whose title (as I argue in *CCKR*) could be translated as *Critique of Discernment*. The twelve chapters that constitute the three main parts of the present book are greatly revised and updated versions of three key chapters that were spread throughout *KCR* (Chapters II, X, and XII). By updating them and bringing them together here in one place, I hope to clarify and strengthen the argument that I first put forward there, that Kant's philosophy has clear and not altogether negative implications for issues relating to mysticism and religious experience.

In the years since *KCR* appeared, I have taught a course entitled "Mysticism and Religious Experience" on several occasions, each time using Kant's philosophy as a framework for discussing the nature and proper understanding of mysticism. This has given me the opportunity to think through and expand upon the extent to which the mystical themes discussed in *KCR* appear in the three *Critiques*. A newly composed Conclusion to the present work provides a systematic overview of the mystical elements embedded in the three *Critiques*, culminating in *RBBR* and *OP*. My contention there (as throughout this book) is twofold: first, nothing in Kant's philosophy militates against the possibility or the value of having mystical experiences, for his philosophy actually guarantees their *possibility* and provides a framework that enables us to understand what is taking place when such experiences occur; and second, his philosophy positively *encourages* such experiences, *if* the person having them interprets them as motivations for deepening one's awareness of conscience.

I interpret Kant's references to "conscience" as referring not to a person's individual opinions regarding what is right and wrong; rather, he refers to these opinions as *moral judgments* and openly admits that we human beings can (and often do) err when formulating such opinions. By contrast, Kant sees conscience, which he infamously claims cannot err (*RBBR* 6.186–87), as a spiritual instinct that constitutes (or is constituted by) all rational beings as a unified whole. As Kant puts it in *CPR*, "if we could intuit the things and ourselves *as they are* we would see ourselves in a world of spiritual natures" (A780/B808)—a world he calls the *corpus mysticum*.[11] In other words, to deepen one's awareness of conscience means to immerse oneself in the idea of a community (i.e., a community of all human beings, and ultimately of all rational beings) wherein everyone works together for the common good. Claims to religious (or any other kind of mystical) experience are, one and all, a sham if they do not produce an ever-deepening awareness of one's individual participation in the community of conscience. This participation prevents the (authentic) mystic from using the freedom that accompanies the experience of transcending the subject–object distinction as an excuse for immoral behavior. Thus, as we shall see throughout this study, especially in the Conclusion, Kant's *moral metaphysics* constitutes the core of his Critical mysticism.[12]

NOTES

1. The literature on the meaning of Kant's famous *Ding an sich* is far too massive to review here. Some, such as Henry Allison, view it as nothing more than a placeholder that plays no substantive ontological role, but merely functions as a necessary presupposition in Kant's epistemology. Others see it as standing for a literally distinct second world, so that every act of knowledge involves a "double affection," whereby we are affected by empirical objects, yet simultaneously affected by a corresponding "thing in itself" (see note 9.5, below). For an overview of the problems associated with Kant's term and a moderate, "perspectival" solution along the lines presented here, see *KSP*, Chapter VI.

2. One of Kant's claims that is most often questioned, by friends and foes alike, is that things in themselves do not exist in space and time. The standard objection is that if we have no knowledge of things in themselves, then how does Kant know that they are *not* spatio–temporal? The thought experiment presented in the main text suggests a suitable response: if, indeed, we could observe, from beginning to end, the "thing" that is the whole space–time continuum, then (just as cosmogonists now assure us) space and time would arise and fall *within* that thing; the thing would not be itself *in* space and time.

3. Volumes Three and Four will deal with science and anthropology (broadly construed, to include political history), respectively.

4. A drawback of the argument for Critical mysticism as presented in *KCR* is that it served as a subordinate part of a broader exposition whose task was to offer an overarching interpretation of Kantian theology and religion. The main body of the present book reworks and updates much of that same material for presentation in a more straightforward way that focuses on this one crucial issue.

5. See *KCR*, Appendix VII.1, for a discussion of the special connotations of Kant's term, *Schwärmerei*. As Manolesco (1969, 19) opines, and as we shall see in Part I of the current study, the model for Kant's lifelong attack on *Schwärmerei* was Swedenborg. But when reading Kant's occasional (often openly negative) comments on mysticism, we must keep in mind the two-edged (Critical) nature of his position. In *PFM* 4.382–83, for example, where Kant ends the book with a reminder that Critical philosophy banishes "mysticism" from theology, replacing it with science, Kant is not refuting the possibility of mystical *experience* as such, but only what he earlier calls "mystical idealism" (375n)—i.e., a theoretical system (such as Swedenborg's) *based on* supposedly objective interpretations of such (necessarily subjective) experiences.

6. Swedenborg's Latin work, *Arcana Coelestia* (*Secrets of Heaven*), was published in eight large volumes from 1746 to 1756.

7. Kant's term is *Bestimmung* (literally, "betuning"), often translated as either "determining" or "vocation," depending on the context. In *CCKR* I use "predetermination" in place of "vocation" whenever Kant's point is that our vocation as human beings is determined (in the sense of being *preset*) by our moral nature.

8. Kant repeatedly assumes, but never presents a detailed argument for, his claim that the thing in itself is unknowable. I demonstrate that this is a basic belief or tenet of faith for Kant in SP–84, revised and republished as Chapter V of *KCR*.

9. As I plan to argue in a forthcoming work co-authored by Brandon Love and Guy Lown, the understanding of Kant's elusive "transcendental object" is greatly hampered by the fact that Kant's two distinct terms, *Objekt* (or *Object*) and *Gegenstand*, are both translated as "object."

10. The American Transcendentalists, most notably Emerson and Thoreau, practiced a form of meditation based on nature. Kant's influence on their thought was mostly indirect, via Samuel Taylor Coleridge, who at one point in the late 1790s was so deeply committed to Kantian philosophy that he considered translating *CPR* into English. Josephson 2015 offers an interesting, though rather morbid, sketch of Kant's influence on these (see especially 207) and other literary figures. Nowadays, the term "transcendental meditation" typically refers to the quite distinct practice introduced to the West by Maharishi Mahesh Yogi and popularized in the 1960s.

11. A809/B837. This phrase is a shortened form of the theological term, *corpus Christi mysticum*, which refers to the church as the mystical body of Christ (see Peters 1993, 35–37).

12. See Lawrence 2001 for a recent study that similarly defends the view that Kant's Critical philosophy constitutes a "moral mysticism" (311, 314). The present book shares Lawrence's stated aim (328): "to disclose the spirit of such mysticism as the hidden heart of Kant's entire philosophy."

I

Swedenborg's Influence on Kant's Critical Awakening

Also, human reason has not been sufficiently inspired [literally given wings] regarding this [i.e., the future destiny of honest people] that it should part such high clouds that obscure from our eyes the secrets of the other world. —*DSS* 2.373, alt.

Chapter One

The Copernican Hypothesis as the Key to Kant's Awakening from Dogmatic Slumber

Kant's life is traditionally portrayed as falling into two distinct periods. The years prior to 1770 form the "pre-Critical" period, while those from 1770 onwards form the "Critical" period. The turning point is placed in the year 1770 because this is when Kant wrote the Inaugural Dissertation (*ID*) for his newly gained position as professor of logic and metaphysics at the University of Königsberg. In this work, entitled *On the Form and Principles of the Sensible and Intelligible World*, he proposed for the first time that space and time should be regarded neither as absolute, self-subsisting containers for physical objects (à la Newton) nor as mere relations between objects that are themselves essentially non-spatiotemporal (à la Leibniz), but as "forms of intuition" that human subjects read *into* experience. This became the basis for what is typically known as the "Copernican revolution" in philosophy, alluding to a metaphor that Kant himself introduced in the second edition Preface to *CPR* (see Bxvi–xviii). While in *ID* Kant had identified a set of forms that the mind imposes onto *objects of sense* in the process of intuiting them, he had not yet made a similar application of his insight to the *objects of thought*. During the 1770s (the so-called "silent decade," when Kant was working so diligently on his first *Critique* that he published almost nothing), Kant eventually came up with his monumental theory of the twelve categories whose architectonic form (as four sets of threefold distinctions) shapes everything we think. Where did Kant come up with this odd, "Copernican" notion that the mind necessarily imposes forms onto everything we experience?

The typical textbook account of Kant's life usually declares that the "pre-Critical" Kant was a Leibnizian rationalist, trained in the dogmatism of the philosophical school that followed Christian Wolff, and was interested as much in speculations relating to natural science as in philosophy, but that sometime around 1770 Kant was suddenly awakened from his "dogmatic slumber" by his reflection on David Hume's philosophy. Indeed, Kant seems to state this explicitly in *PFM* 4.260: "I freely admit that the remembrance of *David Hume* was the very thing that many years ago first interrupted my dogmatic slumber and gave a completely different direction to my researches in the field of speculative philosophy." In a footnote to his revision of Paul Carus' translation of this passage, Lewis White Beck (1950, 8n) suggests that "Kant had probably read Hume before 1760, but only much later (1772?) did he begin to follow 'a new direction' under Hume's influence."[1] Nevertheless, some commentators, such as Manfred Kuehn, go so far as to say not only that "Kant and Hume aim at the very same thing" (Kuehn 1983, 191), but that "all the specific doctrines of Kant's critical enterprise are intimately bound up with Hume's influence on Kant." Although it is difficult to determine the exact nature and date of this dramatic awakening, Kant was familiar with Hume's ideas by the early 1760s; indeed, Kuehn thinks that Kant's 1766 book, *Dreams of a Spirit-Seer* (*DSS*), adopts the skepticism of Hume's empiricist standpoint almost completely. Friedrich Paulsen, by contrast, argues that Kant "did not receive the impetus to his work [i.e., *DSS*] from the English writers, and especially from Hume's epistemological investigations" (Paulsen 1902, 87–88). Rather, Hume's influence came mainly in the early 1770s, "as furnishing an incentive to turn towards his original [i.e., Kant's own unique] position" (93–94), and to a lesser extent, just prior to the writing of *ID* in 1770 (97–99). This supports the view I shall defend in Chapter 3, whereby Hume's "awakening" of Kant refers primarily to the change from *ID* to *CPR*.[2]

DSS is typically interpreted as a minor work of an exceedingly skeptical nature and of relatively little importance in understanding Kant's mature thought. This "strangest and most tortured of Kant's writings" (Ward 1972, 34) is viewed, at best, as a stage he passed out of as quickly as he passed into it, and at worst, as an embarrassment for Kant and Kant scholars alike. The embarrassment could come not only as a result of the rather unorthodox subject matter (visions and other mystical experiences), but (also) because of the flippant attitude Kant adopts from time to time throughout the book (see Chapter 2, below, especially note 2.5). Indeed, regardless of how we interpret the philosophical content of *DSS*, the psychological disposition of its author, who had recently entered his fifth decade, would appear to be that of a man in the midst of what we might nowadays call a midlife crisis. This conjecture is supported not only by Kant's age (early 40s), but also by his cynical dissatisfaction with the status quo. John Manolesco treats "Kant's sudden hatred for speculative metaphysics" as "a deep psychological change due to unrequited love, not by metaphysics but by Swedenborg himself" for not replying to the queries in a lengthy letter Kant had written to him.[3]

This traditional account contains at least as much error as truth. While it is true that Kant never mentions his mature theory of the transcendental ideality of space and time before 1770, it is not true that he owes that theory to Hume (whose theory of space and time bears little resemblance to Kant's). Nor is it legitimate to equate this doctrine (expounded in its official form in *CPR*'s Transcendental Aesthetic) with the term "Critical," as is implied by the dating of the Critical period from 1770. On the contrary, Kant associates his "altered method of our way of thinking, namely that we can cognize of things *a priori* only what we ourselves have put into them" (Bxviii), not with the *Critical method*, but with the new "Copernican" insight, which he believes has enabled him to revolutionize philosophy. His description and use of criticism as a philosophical method is quite distinct from its application to problems in metaphysics by means of the Copernican hypothesis. Thus, when Kant instructed the editor of his minor writings to ignore all those written before 1770 (see Sewall 1900, x), he was not defining the starting point of his application of the Critical method, but rather that of his application of the *Copernican hypothesis* to the task of constructing a new philosophical System. If we must divide his life into two periods at 1770, we should therefore avoid using the term "pre-Critical" (as others have also advised)[4] and refer instead to the "pre-Copernican" and "Copernican" periods. Adopting these new labels will protect us from making inconsistent statements such as that of Gulick (1994, 99), who conflates these two forms of revolution: "Kant's self-designated Copernican revolution ushered in his critical period." Since Kant exhibited Critical tendencies *throughout* his philosophical works (see *KCR* §I.2), his mature years should be named the "Copernican" period.

Before we proceed it is crucial to have a thorough understanding of Kant's mature conception of "Criticism" or "Critique" (*Kritik*), as elaborated in *CPR*. In the first edition Preface, Kant describes his era as "the age of *criticism*" (Axin), during which reason accords "unfeigned respect . . . only to that which has been able to withstand its free and public examination." But this enlightened "way of thinking" can itself be trusted only if it submits to its own "court of justice"—i.e., to Criticism (Axi–xii). Thus "the matter of our critical investigation" (i.e., of the entire Critical philosophy) is reason itself (Axiv), and its first task is "to display the sources and conditions" of the possibility of such Criticism (Axxi). This means the questions addressed to reason cannot be answered by means of

> dogmatically delirious [*schwärmende*] lust for knowledge . . . [that] could not be satisfied except through magical powers in which I am not an expert. Yet

this was also not the intent of our reason's natural vocation; and the duty of philosophy was to abolish the semblance arising from misinterpretation, even if many prized and beloved delusions have to be destroyed in the process.[5]

Instead of depending on the hocus-pocus of dogmatic answers dreamed up in one's philosophical armchair, we can answer reason's questions and thus find solutions to the problems of metaphysics only by first examining "the nature of cognition itself" (Axiv).

In *CPR*'s second edition Preface Kant not only describes more fully the subject matter of the particular type of critique he plans to engage in, but also explains more clearly the nature of the Critical method. Metaphysics will be "purified through criticism but thereby also brought into a changeless state": the purification is "of *negative* utility, teaching us never to venture with speculative reason beyond the boundaries of experience"; but the establishment is *positive* inasmuch as it "removes an obstacle that limits or even threatens to wipe out the practical use of reason" (Bxxiv–xxv). In other words, the scope of reason's speculative (i.e., theoretical) standpoint is narrowed by tying it to sensibility, but this frees metaphysics to be established on the firmer foundation of reason's practical standpoint—i.e., on *morality* (Bxxv). The Critical method, therefore, is intended to establish limits, but to do so for both negative and positive purposes. The former can be seen when Kant refers to "our critical distinction" between "the two ways of representing (sensible and intellectual)" and immediately adds "along with the limitation . . .";[6] likewise, he argues that noncontradictory doctrines of freedom and morality "would not have occurred if criticism had not . . . limited everything that we can *cognize* theoretically to mere appearances" (Bxxix). The positive benefit of such a limitation is that it enables us to avoid "dogmatism" (defined here as "the prejudice that without criticism reason can make progress in metaphysics"), which "is the true source of all [skeptical] unbelief conflicting with morality" (Bxxx). Indeed, Kant goes so far as to say that "criticism puts an end for all future time to objections against morality and religion" (Bxxxi), because his critique will "sever the very root of *materialism, fatalism, atheism*, of free-thinking *unbelief*, of *delirium*, and *superstition* . . . and finally also of *idealism* and *skepticism*" (Bxxxiv, alt.).

Throughout the rest of *CPR* Kant repeats many of these same claims about the nature of criticism in its special, philosophical form. In most of their occurrences the words "critical," "criticism," and "critique" are used in close connection with some mention of the *limitations* of human cognition.[7] An interesting exception is that on several occasions he adds that criticism serves as *a middle way* between the opposite extremes of dogmatism and skepticism (B22–23, A388–89, A756–57/B784–85, A761/B789, A769/B797). Indeed, this epitomizes Kant's association of the Critical method with *synthesis*, which he claims always takes the triadic form of "(1) a condition,

(2) something conditioned, (3) the concept that arises from the unification of the conditioned with its condition" (*CJ* 5.197n). Of course, the most basic example of his use of this threefold pattern is his exposition of the Critical philosophy in the form of three *Critiques*.

This brief overview of Kant's understanding of Criticism reveals that he never associates it directly with the Copernican hypothesis; instead, it relates to several key distinctions. Criticism is, for Kant, the method of striking a middle way between two extremes ("a third step," as he calls it in A761/B789; see also A138/B177, A155/B194, A157/B196, A217/B264, A259–60/B315, A732–33/B760–61, A766/B794). It operates by locating the boundary between what can be cognized (and *proved*) and what can never be cognized (yet remains *possible*)—this boundary line being defined in terms of "the boundaries of all possible experience" (e.g., A89/B121). Thus it is closely associated with the "difference between the transcendental and the empirical" (A57/B81), as well as with that between speculative (theoretical) and practical (moral) "employments of reason," or *standpoints*.[8] Although certain apparently skeptical claims have to be made along the way, the ultimate purpose of Criticism for Kant is positive: to provide a means of constructing the foundation for metaphysics upon solid (nonspeculative, moral) grounds.

Traces of this Critical way of doing philosophy are evident throughout most of Kant's writings, from the earliest essays on metaphysics and natural philosophy to the latest essays on religion, political history, and other subjects.[9] Indeed, the fact that he uses *this method* to develop and expound the implications of his Copernican hypothesis gives lasting value to the theories that arise out of it. There is no need to provide here a thoroughgoing proof of the ubiquity of the Critical method in Kant's writings (but see *KSP* §I.2 and *passim*). Instead, I shall concentrate on *DSS* for the remainder of Part I because, relative to its importance, it tends to be the most neglected and/or misunderstood book in Kant's corpus. The next chapter sketches the contents of *DSS*, after which I shall draw attention in Chapter 3 to its Critical character and discuss its role in Kant's discovery of the Copernican hypothesis. Finally, I shall offer some brief suggestions in Chapter 4 as to the relation between *DSS* and Kant's mature System of Perspectives. This will prepare the way for a proper understanding of Kant's views on mystical experience itself. In Parts II and III I shall therefore consider in more detail the possibility of viewing Kant's entire Critical System as an exposition and defense of the "Critical mysticism" that was first envisaged in *DSS* and (nearly) brought to full fruition in Kant's last, uncompleted work, *Opus Postumum* (*OP*).

NOTES

1. Beck defends his position in Beck 1969, 465–67; see also Wolff 1960. In *ID* and as late as 1772, in a letter to Marcus Herz (*C* 10.129–35), Kant shows no awareness that Hume's skepticism challenges his early conception of causality as an intellectual principle. The supposed reason is that Kant was familiar only with the relatively modest skepticism of Hume's *Enquiry* (1748) until he read James Beattie's *Essay on the Nature and Immutability of Truth* (1772), which contains translations of long passages from the more radically skeptical text of Hume's *Treatise* (1738). Beck later defends this explanation against opponents' conjectures that Kant's friend, J.G. Hamann, who translated part of the *Treatise* in 1771, may have shown his translation to Kant as early as 1768 (Beck 1988, 407–8).

2. Both Paulsen's and Beck's accounts, however, attend only to Kant's recognition of the *need* for a more adequate defense of the philosophical principle of causality. They say nothing positive about the source of one of the most fundamental aspects of Kant's mature philosophical System, his "Copernican" hypothesis. Moreover, as we shall see in Chapter 3, they also fail to account for the unique character of *DSS* and other inadequacies of the traditional view.

3. Manolesco 1969, 14–15; see also Butts 1984, 71–73, and Thorpe 2010, 7–9. Kant himself explicitly states (*DSS* 2.367) that he has "fallen in love" with metaphysics. However, he was likely also suffering from unrequited love of a more literal type, as he was involved in at least two failed love affairs at around this time (Klinke 1952, 39–41; Wallace 1901, 44–45; see especially Gulyga 1987, 54–55).

4. See e.g., Beiser 1992, 36; Dell'Oro 1994, 174. However, neither of these authors recommends a viable alternative to "pre-Critical."

5. Axiii, alt. Kant's word choice in this passage suggests that he was still mindful of his earlier work in *DSS*, which, as will become apparent here in Part I, adopts the same point of view toward delirium and delusion that is expressed here. In fact, Kant uses terms referring to this slumber/dreaming/awakening metaphor at least 16 times in *CPR* (cf. SP–1987a, 34,109,347), most of which echo quite clearly the attitudes adopted in *DSS*. The most significant references are A475/B503, A491–3/B519–21 (2), A757/B785, and A764/ B792 (but see also B1, A112, A201–2/B247, B278, A316/B372, A376–77 (2), A407/B434, A451/B479, A624/B652, and A780/ B808). As we shall see, however, such texts must not be taken as evidence that Kant was completely against all mysticism. Rather, they restate the same problem posed in *DSS*: how one's "beloved delusions" *can* be preserved, if not by dogma and/or magic. We shall examine Kant's *solution* most fully in Parts II and III.

6. Bxxviii. These two modes of representation are similar, though not identical, to the distinction I make between "immediate experience" and "reflective knowledge" in *KSP* §IV.1 (see also §III.2).

7. See e.g., A295–96/B352, A395. SP–87a, 86, lists 168 occurrences of these three words in *CPR*.

8. Indeed, as I argued throughout *KSP*, the making of such perspectival distinctions is the key task of the Critical philosopher (see especially *KSP* §II.1).

9. In the earlier works, of course, the traces are evident retrospectively even though Kant himself would not yet have been conscious of the significance of the naturally Critical tendencies of his way of thinking. In fact, *becoming conscious* of what was *already there* seems to be one of the implications of his much-used metaphor of slumber/dreaming/awakening (see note 1.5). Otherwise a metaphor such as "coming alive" or "giving birth," which (as we shall see) he does use in other contexts, would have been more appropriate.

Chapter Two

The Impact of Swedenborg's Mysticism on Kant's Metaphysical *Dreams*

In *Dreams of a Spirit-Seer* Kant examines the nature and possibility of mystical visions, paying special attention to the claims of the Swedish writer and accomplished scientist-turned-mystic, Emanuel Swedenborg.[1] He examines Swedenborg's visions with two aims in view. His first goal is personal: as his private correspondence testifies, the still-youthful Kant has a strong desire to explore the implications of his lifelong belief in the spirit–world.[2] Kant's interest in the spirit–world is often neglected, if not outright denied, by Kant scholars. Yet, throughout his life he repeatedly affirmed a belief in its reality. Even in *CPR* "spirit" and its cognates appear 18 times in the English text (cf. SP-87a, 353); in the German original, "*Geist*," appears at least 11 times. At one point, Kant affirms his commitment to a surprisingly Platonic view of the eternity of the human spirit (A779–80/B807–8; see also *CJ* 5:468):

> you could propose a transcendental hypothesis: that all life is really only intelligible, not subject to temporal alterations at all, and has neither begun at birth nor will be ended through death; that this life is nothing but a mere appearance, i.e., a sensible representation of the purely spiritual life, and the entire world of the senses is a mere image, which hovers before our present kind of cognition and, like a dream, has no objective reality in itself; that if we could intuit the things and ourselves *as they are* we would see ourselves in a world of spiritual natures with which our only true community had not begun with birth [and] would not cease with bodily death (as mere appearances), etc.

The mystical character of this "transcendental hypothesis" is unmistakable for anyone familiar with a range of mystical writings. Exploring its depth, development, and limitations, once it is subjected to Critique, is the purpose of the present book.

Kant's second (and arguably more important) goal in writing *DSS* was to draw attention to the dangers of speculative metaphysics by comparing it with a form of mysticism whose proponent (Swedenborg, in this case) he calls a *Schwärmer*—a term usually translated as "fanatic" but which I translate as "delirious person" (see Introduction, especially note 5). This analogy, present as it is in the very title of the work, is of utmost importance in understanding how *DSS* relates to the later development of Kant's philosophical System. As noted in the previous chapter, *DSS* is commonly interpreted as evidence of a radically empiricist stage in Kant's development, where he is supposedly adopting something of a Humean position. But his actual intention, as we shall see, is to encourage a *Critical* attitude: while he comes down hard on the misuse of reason by spirit-seers (and metaphysicians) when they regard their respective dreams (and speculations) "as a source of knowledge" (Sewall 1900, 146), he expresses quite clearly his own dream that a properly balanced approach to *both mysticism and metaphysics* will someday emerge.[3] A detailed examination of *DSS* can therefore provide some helpful clues as to Kant's deeper motivations for constructing the Critical philosophy itself.

The mystical experiences considered in *DSS* are not experiences of the presence of God—i.e., "the Infinite Spirit, who is its Creator and Sustainer" (*DSS* 2.321n)—but experiences of lower spiritual beings, who are supposed to be able to communicate with earthly beings in visions and apparitions. Although Kant ridicules those who have such experiences at several points in *DSS*, he reveals his private view of such experiences in two important letters. In a letter to Charlotte von Knoblock (dated 10 August, probably 1763) he admits that he has "always submitted these stories to the test of sound reason and [I] have been inclined to regard such tales with skepticism. . . , until I became acquainted with the stories about Herr Swedenborg."[4] After recounting several impressive stories, Kant tells how Swedenborg was once able to describe in precise detail a fire that "had just broken out in Stockholm," even though he was fifty miles away in Göteborg (10.46–47). He says this "incident seems to me to have the greatest weight of any of these stories and really removes any conceivable doubt" about Swedenborg's "extraordinary gifts." In a subsequent letter (8 April 1766) to Mendelssohn, Kant explains that he clothed his thoughts with ridicule in *DSS* in order to avoid being ridiculed by other philosophers for paying attention to mystical visions—hardly taken seriously by most Enlightenment philosophers (see *DSS* 2.353–54). He admits (*C* 10.70):

> my mind is really in a state of conflict on this matter. As regards the spirit reports, I cannot help but be charmed by stories of this kind, and I cannot rid

myself of the suspicion that there is some truth to their validity, regardless of the absurdities in these stories and the fancies and unintelligible notions that infect their rational foundations and undermine their value.

Toward the end of the same letter he draws a Critical conclusion (*C* 10.72), that there may be "boundaries imposed upon us by the limitations of our reason, or rather, the limitations of experience that contains the *data* for our reason." Relating this to the problematic nature of Swedenborg's "powers," he says "they can only be the product of poetic invention. But this invention (an heuristic fiction or hypothesis) can never even be proved to be possible . . . (which has its plausibility only because no impossibility can be derived from the concept either)." He calls "Swedenborg's daydreams" *delusions*, yet admits: "I myself tried to defend them against someone who would argue that they are impossible."[5]

Mendelssohn captures the strangeness of Kant's mood in *DSS* when he writes in a book review (trans. Johnson 2003, 123): "The joking profundity with which the work is written leaves the reader in doubt whether Mr. Kant wants to make metaphysics laughable or spirit-seeing plausible." The answer, as we shall see, is *both* and *neither*: making uncritical approaches to both issues look ridiculous prepares the way for the Critical method to reveal the plausibility of both. For *DSS* adopts an entirely Critical method, and so first poses the problem (though somewhat obscurely) that is to be solved by Kant's mature philosophical System. That Kant is intentionally using Swedenborg's visions as a *test case* for the application of his well-formed Critical method, before launching into its application to all of metaphysics, is indicated in his April 8, 1766, letter to Mendelssohn (*C* 10.71), where, alluding to "some important insights . . . that will establish the proper procedure for metaphysics," he invites *Mendelssohn* to use this new (Critical) method "to draw up the plans for this heretofore haphazardly constructed discipline with a master's hand."[6] Clearly, Kant believed something significant was happening in Swedenborg's mystical experiences—significant enough to merit a comparison with the tasks of metaphysics, "the dream science itself" (*C* 10.70), to which he elsewhere admits to being hopelessly "in love" (see note 1.3, above). The problem this set for him was to describe "[w]hat exactly is this thing which, under the name of *spirit*, people claim to understand so well" (*DSS* 2.319).

In the Preface to *DSS* Kant hints at the Critical nature of his inquiry by asking two opposing questions regarding how the philosopher should respond to eyewitness accounts of stories involving apparitions, then offers a "third way out": he asks (1) "Is he completely to deny the truth of all such apparitions?" or (2) "Is he to admit the probability of even only one of these stories?"; he then concludes that (3) the philosopher should "concern oneself only with what is *useful*."[7] The treatise itself consists of seven chapters, grouped into two parts: Part One contains four "dogmatic" chapters and Part Two contains three "historical" chapters. The correspondence between these two parts and the structure of the System he was soon to begin elaborating is evident by the fact that Part One ends with a chapter on "Theoretical Conclusions" and Part Two ends with a chapter on "Practical Conclusions" (2.349, 369), thus foreshadowing the distinction between the standpoints of the first and second *Critiques*.

The theoretical part begins in Chapter One, under the heading "a tangled metaphysical knot, which can be either untied or cut as one pleases" (*DSS* 2.319), by discussing what a *spirit* is or might be. Kant confesses (320):

> I do not, therefore, know whether spirits exist or not. And, what is more, I do not even know what the word "spirit" means. However, since I have frequently used the word or heard others use it, it follows that something or other must be understood by the term, irrespective of whether this something be a figment of the imagination or something real.

To this he adds the rather Wittgensteinian remark (321n): "It follows that the concept of the spirit–nature cannot be treated as if it were a concept derived by abstraction from experience," though its "hidden sense" can be drawn "out of its obscurity by comparing it with all the different kinds of cases in which the expression is employed and which either agree with or contradict that meaning." He then argues that a spirit must be conceived as a simple, immaterial being, possessing reason as an internal quality (321–22). After considering some of the difficulties associated with this concept, he adopts an entirely Critical position: "We may, accordingly, accept the *possibility* of immaterial beings without any fear that we shall be refuted, though there is no hope either of our ever being able to establish their possibility by means of rational argument" (324, emphasis added).

If one assumes "that the human soul was a spirit" (*DSS* 2.324), even though this cannot be proved, then the problem arises as to how it is connected with the body (324–26). Kant rejects the Cartesian focus on a mechanism in the brain in favor of "ordinary experience":

> But no one is immediately conscious of a particular place in his body; one is only immediately conscious of the space which one occupies relatively to the world around. I would therefore rely on ordinary experience and say, for the time being: Where I feel, it is there that *I am*. I am as immediately in my finger-tip as I am in my head. It is I myself whose heel hurts, and whose heart beats with emotion.[8]

Kant further notes (326n) that

> The current opinion of the soul[,] which assigns it to a place in the brain, would seem to have originated chiefly from the fact that, when one engages in

deep thought, one has the distinct feeling that the nerves of the brain are being strained. But if this conclusion were correct, it would also prove that the soul was situated in other places as well. For example, in anxiety or joy, the sensation seems to have its seat in the heart. Many emotions, indeed the majority of them, manifest their chief force in the diaphragm. Pity moves the intestines, and other instincts express their origin and their sensibility in other organs.[9]

Here we see a good example of Kant's awareness of and concern for the condition of his own body—a common character trait exhibited by those who are adept at meditation. Unfortunately, interpreters tend to excuse this concern as stemming *merely* from his eccentric ideas about how he could maintain his own health through sheer will power and self-determination (see e.g., *MH* and Part III of *CF*). Yet it seems also to reflect the importance he placed on fostering a meditative awareness of his *immediate experience* overall: Critique, for Kant, is ultimately not an abstract function of the mind or brain, but a *disciplined experience* that requires the whole body to participate as well.

The first chapter of *DSS* concludes (2.237): "I must confess that I am very much inclined to assert the existence of immaterial natures in the world, and to place my own soul in the class of these beings." Although he concedes that the various questions concerned with such a belief "far transcend my powers of understanding" (328), he adds (327n): "The principle *of life* is to be found in something in the world which seems to be of an immaterial nature. For all *life* is based upon the inner capacity to determine itself *voluntarily*." Here we see preliminary glimpses not only of the transcendental description of spiritual "life" conveyed in the passage from A779–80/B807–8, quoted above, but also *CPrR*'s reflections on a special form of practical freedom.

After confirming the metaphysical possibility of (and his personal belief in) spirits, Kant presents in Chapter Two "a fragment of occult philosophy, the purpose of which is to reveal our community with the spirit–world" (*DSS* 2.329). He begins by positing an "immaterial world" that is conceived as "a great totality . . . , an immeasurable but unknown hierarchy of beings and active natures, in virtue of which alone the dead stuff of the corporeal world is animated."[10] Considered as a member of both the material and the immaterial world, the human being has a soul and a body that together "constitute a personal unity" (332). Kant conjectures that purely immaterial beings may be "able to exercise an influence on the souls of human beings, for the latter are beings of the same nature as themselves. And it is also likely that they do, at all times, stand in reciprocal communion with human beings," though the results of such intercourse cannot ordinarily "be communicated to other spirit–beings," nor "be communicated to the clear consciousness of human beings" (333). As evidence for such a communion of spirits, Kant examines the nature of morality. Using one of his favorite geometrical metaphors (that of intersecting lines), he says (335): "The focal point[,] at which the lines which indicate the direction of our drives converge, is therefore not merely to be found within us; there are, in addition, other forces which move us and which are to be found in the will of others outside ourselves." The fact that our actions are motivated not only by selfishness, but also by duty and benevolence, reveals that "we are dependent upon the *rule of the general will*" (335); and "this *sensed dependency*"—i.e., our "moral feeling"—suggests that "the world of all thinking beings" is governed by "*moral unity* and invests it with a systematic constitution, drawn up in accordance with purely spiritual laws." Thus, "since the moral character of the deed concerns the inner state of the spirit" (336), its effect can be fully realized not in the empirical world, but only "in the immediate community of spirits."

In reply to the possible objection that, given this view of the spirit-world, "[t]he rarity of [spiritual] phenomena" seems "extraordinary," Kant stresses that "the representations of the one world are not, on account of their different constitution, the accompanying ideas of the representations belonging to the other world"; so even if we have a "clear and intuitive" spiritual conception, this cannot be regarded as "an intuitive empirical concept."[11] However, he freely admits (*DSS* 2.338–39) that a person, being both material and immaterial, can sometimes gain awareness,

> even during this present life, of the influences which emanate from the spirit–world. For these influences can enter the personal consciousness of man, not, it is true, directly, but, nonetheless, in such a fashion that they . . . excite those images which are related to them, and awaken representations which bear an analogy with our senses. They are not, it is true, the spirit–concept itself, but they are symbols of it. . . . It is thus not improbable that spirit–sensations may enter consciousness, if they arouse images in our imagination which are akin to them.

Even "the higher concepts of reason" need to "assume, so to speak, a corporeal cloak in order to present themselves in a clear light," as when "the geometer represents time by a line" (*DSS* 2.339). An actual apparition, which might "indicate a genuine malady, for it presupposes a modification in the balance of the nerves" (340), is unusual because it is based not on a simple analogy, but on "the illusion of the imagination," in which "a true spirit-influence" is perceived through "images . . . which assume the semblance of sensations." Kant warns that in an apparition "delusion and truth are mingled together," so it tends to deceive "even though the original representation *may have been based upon a true spirit-influence*" (340, emphasis added).

In truly Critical fashion Kant now adopts the opposite perspective in Chapter Three, presenting an "anti-cabbala"—that is, "a fragment of ordinary philosophy, the purpose of which is to cancel community with the spirit–world" (*DSS* 2.342). Here Kant first states the analogy between metaphysicians ("*dreamers of reason*") and visionaries ("dreamers of *sense*"): in both cases the dreamer imagines a private world "which no other normal person sees" (342–43), yet "both types of image are, in spite of the fact that they delude the senses by presenting themselves as genuine objects, hatched out by the dreamer himself." In order to help such dreamers "awake completely, that is to say, . . . open their eyes to a view which does not exclude agreement with the understanding of other human beings" (342), he proposes an alternative description of what is happening in an apparition. The problem is to explain *how* visionaries "transpose the illusion of their imagination and locate it outside themselves, and do so in relation to their body, of which also they are aware by means of the outer senses" (343–44). He suggests that in external sensation "our soul, in its representation, transposes the object of sensation, locating it at the point at which the various lines, which are caused by the object and which indicate the direction of the impression, converge," whereas in a vision this "*focus imaginarius*" is located not outside of the body but "in the brain" (344–45). The difference between the fantasy of a sane person (see 346n) and the delusion of an insane person is that only the latter "places mere objects of his own imagination outside himself, taking them to be things which are actually present before him" (346). So "the malady of the fantastical visionary does not really affect the understanding but rather involves the deception of the senses" (347). Kant concludes that by this simpler interpretation "the deep speculations of the previous chapter are rendered wholly superfluous. . . . Nor would it be necessary, if this was how things stood, to range so far afield, and, with the help of metaphysics, to seek out mysteries in the fevered brains of deluded delirious [persons]."[12]

The fourth and final chapter of Part One presents the "theoretical conclusion established on the basis of all the observations contained in the first part" (*DSS* 2.348). Kant begins with a penetrating description of his own method of philosophizing (which he eventually came to call "Criticism" or "Critique"), according to which one always checks "[t]he bias of the scales of understanding" through a procedure whereby "the wares and the weights are made to change pans" (349). He uses this metaphor to make two points. First, it suggests the importance of being willing to give up all prejudices, submitting one's private beliefs instead to the universal force of reason's light (349):

> nothing is important or venerable for me except that which, having followed the path of honesty, occupies its place in a tranquil mind open to any argument. Whenever I encounter something which instructs me, I appropriate it. . . . I formerly used to regard the human understanding in general merely from the point of view of my own understanding. Now I put myself in the position of someone else's reason, which is independent of myself and external to me, and regard my judgements, along with their most secret causes, from the point of view of other people.

This testimony to Kant's special method of discovering philosophical truth prefigures the three-step path to truth-seeking that Kant first elaborates explicitly in *CJ* 5.294: "1. To think for oneself; 2. To think in the position of everyone else; 3. Always to think in accord with oneself." Wood (2008, 17) claims that Kant did not formulate this threefold touchstone for truth until "around 1788"; yet in this part of *DSS* Kant portrays very similar features—putting all one's desires in abeyance, choosing a lifestyle that is imbued with sincerity, and "a tranquil mind" that always seeks to adopt "the point of view of other people"—as among the chief characteristics of what I am calling his Critical mysticism. The exposition in *DSS* thus exemplifies Kant's perspectival (Critical) shift by holding together (in Chapter Four) the merchandise of Kant's own prejudices concerning the spirit-world (Chapter Two) and the dead weight of a reductionist explanation (Chapter Three).

The second point of the analogy is the crucial one: we must recognize "the bias of the scales of understanding" and so move the merchandise from the speculative pan to the pan "which bears the inscription: *Hope of the Future*" (*DSS* 2.349)—a shift that prefigures Kant's later change from the standpoint of the first *Critique* to that of the third (cf. *KSP* 37n, 307)—where "even weak reasons . . . cause speculations, which are in themselves of greater weight, to rise on the other side" (*DSS* 2.349). As he prepares to cross the threshold into the construction of his mature philosophical System, Kant stresses the overriding importance of what I call the "judicial" standpoint (see *KCR*, note I.17): "This is the only defect [of the scales of reason], and it is one which I cannot easily eliminate. Indeed, it is a defect which I cannot even wish to eliminate" (*DSS* 2.349–50).

On this basis, Kant concludes that, even though "when placed in the scale-pan of speculation, such things seem to weigh no more than empty air," the dreams of *both spirit-seers and metaphysicians* "only have a significant weight when placed in the scale-pan of hope" (*DSS* 2.350). While admitting "I am completely ignorant about all these matters" of how the immaterial can interact with the material, he claims: "The theory can be completed, albeit in the *negative* sense of the term, by securely establishing the limits of our understanding" (351). The assumed spiritual principle of life "can never be positively thought, for, in the entire range of our sensations, there are no *data* for such positive thought."[13] Human ignorance therefore "prevents my venturing wholly to deny all truth to the many different ghost-stories which are recounted" (351), yet he "ascribe[s] some credence to all of them taken together." However, as Kant clarifies in a footnote (350n), our speculative ignorance "does nothing to destroy our confidence that the concepts which have sprung from this source are correct." For example, the "inner sentiment" that death is "nothing but a transformation" leads "precisely where reason would lead, if it were more enlightened and more extensive." Kant is saying that our immediate experience, our *encounter* with the totality of what is, can provide existential certainty for a position that cannot be proved theoretically—a certainty that Kant will later call "rational faith" (see *KCR*, note IV.15).

As I have argued in *KSP* §V.1, this subordination of speculative knowledge to practical faith is the key to the justification of the Copernican hypothesis itself. Thus, Kant's concluding comment in Part One, that "the whole matter of spirits" will "from now on be of no concern to me," because "I hope to be able to invest the modest abilities of my understanding in a more profitable fashion in the objects which are left" (*DSS* 2.352), is a hint that he is already beginning to formulate a plan for constructing a System of Perspectives based on the Critical method of reasoning which, as we shall see, is steeped in a meditative openness to an *experience* of reason's humbling influence on one's thinking.

Having promised not to *philosophize* on spirits any longer, Kant now provides, in the first chapter of the second ("historical") part, an account of three stories concerning the spiritual powers of Swedenborg, "the truth of which is recommended to the reader's own free examination" (*DSS* 2.353). He claims to adopt "a completely impartial spirit" regarding "the reader's judgement, whether favourable or unfavourable" (354), admitting that in any case (353–54) "stories of this kind are probably only ever believed secretly, whereas publicly they are dismissed with contempt by the incredulity which is currently in fashion." Of course, what Kant doesn't tell the reader is that, as revealed by the letters excerpted in the previous chapter, he was—if not one of those persons who "believed secretly"—at least one who had been (and possibly still was) privately intrigued by what these very stories seemed to suggest about the reality of a spiritual world.

In the second chapter of Part Two Kant provides a summary of Swedenborg's own explanation of his "ecstatic journey . . . through the spirit-world" (*DSS* 2.357) and notes its similarity to "the adventure on which we have embarked above [i.e., in Part One] in the airship of metaphysics" (360). The position Swedenborg develops "bears such an uncommon likeness to the philosophical figment of my imagination," Kant explains, that he feels the need to "declare . . . that, as far as such seductive comparisons are concerned, I understand no joke [*keinen Spaß verstehe*]" (359, alt.). Apparently to cover up his own secret fascination with Swedenborg's work, Kant ridicules his "hero" for writing an eight-volume work that "is completely empty and contains not a single drop of reason" (360)—a good example of the occasional harsh or frivolous statements that later embarrassed him (see note 2.5). The summary turns out to be so close to the views Kant had expounded in Chapter Two of Part One that he concludes it by reassuring the reader that

> I have not surreptitiously added to the daydreams of our author by including any of my own. I have made a faithful selection, offering it to the reader who is

careful of his comfort and his purse (he may not be *that* ready to satisfy his passing curiosity by sacrificing £7 sterling).[14]

The chapter ends with an apology for tricking the reader: "by following a tiresome detour, I have conducted him in his enquiry and in his thirst for knowledge to precisely the point of ignorance from which he set out in the first place" (*DSS* 2.367); but he adds (368), "I have wasted my time in order to save it. I have deceived my reader in order to benefit him." After confessing his unrequited love of metaphysics, Kant insists that metaphysics as a rational inquiry "into the hidden properties of things" (i.e., what Kant calls *speculative* metaphysics in *CPR*) must be clearly distinguished from a new (i.e., *Critical*) approach to "metaphysics [as] a science of the *limits of human reason*" (368):

> So far we have been wandering, like *Democritus*, in empty space, whither the *butterfly-wings* of metaphysics have raised us, conversing there with spirit-forms. Now, when the *styptic* power of self-knowledge has folded those silken wings, we find ourselves back on the humble ground of experience and common sense, happy if we regard it as the place to which we have been assigned: the place from which we may never depart with impunity, the place which also contains everything which can satisfy us, as long as we devote ourselves to what is useful.

Far from indicating a temporary conversion from dogmatic rationalism to skeptical empiricism, as is often assumed about *DSS*, this passage, interpreted in its proper context, reveals that Kant already has a clear conception of the Critical *method*, and is nurturing the seed that was to grow into his complete philosophical System.

Any doubt about the Critical character of *DSS* is dispelled by the "practical conclusion drawn from the treatise as a whole," given in the final chapter of Part Two (*DSS* 2.368). Kant begins by distinguishing between what science *can* understand in order to achieve *knowledge* and what reason *needs* to understand in order to achieve *wisdom*—a distinction that pervades the entirety of his mature System. By identifying what type of knowledge is impossible to attain, the philosopher can establish "the limits imposed upon [science] by the nature of human reason," so that "even metaphysics becomes . . . the *companion of wisdom*" (369). Kant then introduces (what I call) the principle of perspective (see *KSP*, Chapter II) as the guiding principle of this new way of philosophizing: "if this philosophy should subject its own procedure to judgement, and if it should have knowledge not only of the objects themselves but also of their *relation to the human understanding*" (369, emphasis added), thus establishing the *perspective* from which the object is viewed, then "its frontiers will contract in size and its boundary-stones will be securely fixed. And those boundary-stones will never again permit enquiry to leave the realm which is its home, and cross the boundary to range abroad." This is followed by a warning (370) against the failure to distinguish between philosophical relations (i.e., those based on concepts and known by reflection) and "relations which are fundamental" (i.e., those that "can only be derived from experience")—the distinction that forms the basis for all other Critical distinctions.[15]

That Kant is here referring to immediate experience, not to empirical cognition, is evident when he says (*DSS* 2.370): "I know, of course, that thinking and willing move my body, but I can never reduce this phenomenon, as a simple experience, to another phenomenon by means of analysis; hence, I can recognise the phenomenon but I cannot understand it." He reaffirms that the human power of reflection makes it natural to "think of myself as an incorporeal and permanent being"; yet, because our immediate experience as earthly beings relating to other earthly beings depends on "corporeal laws," we physical beings can never know for certain whether there are also "pneumatic laws" that would enable us to "think independently of the body" (370–71). Concerning the establishment of "new fundamental relations of cause and effect"—i.e., of an immediate experience not of corporeal nature but of spiritual nature—Kant claims "it is impossible ever to have the least concept of their possibility" (371); "inventing these relations in a creative or chimaeric fashion," perhaps through reference to a Swedenborgian type of spiritual causality (cf. what Kant calls *noumenal* causality in the *Critiques*), cannot establish knowledge (much less scientific "proof") precisely because the "alleged experiences" are not governed by corporeal (cf. a priori) laws, which alone are required for a knowledge-claim to be "unanimously accepted by the majority of people" (371–72).

This final chapter ends with a concise (and surprisingly Critical) explanation of the positive aspect of this otherwise negative conclusion. The fact that "philosophical insight in the case under discussion is *impossible*" need cause no concern (neither for the metaphysician nor for the mystic), as long as we recognize that "it is superfluous and *unnecessary*," because reason does not need to know such things (*DSS* 2.372). "Science in its vanity" fools us into believing that "a proof of all this from experience" is required. "But true wisdom is the companion of simplicity, and since, in the case of the latter, the heart commands the understanding, it normally makes the elaborate apparatus of learning superfluous, its purpose needing only the means which lie within the reach of everyone." The true philosophy, which Kant always believed would confirm common sense and therefore would be attainable for everyone (unlike a speculative dependence on theoretical proofs or mystical apparitions, each available to only a few individuals), should be based on "immediate moral prescriptions" (372)—that is, on a "moral faith" (373) that "leads [the "upright soul"] to his true purposes." Thus, *DSS* concludes (373) by defending the position Kant will later elaborate in his practical and religious systems, that it is more appropriate "to base the expectation of a future world on the sentiments of a nobly constituted soul than, conversely, to base its noble conduct on the hope of another world."[16]

NOTES

1. Swedenborg (1688–1772) was not only the founder of crystallography, but also made significant advances in a wide range of scientific, technological, and economic fields. For an account of such accomplishments, see Florschütz 1993, I.1.1, and Laywine 1993, 57–58.

2. The evidence directly relevant to *DSS* will be discussed later in this chapter. For a broader-ranging demonstration of the importance of "spirit" throughout Kant's writings, see Shell 1996. For a study focusing on Kant's use of "spirit" as a specifically *aesthetic* principle (and one that thereby lies at the core of his mature philosophical project), see Völker 2009.

3. The subtle difference between this and the usual interpretation can be illustrated by quoting W.H. Werkmeister's claim that in *DSS* Kant concludes "that metaphysics ought to abandon its dogmatic speculations about God, the life hereafter, and similar topics" (Werkmeister 1980, 64). This is correct, provided we understand, as Werkmeister himself hints elsewhere (cf. note II.6), that abandoning dogmatic speculation does not entail altogether abandoning rational belief in God, etc.—as is assumed by those who regard *DSS* as evidence of a skeptical phase in Kant's development. Kant abandons speculation not in order to swing over to the skepticism of unbelief, but in order to make room for a Critical *reformation* of his beliefs.

4. *C* 10.43–44. On the year this letter is assumed to have been written, see Sewall 1900, 160, Broad 1953, 117–18, and Rabel 1963, 74.

5. For a provocative paraphrase of this passage, see Rabel 1963, 74. Laywine 1993, 60–61, gives a good summary of the first three visions Swedenborg made public, each mentioned in Kant's letters. Kant's tendency in *DSS* to ridicule views toward which he was in fact sympathetic may be what led him to suggest this book be excluded from his collected minor writings (see Sewall 1900, x; Manolesco 1969, 7). Paulsen (1902, 84) admits that the "spiritology" in *DSS* "is not intended [by Kant] to be entirely without seriousness," inasmuch as it foreshadows the important "two worlds" doctrine later propounded in *CPR*. Later he relates this to "Kant's Platonism," already evident in *DSS*, calling it "an ethical and religious view of the world on the basis of objective idealism" (Paulsen 1902, 310). While Paulsen may be mistaken to refer to Kant's idealism as *objective*, he is certainly correct to see in it a fundamentally religious worldview.

6. *C* 10.70. See also Laywine (1993, 72–100) and Werkmeister (1980, 44,84) for similar views of the prefiguring role of *DSS*. Werkmeister (1980, 45) quotes Borowski's biography of Kant as saying "the attentive reader found already here [in *DSS*] the seeds of the Critique of Pure Reason and of that which Kant gave us later." Unfortunately, he gives no details as to just which aspects of *DSS* constitute these "seeds." Manolesco (1969, 13) uses the same metaphor (*DSS* "contains . . . many of the seeds of Kant's Critical Philosophy"), then lists some examples (17–18): Kant's "theory of spirits is almost an exact replica, expressed in philosophical language, of Swedenborg's own thesis. . . . Swedenborgian doctrines . . . provided him with fundamental metaphysical starting points for his later views on the soul, on the dualism of mind and matter, on his conception of noumena and phenomena, on inner sense and its connection with the unity of apperception." I discuss such parallels more fully in Chapter 3. While Michelle Grier is correct to emphasize that in *DSS* Kant does not equate but actually "*distinguishes* Swedenborg's 'dreams' from the 'reason-dreams' of the metaphysician" (2002, 9; see also 10–14), this does not take away from the fact that he also argues for a metaphorical relationship between them. In order to establish the applicability of a metaphor, one must show that the two things being compared have differences as well as similarities. Along these lines, W.P. Kiblinger supports the position I am defending here by arguing that Kant applies his distinction between "brooding and healthy reason" (2015, 200f) to both metaphysicians and mystics throughout his career, beginning in *DSS*.

7. *DSS* 2.317–18. McCarthy 1982 makes the interesting suggestion that Kant's mature philosophy replaces "Christus" (Latin for "anointed") with "Crestus" (Latin for "useful"). If so, Kant's third point can be regarded as a foretaste of what is to come. We must keep in mind, however, that "useful" for Kant means "useful in bringing about goodness"; it is not a sudden leaning toward utilitarianism (cf. *LM* 29.846). McCarthy shows his implicit awareness of the moral aspect of the Kantian "useful" when he says his (like Kant's) concern is with "the role of Jesus the (morally) 'Useful'" (McCarthy 1982, 192). What McCarthy ignores is that the "Crestus" need not exclude the "Cristus"; as we shall see in Part III, both can (and should) work together as complements.

8. *DSS* 2.325; see also *LM* 28.146–47 and Laywine 1993, 52,159. Laywine makes a good case for viewing soul–body interaction as the chief philosophical concern around which most of Kant's pre-Copernican writings revolved. She argues that, prior to *DSS* Kant was (at least implicitly) committed to a theory of "physical influx," whereby the soul has quasi-material characteristics, such as impenetrability, and that in the process of grappling with Swedenborg's vulgar version of the same view, Kant recognized the need to give it up. I summarize and assess Laywine 1993 in *KCR*, Appendix II.2.

9. I argue in SP–16b that the position on the mind–body problem that Kant adopts here is potentially consistent with, but at the same time requires some important restrictions on, the contemporary position known as "eliminative materialism." One of the intriguing features of Kant's perspectival method is that it enables him to embrace (or at least, accommodate) philosophical positions as diverse as materialism and spiritualism.

10. *DSS* 2.330. Concerning this hierarchy of immaterial beings, Kant adds that "their relation to each other through the mediation of matter would only be contingent" (330). Since an "undisputed characteristic mark of life" is "free movement" (including growth), Kant infers that both plants and animals also have an immaterial nature (330). To illustrate the close connection between plants and animals, Kant appeals to Boerhaave's metaphor: "The animal is a plant which has its root in its stomach (inside itself)." He then opines that the converse is also true: "The plant is an animal which has its stomach in its root (outside itself)." But he warns that "these conjectures, which are regarded as dusty and outmoded whims, are also exposed to fashionable mockery"; because "the appeal to immaterial principles is the resort of lazy philosophy . . . , explanation of this sort is to be avoided at all costs" (331).

11. *DSS* 2.337–38. In this context Kant also develops an interesting theory of (literal) dreams. He conjectures that the spiritual conceptions that arise in the deepest, dreamless sleep "may be clearer and more extensive than even the clearest of the representations we have when we are awake. For this is what is to be expected of a being, as active as the soul, when the external senses are in a state of perfect rest. But since the body of the person is not sensed at the time, the accompanying idea of the body is lacking on awakening" (338n). When a person dreams, by contrast, "to a certain degree he has clear sensations, and weaves the actions of his spirit into the impressions of the external senses." Unfortunately, Kant does not acknowledge the importance of this connective function of dreams, so instead of regarding them as revealing profound symbols of spiritual conceptions, as Jung (using Kant as his philosophical springboard) has since suggested (see *KCR*, Appendix II.1), he ridicules them as being "only wild and extravagant chimeras" (*DSS* 2.338n). Carl du Prel develops an elaborate theory of "somnambulism" (including hypnotism) based explicitly on Kant's philosophy (see e.g., Du Prel 1889, 1.xxvi, 5–7, 62, 71, etc.). He agrees with Kant on many specific points (see e.g., 1.57–58). For example, in Du Prel 1889, 1.44, he says: "With the deepening of sleep must diminish the confusion of the dream." In arguing for "the scientific importance of dream," he claims this clarity can be explained best by assuming that in deepest sleep the center of control changes from the brain (the focus of consciousness) to the solar plexus (the focus of the unconscious), and that the more control exercised by the latter, the more significant the dream will be (1.27–44, 68–69). Given Kant's assumption that "what I think as spirit is not remembered by me as human being" (*DSS* 2.338), Du Prel's mapping of Kant's position onto the notion of the unconscious, as adopted by post-Kantian psychology, seems plausible.

12. *DSS* 2.348, alt. The concluding paragraph of Chapter Three, containing these comments, also includes some harsh ridicule of those who adopt the perspective of Chapter Two. Kant suggests, for instance, that although visionaries are not necessarily insane, "I have connected

the two by supposing madness to be a natural effect of such a community. . . . I do not, therefore, blame the reader at all if, instead of regarding the spirit-seers as semi-citizens of the other world [a view Kant himself seems to regard as plausible], he simply dismisses them without ado as candidates for the asylum" (348).

13. *DSS* 2.352. This position has an obvious affinity with the doctrines of the positive and negative noumenon developed in *CPR* (see *KSP* §VI.3).

14. *DSS* 2.367. Calculating the equivalent value in today's currency of £7 in the 1760s is far from straightforward, but it was roughly equivalent to a month's salary for a teacher. Kant's reason for stating the price of Swedenborg's book in British pounds might have been that Swedenborg commissioned John Merchant to make English translations of each (Latin) volume, starting in 1750. However, either the price in Prussia was far greater than in England or else Kant greatly exaggerated what he paid—or perhaps he got cheated—because the title page of the original edition of Merchant's translation of Volume I states the price as "Eight-pence."

15. For a fuller explanation of this fundamental distinction between immediate experience (which, as such, produces no knowledge) and the various reflective forms of experience (which do produce knowledge), see *KSP* §IV.1.

16. Compare this closing statement, for example, with the final sentence of *RBBR* (6.201–2): "So far, however, we have not seen that those who in their opinion are exceptionally favored (the chosen) outdo in the least the natural honorable man, whom one can trust in interactions, in business, and in need; we have seen, rather, that on the whole they probably cannot withstand the comparison with him, [which] proves that the right way to advance is not from pardoning grace to virtue, but rather from virtue to pardoning grace."

Chapter Three

Kant's Awakening

The Copernican Hypothesis as the Key to Critical Mysticism

In the preceding chapter we saw that the main features of Kant's Critical method, together with anticipations of several of his mature doctrines and distinctions, are prefigured in *DSS*. The method of choosing the middle path between two extremes is exemplified by Kant's advice in the Preface to "hold on to the useful"—though this is not how he would later describe his Critical means of steering between the extremes of dogmatism and skepticism (cf. note 2.3, above). His mature distinction between the theoretical and practical standpoints, whose most obvious application is to the distinction between the first two *Critiques*, is foreshadowed by the conclusions to the two parts of *DSS*, the first being theoretical and the second, practical. The attitude expressed in the first chapter, that "spirits" are theoretically possible but can never be proved to exist, is reminiscent of the hypothetical perspective adopted in the Dialectic of *CPR*, where the "ideas of reason" (God, freedom, and immortality) are treated similarly.[1]

Even the second chapter, where Kant lets his metaphysical imagination run wild, contains an interesting parallel: Kant's suggestion that the inner state of spirits is primarily important in its connection with *morality* prefigures his later decision to regard morality as the proper foundation for metaphysics. (He emphasizes the same point in the last chapter of *DSS*, by saying the true basis for belief in spirits rests on morality rather than speculation.) And the skepticism Kant employs in Chapter Three is not unlike the cautious approach he adopts in the Dialectic of *CPR*—in both cases as a temporary measure to guard against unwarranted speculation.[2] The subordination of the theoretical (i.e., speculative) to the practical and the judicial, as hinted by

Kant's expressed preference for the "useful" (see note 2.7), is forcefully emphasized by his reference to the "scales of reason" in the fourth chapter. His use of this analogy to emphasize the philosophical legitimacy of hope for the future in spite of our theoretical ignorance foreshadows both *CJ* and *RBBR*.[3] Throughout Part One of *DSS*, and again in the second chapter of Part Two, Kant describes his new view of the first and foremost task of metaphysics in exactly the same terms as he would use in *CPR*, some fifteen years later: metaphysics must begin as a *negative* science concerned with establishing the limits of knowledge. And in the book's final chapter we meet not only the distinction between immediate experience and reflective knowledge, so crucial to Kant's System (see note 2.15), but also the equally important notion that reason does not *need* to have a theoretical understanding of mystical experiences (or of metaphysical propositions), as long as we take into consideration the common moral awareness of all human beings—what he later dubs *conscience*.

If Kant was in possession of so many aspects of his Critical philosophy by 1766, why did he take fifteen more years to write *CPR*? This is particularly perplexing in light of the fact that after 1781 Kant published at least one major work nearly every year until 1798. The standard account of Kant's development renders this problem slightly less difficult, because the "Critical awakening" is regarded as not happening until the late 1760s or early 1770s. On this view Kant had a great deal of trouble formulating his ideas for *CPR*, yet *after* it was completed he suddenly realized the need for a second *Critique*, and *after* that, the need for a third. However, the fact that Kant could apply so many of his mature Critical tools in 1766 to write *DSS* makes it difficult to believe that he would fumble around for fifteen more years, then suddenly turn into a prolific genius. Rather, it suggests that Kant may have wanted to have the basic (architectonic) plan for his entire System more or less complete *in his mind* before even *starting* the long task of committing it to paper. The need for a fifteen year gap (including his long "silent decade") between *DSS* and *CPR* becomes more understandable if we regard Kant as formulating in his mind during this time not just *CPR*, but his entire System—though obviously, the details concerning the precise form it would take had not entirely crystallized by 1781.[4] The traditional view fails to take account of the fact that writers do not always say everything they know about their plans for future undertakings, and also ignores the importance of Kant's emphasis on establishing and maintaining specific architectonic patterns.[5]

One aspect of Kant's transcendental philosophy that is conspicuously absent in *DSS* is the cornerstone of the whole System, the Copernican hypothesis—i.e., the assumption that a posteriori objectivity is based on a priori subjectivity, rather than vice versa (see *KSP* §III.1). This had begun to dawn on him by 1770, when he wrote *ID*, where he argues for the first time that time and space are "forms of intuition" rather than being properties inherent in empirical objects. Thus the crucial question is: if Criticism was the distinguishing character of Kant's life-long philosophical method, which he developed and refined slowly but surely throughout his career, then what was the source of the sudden insight that he later called his "Copernican" hypothesis? Frederick Copleston (1960, 196) conjectures that the new insight might have come as a result of his reading of the *Clarke-Leibniz Correspondence*, newly published in 1768. Others would cite Hume as responsible for all such major changes in Kant's position (see note 1.1). What has long been ignored in English Kant-scholarship is the significant extent to which some of the details of the Critical philosophy, not the least being the Copernican hypothesis itself, actually correspond to the ideas developed by Swedenborg. Kant himself acknowledges this correlation in *DSS*, but repeatedly emphasizes that the ideas he presents as his own were developed independently of his acquaintance with Swedenborg's writings (*DSS* 2.359, 360, 366). However, the extent of the parallels between his subsequent theories (especially those in *ID*) and Swedenborg's is sufficient to merit the assumption that, in spite of his ridicule in *DSS*, Kant actually adopted much of Swedenborg's "nonsense" (360) into his own thinking![6]

A good example of the resonance between Kant's mature views and Swedenborg's ideas is brought out in Kant's summary of Swedenborg's position, highlighting the distinction between a thing's true or "inner" meaning and its outer manifestation. How closely this coincides with the position Kant eventually defends in his mature writings on religion becomes quite clear in *DSS* 2.364 when he says: "This inner sense is . . . the origin of the new interpretations which [Swedenborg] has wished to make of the Scriptures. For the inner sense, namely, the symbolic reference of all the things recounted in the Scriptures to the spirit–world is . . . the kernel of their value, the rest being but the husk." In *RBBR* Kant uses essentially the same metaphor—often referring to the husk as the "vehicle" or "channel" through which the "seed" or "germ" of religious truth is conveyed to the people—to refer to his own attempt to strip historical religion down to the "bare religion" at its core by exposing it to the light of reason (see e.g., *CCKR*, 46n, 304–7, and Part III); a key difference is that he derives the "inner sense" from practical (i.e., moral) reflection, which, as we shall see, serves as the Critical corrective on Swedenborg's visionary (delirious) "dreaming" about a literal spirit–world.

A more detailed examination of Swedenborg's own epistemological distinctions would reveal numerous other corresponding theories. For example, the Copernican hypothesis itself, which marks the main difference between *DSS* and *ID*, has its roots at least partially in Swedenborg. For, as Hans Vaihinger puts it in his discussion of Lind 1892, the relationship of Kant's "transcendental subject . . . to the Spiritual Ego of Swedenborg is unmistakable" (Vaihinger 1895, 556; trans. Sewall 1900, 25); indeed, Vaihinger surmises that Kant may well have taken his "doctrine of two worlds from Swedenborg direct" (Sewall 1900, 24; see also 12–14). Thus there are good grounds for regarding Swedenborg's "spiritual" perspective as the mystical correlate of Kant's transcendental perspective in Critical metaphysics. Such a perspectival relationship is hinted at by Sewall (1900, 22–23): "Neither of the two great system builders asks the support of the other. . . . As Kant was necessarily critical, this being the office of the pure reason itself, so was Swedenborg dogmatical, this being the office of experience."

Frank Sewall appends to the 1900 translation of *DSS* various extracts from Swedenborg's writings,[7] providing evidence that Swedenborg's ideas often anticipate (from his own mystical perspective), and therefore may have influenced the development of, many of the new ideas Kant advances in his Critical philosophy. The roots of Kant's transcendental idealism can be seen in Swedenborg's spiritual idealism: "spaces and times . . . are in the spiritual world appearances" (Swedenborg 1760, §104); "in heaven objects similar to those which exist in our [empirical] world . . . are appearances" (§106); "appearances are the first things out of which the human mind forms its understanding" (Swedenborg 1763, §40). Claims reminiscent of Kant's view of the intelligible substratum of nature are also evident: "nothing in nature exists but from a spiritual origin" (Swedenborg 1760, §94); "nature serves as a covering for that which is spiritual" (§95); "there exists a spiritual world, which is . . . interior . . . to the natural world, therefore all that belongs to the spiritual world is cause, and all that belongs to the natural world is effect" (§94); "Causes are things prior, and effects are things posterior; and things prior cannot be seen from things posterior, but things posterior can be seen from things prior. This is order" (Swedenborg 1763, §119).

Swedenborg even makes claims that correspond quite closely to Kant's "Analogies of Experience," especially the First Analogy, whose "Principle of Persistence" states in the first edition (A182): "All appearances contain that which persists (*substance*) as the object itself, and that which can change as its mere determination, i.e., a way in which the object exists." Compare this with Swedenborg's claim: "Material things . . . are fixed, because, however the states of men change, they continue permanent" (Swedenborg 1760, §105). Similarly, Kant's Second Analogy, which in the second edition he labels as the "Principle of temporal sequence according to the law of causality," says (B232): "All alterations occur in accordance with the law of the connection of cause and effect." Along the same lines, Swedenborg says: "The reason that nothing in nature exists but from a spiritual origin or principle is, that no effect is produced without a cause" (Swedenborg 1760, §94).

Such parallels extend beyond the theoretical to the practical and judicial standpoints as well. Kant grounds morality in the human will, one's inward "conviction" (*Gesinnung*; see note 5.1, below) being what determines each person's good or evil nature, and goodness being associated with an emphasis on *inwardness*. Swedenborg suggests a similar grounding, "the will being the very nature itself or disposition [*indoles*] of the man" (Swedenborg 1758, §508.7); "heaven is within man" (§319). Like Kant with his contrast between the theoretical and practical standpoints, Swedenborg treats the natural and the spiritual as two standpoints that we as human beings can adopt and argues that each carries with it a different set of limiting conditions that will produce, in turn, a different outcome for the person who adopts them. Indeed, Kant's criticism of mystical visionaries as wrongly taking imagined symbols to be real sensations cannot be charged against Swedenborg, who warns (Swedenborg 1763, §238): "So long as man lives in the world he knows nothing of the opening of these degrees within him, because he is then in the natural degree . . . ; and the spiritual degree, which is interior, communicates with the natural degree, not by continuity but by correspondences and communication by correspondences is not sensibly felt." Indeed, in his *magnum opus* (see Introduction, note 6), Swedenborg 1746–1756 repeatedly warns against the mistake of confusing his visions of the spirit–world with the "fantasies" that most so-called "visionaries" experience, which are "nothing but illusions" conjured up from the "appearances" of outward objects, especially "if the object be in a dark place" (§1967). By contrast, "genuine visions" are "visions or sights of such things in the other life as have real existence, and are nothing but actual things that can be seen by the eyes of the spirit and not by the eyes of the body" (§1970).

By calling attention to these parallels, I do not mean to suggest that Kant merely adopted Swedenborg's positions as he found them; rather, to the extent that his own thinking was influenced by his fascination with Swedenborg's experience and by his reading of Swedenborg's writing, Kant undoubtedly transformed the ideas he found there in certain key respects. Perhaps most importantly, whereas Swedenborg assumed we can have empirical cognition of both natural and spiritual causality, Kant argues in *CPR* that only *phenomenal* causality can play a legitimate role in the formation of empirical cognition; noumenal causality, as the foundation of his theory of freedom, does give rise to practical cognition, but as such it is barred from having a direct influence on our cognition of nature. Still, the fact that before reading Swedenborg he did not write about such matters, whereas afterwards such "Copernican" ideas (i.e., a focus on the mind's role in determining whether the source of causality is natural or spiritual/noumenal) occupied a central place in his writings, makes it very likely that Swedenborg had a significant influence on Kant's formulation of the Copernican hypothesis. I am not claiming that Kant owes his recognition of the importance of the Copernican hypothesis *entirely* to Swedenborg, but only that his influence has been much neglected, and merits further exploration.[8]

If Swedenborg did exercise an important influence on Kant, then why does Kant seem to give Hume all the credit, for instance, in the oft-quoted passage from the Introduction to *PFM*? Perhaps Kant did not feel constrained to acknowledge the influence of a writer who was not recognized as a bona fide philosopher; indeed, he might have even felt *embarrassed* about the influence, since Swedenborg's reputation was hardly respectable among Enlightenment philosophers. Kant's request (mentioned in Chapter 2, above), that his writings prior to 1770 not be included in his collected minor writings, might therefore reflect his desire to protect his reputation from too close an association with the likes of Swedenborg. In any case, Kant's claim that the ideas he expresses in *DSS predate* his reading of Swedenborg surely suggests that Swedenborg probably stimulated him to think through his own previously formulated ideas more carefully, and in the process of being transformed by that re-examination, Kant's ideas ended up looking more like some of Swedenborg's ideas than they ever would have, had he not encountered Swedenborg's work.

Does the *PFM* passage therefore represent a false confession on Kant's part? Certainly not. In order to understand that passage properly, and so to give an accurate answer to the question of the relative influence of Hume and Swedenborg on Kant, it will be necessary to distinguish between four aspects of Kant's development that are often conflated:

1. The general *Critical method* of finding the boundary conditions that define the "middle way" between unthinking acceptance of the status quo (dogmatism) and unbelieving doubt as to the validity of the entire tradition (skepticism).
2. The general *Copernican insight* that the most fundamental aspects of human knowledge (the ones that make it objective) have their source in the human subject as a priori forms, not vice versa. (That is, time, space, etc., are not absolute realities rooted in the object, as philosophers had previously assumed.) This, of course, was the seed that (when fertilized by the Critical method) gave rise to "transcendental philosophy"[9] and through it, to the entire Critical System.
3. The *particular application* of (1) to itself (i.e., reason's self-criticism, through locating the sources of its insights in specific mental capacities), which Kant calls "critique" from 1781 onwards.
4. The *particular application* of (2) to the problem of the necessary connection between a cause and its effect, which provides the occasion for the most influential of Kant's various transcendental arguments.

As stated above in Chapter 1, we can detect (1) operating in varying degrees in almost all of Kant's writings (see note 1.9). Indeed, his lifelong acceptance of (1) is the intellectual background against which alone his great philosophical achievements could have been made (and as such, is the source of his genius). Although his ability to make conscious use of this method certainly developed gradually during his career, receiving its first full-fledged application in *DSS*, neither Swedenborg (the dogmatist) nor Hume (the skeptic) can be given full credit for this. The Critical method is not something Kant *learned* from these (or any other) philosophers, but is rather the natural *Dao* through which Kant read, and in reading, transformed, their ideas.[10] If anyone is to be thanked for (1), it should be his parents, and in particular, his mother.[11]

Kant's recognition of (4) as one of the crucial questions to be answered by his new philosophical System, is, by contrast, clearly traceable to Hume's influence. In fact, his discussion of Hume's impact on his development in *PFM* 4.260 undoubtedly refers primarily (if not solely) to this narrow sense of awakening: Kant is probably telling us nothing more than that his "remembrance" of Hume helped him recognize that causality cannot be treated as a purely intellectual principle (as he had done in *ID*), but must be justified (if at all) in some other way (namely, as a transcendental form of cognition, just as were space and time in *ID*). The fact that Kant uses the term "recollection" indicates a fairly late date (probably 1772; see note 1.1) for this dramatic event. For Kant is suggesting that (4) came to him as a result of *remembering* the skepticism of Hume ("the first spark of light") that had begun influencing his thinking about ten years before. However, if Kant's famous "awakening" is only a dramatized account of his discovery of (4), then such references to Hume do not answer the more fundamental question, the answer to which we have been seeking here: Where did Kant get the idea of using (2) as the basic insight for solving *all* such philosophical problems?

Kant's discovery of (2) came in several fairly well-defined steps, mostly from 1768 to 1772. Prior to 1768 there is little (if any) trace of the theory he eventually came to call the "Copernican hypothesis." Between 1768 and 1772 he applied the insight to intuitions but not to concepts. In 1772 he realized that concepts too must be regarded from this Copernican Perspective. As a result of this somewhat unsettling discovery—unsettling because in early 1772 he believed he was within a *few months* of completing *CPR*—he spent *nine more years* (from 1772 to 1781) working out in his mind the thoroughgoing implications of this insight for his plan to construct a philosophical System. It is plain enough to see how Hume's ideas could have caused the final (and crucial) change in the extent of Kant's *application* of (2) in 1772, because Hume employs some of his most powerful arguments to support his skepticism regarding the a priori basis of the idea of necessary connection. Kant's reflections in 1772 on the full force of these arguments awakened him to an awareness of the incomplete nature of his application of (2) in *ID* and gave him the idea of applying (2) to concepts as well as to intuitions.

But where did the Copernican hypothesis come from in the first place? It could not have come from Hume, inasmuch as nothing like it appears in Hume's doctrines of space and time (or anywhere else in Hume's works). Hume's explanation for our belief in all such "objective facts" is always to reduce them to logic and/or an *empirical* kind of subjectivity (as he does in the final paragraph of his *Inquiry*); he never so much as hints at the possibility of any third way, such as is given by Kant's theory of *transcendental* subjectivity. There are, to my knowledge, only two likely explanations, which probably both worked together to awaken Kant to his Copernican insight sometime between 1766 and 1768. The first is his reading of Swedenborg's writings, especially his massive work, *Arcana Coelestia*, which Kant read in 1765–66, just before writing *DSS* (see *DSS* 2.318 and Sewall 1900, 14n); and the second is his reading of the *Clarke–Leibniz Correspondence*,[12] together with his consequent discovery of the antinomies of reason (see below). If this account of Kant's development during these portentous years is correct, then Kant's description of (4) as an awakening from *dogmatic* slumber is a somewhat over-dramatized account, whose purpose is not to emphasize a sudden break from lifelong dogmatism (cf. note 3.10), but only to explain how Hume saved him from settling for the half-baked *form* of (2) that he had originally distilled from the ideas of Leibniz and Swedenborg— both of whom *he regarded as dogmatists*. Thus, if we look at the overall picture, we see that Hume's influence has, in fact, been overrated; it fulfills only one specific role in Kant's long process of development.

This interpretation of Kant's development gives rise to two further questions regarding Kant's use of his slumber/dreaming/awakening metaphor. For he uses it not only in relation to Hume's influence, but also in many other contexts. In a letter to Christian Garve (21 September 1798), for instance, he confides that his discovery (c.1768) of "the antinomy of pure reason . . . is what first aroused me from my dogmatic slumber and drove me to the critique of reason itself."[13] How can this account of Kant's "awakening" be made compatible with his (better known) references to Hume? Although interpreters have often struggled with this question, the answer seems obvious once we distinguish between the four *aspects* of Kant's development listed above. Kant's comments must refer to *different stages* in the long-term experience of Critical awakening: the awakening by Hume refers to (4), while that for which the antimony is responsible refers to (3). Accordingly, Kant says the antinomy showed him the need for a critique of reason, whereas he says Hume's stimulus "gave a completely different direction" (*PFM* 4.260) to his speculative research, thus implying he had already begun working on that critique. The tendency to regard these as referring to the same experience arises only because Kant uses the same metaphor to describe both stages in his development.

The second question arises once we recognize the obviously close connection between Kant's metaphor of being awoken from sleep and the metaphor of *dreaming* that permeates the entirety of *DSS*, starting with its title. Whether an interpreter thinks Kant's awakening *really* happened only in 1768 (via the antinomies) *or* only in 1772 (via Hume's skepticism)—or, as argued above, at both times—Kant's comments might be construed to imply that *DSS* must itself date from the period of "dogmatic slumber" from which he only *later* awoke. Yet even those who do not fully appreciate the *Critical* elements in *DSS* agree that it is not the work of a sleeping dogmatist! So how could Kant's metaphor apply to anything that happened *after* he wrote this book? Without presuming to give the final answer to this complex question regarding Kant's development, I shall venture to offer a plausible suggestion, based on the four types of awakening outlined above.

Criticism is the experience of forging a middle path between dogmatism and skepticism. It is the tool Kant believed he could use to preserve the *truth* and *value* of the other two, opposing philosophical methods, while doing away with the errors into which each inevitably falls. The Critical mind will therefore always allow itself to be "tempted," as it were, by the two extremes it ultimately seeks to overcome; but in the process of becoming more and more refined, it will appear at one moment to be more dogmatic and at another to be more skeptical—just as we observed Kant's mind to be in the text of *DSS* (see Chapter 2, above). In other words, the Critical method does not *do away* with skepticism and dogmatism, so much as use them as opposing forces to guide its insight further along the circuitous path toward the central point of pure Critique. Now, in order to stay healthy a human being needs both sleep and waking; and in the same way, we could develop Kant's analogy one step further by saying the healthy (Critical) philosopher needs regular doses of both dogmatism and skepticism. Skepticism functions like an alarm clock to remind philosophers when it is time to stop their dogmatic dreaming and return to the normal waking life of criticism. The Critical philosopher will naturally have many experiences of this type, just as a normal person may be surprised to wake up in the middle of a dream, yet will dream again after falling back to sleep. Thus, the confusion caused by Kant's various references to his awakening from dogmatic slumber may be best explained by regarding each as equally legitimate and equally important milestones in his development.

We have seen that Hume's influence was never such as to *convert* Kant to skepticism, but served only as "the first spark of this light" (*PFM* 4.260) to kindle his awareness of the need to reflect on the rationality of his cherished beliefs. This *limited* view of the influence of Hume on Kant comes out quite clearly in almost all Kant's references to Hume or skepticism. In A757/B785, for example, Kant again uses his favorite metaphor to describe the relation between dogmatism, skepticism, and criticism: "[skepticism] is at best only a means for awaking [reason] from its sweetest dogmatic dreams, in order to undertake a more careful [i.e., Critical] examination of its condition." Kant's attempt in *DSS* to examine mysticism and metaphysics with a Critical eye should therefore be regarded as resulting from one of his first major awakenings (perhaps partly as a result of his *initial* reading of Hume, in the early 1760s). Ironically, although he disagreed with the *dogmatic use* to which Swedenborg put his ideas, Kant's reading of *Arcana Coelestia* in the mid-1760s seems to have prompted him to consider valuable *hypotheses* that could be purified in the refining fire of Criticism. The antinomies then awoke him (in 1768) to the realization that reason's Critical method must be applied not only to problematic objects of possible empirical cognition (such as mystical experiences and metaphysical theories concerning the soul), but also *to reason itself* in *all* of its endeavors. And just when he thought he was on the verge of perfecting this self-criticism of reason (in 1772), Hume awoke him once again to the realization that his Copernican insight must be used to limit not only intuition but also the concepts arising out of human understanding. We can conclude, therefore, that although Hume was instrumental in awakening Kant to the *limits* of dogmatism, Swedenborg's mystical speculations were responsible in a more direct way for the initial formation of his Copernican hypothesis.

NOTES

1. This emphasis on the useful in *DSS* may be a holdover from Kant's Wolffian education, for Wolff also stressed the importance of "the useful" (see Copleston 1960, 112, for details). Kant did not abandon this emphasis in his mature writings, but rather transformed it into the hypothetical perspective in his theoretical system and into the practical standpoint of his overall System (see *KSP* §II.3 and §IV.3). He employs the same strategy in the final chapter of *DSS* to address the issue of the possibility of a spiritual influence on the body: such influences are possible but cannot be proved because they are not governed by corporeal laws. This is directly parallel to Kant's mature attitude toward what he calls "noumenal causality," which cannot be regarded as knowable because it does not fall under the a priori principles of the possibility of experience yet must be presupposed in order to explain how morality is possible.

2. Indeed, as we saw in Chapter 2, Kant even uses the analogy of awakening in the skeptical chapter (*DSS* 2.342), so in 1766 he was already thinking of skepticism as a useful tool for stimulating philosophers to reconsider their dogmatism. This fact, as we shall see later in this chapter, raises serious questions about the traditional view that Kant's "awakening" by Hume did not happen until 1768, or perhaps even 1772 (see note 1.1).

3. Moreover, Kant uses the same analogy in A767/B795, where he refers to "the assay–balance of criticism" (see also A589/B617, A783/B811). And he uses the corresponding metaphor of "weighing" two opposing arguments in A388–9, A587/B615, A589/B617, A637/B665, and A750/B778, as well as in *CPrR* 76.

4. As early as 1764 Kant recognized a special relationship between metaphysics, moral philosophy, and philosophy of religion (see *OFBS* 2.246n). And by early 1766, when *DSS* was in press, he must have already been working on (or at least sketching plans for) two of his later systematic works, because in a letter to Kant dated February 3, 1766, Lambert states that he is waiting "impatiently" for "the publication of both your 'Foundations of Natural Philosophy' and the 'Foundations of Practical Philosophy'" (*C* 10.67)—titles very close to those that Kant used for the books that eventually became *MFNS* (1786) and *GMM* (1785), respectively. In

June 1771 Kant affirmed in a letter to Marcus Herz that his project would have to address the topics of metaphysics, morality, *and aesthetics*. And a follow-up letter to Herz, dated February 21, 1772, shows he already conceived of his task as including work on "the principles of feeling, taste, and power of judgement" in addition to its theoretical and moral aspects (*C* 10.129–30). Although he apparently had not yet decided to devote a separate *Critique* to each subject, he *had* already thought of the title "Critique of Pure Reason" (10.126). For a concise summary of the importance of these two letters to Herz, see Copleston 1960, 203–7.

5. I examine the details of the architectonic structure of Kant's System in *KSP* §III.3–4. I give a brief summary of those sections in *KCR* §III.1; see also Appendix III.1. For a general defense of the dangers of putting too much weight on matters of historical development in understanding phenomena of emergence, such as the ideas put forward by a creative genius, see SP-07.

6. *DSS* 2.357–8. For an early argument along these lines, see Sewall 1900, 24–27, 31–33. For more recent studies of the Kant–Swedenborg relationship, see Johnson 2002 and 2003.

7. These extracts appear in Sewall 1900, 123–54 (Appendix I).

8. Laywine 1993 makes significant headway in this direction (cf. note 2.8), though she reaches some rather questionable conclusions. (For a detailed discussion of her interpretation, see *KCR,* Appendix II.2.) For a good overview and critique of the two main interpretations of *DSS*, which the author calls the "anti-metaphysical and self-critical readings," see McQuillan 2015; unfortunately, he neglects the option I presented in *KCR*, which could be called the "Critical reading" of *DSS*. Alberg 2015 explores another much-neglected option, arguing (mostly on the basis of indirect evidence) that Rousseau played a greater role in the exposition of *DSS* (and so also, presumably, on Kant's discovery of the Copernican hypothesis) than is normally considered.

9. This distinction between Kant's Critical method and the *transcendental* orientation of his philosophy is often ignored by Kant-scholars, who tend to conflate the terms by talking about Kant's "transcendental method"—a phrase Kant himself never uses. This type of interpretive error lies behind Ernst Cassirer's claim that in *CPR* "Kant is presenting a completely novel *type of thinking*, one in opposition to his own past and to the philosophy of the Age of Enlightenment" (Cassirer 1981, 141). This notion of a complete opposition between Kant's past (wherein he is portrayed as being unknowingly duped by his dogmatic upbringing) and his Critical outlook (which is supposed to have sprung as suddenly as the ringing of an alarm clock from his reading of Hume) typifies the mythical account of Kant's development against which I am arguing here in Part I. In *CPR* Kant is not negating his past, but pressing it to its proper limit; he is separating the wheat from the chaff of his own background and of his Age (see e.g., Axin) by bringing into full view the Critical method that had characterized his way of thinking from the start of his career. One exception to the tendency of past Kant-scholars to overlook the foregoing point is J. Fang, who calls attention (in Fang 1967, 112–13) to the mistake of regarding Kant's *method* as transcendental. He also recognizes the importance of distinguishing between the Critical method and the transcendental character of Kant's mature philosophy: the "critical method" is already "*partially* revealed" (i.e., applied) in 1770, but "concerns itself with 'limits' alone . . . and not yet with 'sources,'" as it does in its transcendental application (118–19). With intimations of Einstein, Fang then suggests (121) that "the *special* critical method of 1768–69, viz., 'to determine the validity and bounds of intuitive principles,' had to be generalized, and when it was finally 'broadened,' the *general* critical method was to discover and justify . . . the sources, the extent, and the limits of the human faculty of knowledge or metaphysic in general—the main task of the *Critique*." Unfortunately, Fang does not work out in any detail the significance of this distinction (which relates more to Kant's gradual application of his Copernican insight than to the Critical method as such), nor does he mention *DSS* as relevant to the development of Kant's Critical method. In the main text I have reversed Fang's special–general polarity.

10. This implies that the traditional view of *DSS* as a temporary excursion into Humean skepticism (see Chapter 1) is entirely unjustified, based as it is on a shallow reading of the text and a neglect of the ubiquity of the Critical method in Kant's writings. Hume's influence on Kant in the early 1760s was only one of many influencing factors acting together as grist for the Critical mill. Interestingly, neither Hume nor Swedenborg is included in Werkmeister's de-

scription of "the complexus of ideas which is the basis for all further development of Kant's philosophy" (Werkmeister 1980, 15).

11. Kant's biographers consistently report the strong influence he felt his mother had on his general personal and intellectual development. I discuss her influence further in Chapter 8, below.

12. In fact, the influence of Swedenborg is quite compatible with the influence of Leibniz. For Swedenborg himself studied Descartes, Leibniz, and Wolff, much as Kant did in his early years (see Jonsson 1967, 47). (In §335.7 and §696 of *The True Christian Religion* Swedenborg describes visions he had of Aristotle, Descartes, and Leibniz, together with nine of their followers, among whom was Wolff.) Thus, Kant's reading of Swedenborg may well have worked *together* with his reading of the *Clarke–Leibniz Correspondence* to point him toward the Copernican hypothesis.

13. *C* 12.255. See note 1.5 for a list of references to this metaphor in *CPR*.

Chapter Four

Kant's Metaphysical Dream

A System of Critical Philosophy

A clear understanding of Swedenborg's influence on Kant, and of the function of *DSS* as the prolegomenon to Kant's mature Critical System, makes it not so surprising that Sewall 1900 says mystics "from Jung–Stilling to Du Prel" have always "claimed Kant as being of their number" (16–17, 32). Indeed, Du Prel 1889 stresses Kant's positive attitude toward Swedenborg (2.195–98, 243, 290) and argues that in *DSS* "Kant ... declared Mysticism possible, supposing man to be 'a member at once of the visible and of the invisible world'" (2.302). He even suggests that "Kant would confess to-day [i.e., in the 1880s] that hundreds of such facts [based on mystical experience and extra-sensory powers] are proved" (2.198). The latter may be going too far, but so is the extreme opposite conclusion drawn by Vaihinger (1892, 513; trans. Sewall 1900, 19) that "Kant's world of experience ... excludes all invasion of the regular system of nature by uncontrollable 'spirits;' and the whole system of modern mysticism, so far as he holds fast to his fundamental principles, Kant is 'bound to forcibly reject.'"

Kant is forced to reject mysticism *only* as a constitutive component of his theoretical system (i.e., of *CPR*); his practical and judicial systems, especially as set forth in the second and third *Critiques* and in *RBBR*, remain open to nontheoretical interpretations of mystical encounters. Sewall 1900 reflects Kant's purposes more accurately when he says (20–21):

> The great mission of Kant was to establish ... [that reason] can neither create a knowledge of the spiritual world, nor can it deny the possibility of such a world. It can affirm indeed the rationality of such a conception, but the *reality* of it does not come within its domain as pure reason.

Kant's qualified rejection of mysticism therefore "refers only to the practices (of spiritism), and to the *Mysticism of the Feelings*; it does not apply to the rational belief of Kant in the '*corpus mysticum* of the intelligible world.'"[1] Indeed, Kant affirms his belief in the notion of a "*corpus mysticum*" at several points even in *CPR*, as in his above-quoted claim that "if we could intuit the things and ourselves *as they are* we would see ourselves in a world of spiritual natures with which our only true community had not begun with birth [and] would not cease with bodily death" (A780/B808; see also A393–4).

Kant therefore has two distinct, though closely related, purposes in *DSS*. The first is to reject uncritical (delusory or delirious) forms of mysticism, not in order to overthrow all mysticism, but in order to replace it with a refined, *Critical* version, whereby the mystical encounter revitalizes our experience of *this* world and our reflection on it from various perspectives. This perspectival element in Kant's philosophy is hinted at by Vaihinger (1892, 512–13; trans. Sewall 1900, 15,18) when he says Kant believes:

> The other world is . . . not another place, but only another view of even this world. . . . [It] is not a world of other things, but of the same things seen differently by us. . . . But the wildly fermenting must of the Swedenborgian Mysticism becomes with Kant clarified and settled into the noble, mild, and yet strong wine of criticism.

Unfortunately, the general mystical thrust of Kant's Critical System has been grossly neglected by most Kant scholars. In the remainder of this monograph I shall attempt to set right this neglect by examining the extent to which Kant's critique of mysticism in *DSS* paves the way for a full-blooded "Critical mysticism" in his mature philosophical System.

An exception to this general neglect of Kant's interest in mysticism came in the waning years of the nineteenth century, especially due to the work of Carl Du Prel. Sewall 1900, x (*sic*; page number should read 'ix') lists several works written between 1889 and 1895 that do focus on Kant's mystical tendencies. The most significant of these is Du Prel's Introduction to his 1889 edition of *Kant Vorlesungen über Psychologie*, entitled "Kant mystische Weltanschauung," which Vaihinger (1892, 431) assesses as containing a significant element of truth regarding Swedenborg's influence on Kant. Sewall 1900 (13–14n) translates the following passage from pages vii–viii of Du Prel's work:

> 'Dreams' . . . has been interpreted as a daring venture of Kant's genius in making sport of superstition; the accent has been laid on Kant's negations, and his affirmative utterances have been overlooked. The 'Lectures on Psychology' now show . . . that these utterances were very seriously intended; for the affirmative portions of the 'Dreams' agree very thoroughly with the lengthier

exposition of the 'Psychology,' and the wavering attitude of Kant is here no longer perceptible.

Scholarly attention to Kant's lectures in general began to mushroom about a century after those words were written, yet to this day few scholars have explored (or even considered) the claim that Kant's lectures on metaphysics (from which Du Prel excerpted the psychology lectures that he published) exhibit mystical tendencies, as Du Prel claimed.[2]

Kant's second purpose in clearing from the path of metaphysics the obstructions created by the speculative claims of mystical experiences is to prepare the way for his own attempt to provide a metaphysical System that could do for metaphysics what *DSS* does for mystical visions. I have intentionally presented this as the *second* purpose, because the text of *DSS* clearly regards it as such. Nearly all interpreters read into the text their own *exclusive* interest in Kant's metaphysics, and thereby treat the whole topic of mystical visions as a mere (perhaps ill-chosen) illustration. How easy it is to forget that even the title specifies the *main* topic as focusing on visionary dreams, and explicitly depicts *metaphysics* as a secondary illustration!

Johan Gerding is an exception: he stresses that Kant is dealing with what we now call the parapsychological (or "psi" for short). However, he takes *DSS* as a "fundamental denial of psi" (Gerding 1994, 141), claiming "Kant explicitly states that psi phenomena cannot exist." But this is too strong. As we have seen, Kant's conclusion is that we cannot construct a *science* from such mystical encounters: he openly admits that psi *do exist* as immediate experiences; the problem is that we cannot *understand* them. Gerding goes so far as to claim that for Kant "psi cannot even be hypothetical" (144) and that "Kant does not allow psi to be even possible." He suggests we could avoid excluding psi from transcendental philosophy by tracing them to "an unknown capacity of the human mind" (144–45), but this renders them uninformative: "Psi information from a transcendent world therefore is not possible." He defends his position by arguing that a case of Extra Sensory Perception (ESP), for example, "has to be verifiable for living human beings" in order to be regarded as genuine (145). This still leaves the *process* unknowable: we can know *that* something happens without knowing *how* it happens. His own position, offered in conclusion, is more balanced: "the Kantian transcendental philosophy does not exclude paranormal phenomena when they are interpreted as anomalous phenomena, which happen to living human beings." What Gerding fails to recognize is that a perspectival interpretation of *DSS* enables us to see this as precisely Kant's own view! The error is to think Kant himself did not recognize that psi can be entirely possible while nevertheless remaining mysterious.

In a more measured and systematically complete study of the epistemological status of Kant's claims in *DSS*, Ayon Maharaj distinguishes between "direct" and "indirect" mystical experiences, as well as between several types of each. A "direct mystical experience" ("DME") is one that claims to make contact with "a supersensible entity by means of non-sensible intuition" (Maharaj 2017, 313); Kant resoundingly denies the legitimacy of such experiences from *DSS* onwards, although he might allow the possibility of DME of "a supersensible entity that has assumed a physical form" (313)—an option that Maharaj regards as beyond the scope of his study. The rationale for Kant's denial is that he interprets Swedenborg's extraordinary experiences as "indirect mystical experiences" ("IMEs"), in which a person contacts "a supersensible entity through the perception of something sensible—such as an image or a feeling—that is caused by that supersensible entity" (313). Maharaj argues that for Kant, both in *DSS* and in his later writings, IMEs can be veridical, as when Kant allows that Swedenborg's visions may be cases of "a genuine spiritual–influence" (*DSS* 2.340) but warns that they are "both morally dangerous and philosophically untenable" (Maharaj 2017, 314). Maharaj further demonstrates that Kant's interest in both DME and IME persisted throughout his Critical period; indeed, Kant's own mature theory of noumenal causality preserves and formalizes his concession that IMEs are possible. Maharaj astutely observes how the DME–IME distinction clarifies what is so misleading about Kant's tendency to dismiss mysticism outright (321): what Critical principles definitely rule out is only non-sensible DME, yet many mystics explicitly interpret their experiences as IME, whose possibility (as we shall see) is actually *protected* by Critical principles, provided they are not regarded as self-authenticating (334–35).

The Critical dream that Kant envisaged in *DSS* was to serve as a seed planted in his reason, which eventually matured into the tree of Critical philosophy; only when this tree finally bears fruit does the mystical seed that gave birth to the System appear once again (i.e., in Kant's final work, *OP*). Accordingly, Kant's Critical labors can be regarded as an attempt to build a rational System that *preserves* the true mystical dream, thus putting mysticism in its proper place: Critique, understood as the mystical experience of baring all in reason's light, belongs at the *center* of metaphysics. In this sense, at least, Kant would agree with Du Prel (1889, 1.70) when he says: "dream, not waking . . . is the door of metaphysic, so far as the latter deals with man.

NOTES

1. Sewall 1900, 25, quoting Kant in A808/B836. Detailed evidence in support of Kant's lifelong belief in a spirit–world is provided by Manolesco 1969.
2. For some passages relevant to Du Prel's point, see *LM* 28.207–8, 241, 753; 29.759–61, 764, 950, 953. *LM* 28.207 offers something like a definition of mysticism: "*If I maintain thinking beings of which I have intellectual intuition, then that is mystical.*" Kant sometimes explicitly calls Plato "a mystical philosopher" in this sense (e.g., at 28.232).

II

Kant's Critical Philosophy as a Critique of Mysticism

The sum of all these reflections leads us to a concept of the Highest Being, which captures everything in itself—what one can only propose to be able to think—when man, made out of dust, dares to cast an exploring eye behind the curtain which conceals from created eyes the secrets of the unfathomable. God is all-sufficient. What there is, be it possible or actual, is only something in so far as it is given through Him. A human language can let the Infinite talk to itself in this way: *I am from eternity to eternity; outside of me is nothing; except that, in so far as it be through me, something is.* This thought, the most sublime of all, is still very neglected, or for the most part has hardly been touched. —*OPA* 2.151, alt.

Chapter Five

Does Mystical Experience Always Prompt Delirium?

Part I examined the Critical character of Kant's *Dreams of a Spirit-Seer* and its role in preparing the way for his Critical System. I argued that, although Kant wrote it during the so-called "pre-Critical" period, *DSS* contains the essential ingredients of the Critical method and that the only key element of Kant's mature thinking that is altogether missing, namely the decisive "Copernican" insight, is at least hinted at in the works of Swedenborg, whose views Kant was critiquing in *DSS*. I also suggested, but left undeveloped, the idea that Kant himself did not have an entirely negative opinion of mysticism, but rather hoped through his Critical philosophy to provide a secure foundation not only for metaphysics, but for mysticism as well. The purpose of Part II will be to defend this idea more thoroughly by demonstrating the extent to which a mystical worldview can be seen operating throughout Kant's mature philosophical writings, especially in those composing the Critical System itself (see *KSP* §III.4). I begin in this chapter by distinguishing between several kinds of mystic, depending on what type of experience one regards as genuinely "mystical." The next chapter examines more thoroughly Kant's reasons for rejecting what he calls "delirious" (*schwärmerischer*) mysticism. Chapter 7 then demonstrates that Kant himself develops a special *Critical* type of mysticism. And Chapter 8 concludes Part II by examining various factors that shaped this worldview, especially the systematic relationship between four of his favorite meditative metaphors. Part III will then show how Critical mysticism served as a crucial motivating factor in the last few years of Kant's life (especially while writing *OP*), to the extent that the ultimate "need of reason" is paradoxically fulfilled by the mystical "death" of reason itself.

A good general definition of mysticism is suggested by Albert Schweitzer's description of the mystic (Schweitzer 1931, 1) as "a human being looking upon the division between earthly and super-earthly, temporal and eternal, as transcended, and feeling himself, while still externally amid the earthly and temporal, to belong to the super-earthly and eternal." Schweitzer 1951 makes a rather different distinction between two worldviews: a "life affirmation" that "is dualistic and doctrinaire" (i.e., ethical) and a "life negation" that "is monistic and mystical" (10). Pegging Kant as "dualistic," he places him along with most other Western philosophers in the former class (12). Schweitzer's ideal worldview is a combination of the two basic types, in the form of "[t]he enlightened ignorance of ethical mysticism" (263). He sees Kant as exemplifying the ethical side of this ideal (264); I shall demonstrate that Kant's System makes room for the monistic, mystical side as well. Considered in this light, Schweitzer's position can be taken as an illustration of Kantian (Critical) mysticism.

Schweitzer distinguishes between "primitive" mysticism, based on a "magical act" leading to supposed oneness with God, and "developed" mysticism, whereby this union "takes place through an act of thinking" (Schweitzer 1931, 1–2). He argues that Paul the Apostle does not have "the usual mentality of a mystic. The exoteric and the esoteric go hand in hand. . . . [For] mysticism is combined with a non-mystical conception of the world" (25). Schweitzer's interpretation of Paul's mysticism of "being in Christ" is strikingly similar to the interpretation of Kant's mysticism that I will offer throughout the remainder of this book. Both forge a middle path between the extremes of magical and intellectual mysticism, and in so doing they avoid the greatest "danger of all mysticism," which (for both Kant and Schweitzer) "is that of becoming supra-ethical" (297). From Schweitzer's definition at least three sorts of mysticism can therefore be inferred, depending on how a person believes the eternal can be encountered. First, the mystic might believe that our membership in a "super-earthly" realm makes it possible for us to engage in non-physical forms of communication with other spirits, especially those that are no longer tied to a body. This is the type of mysticism practiced by Swedenborg and condemned by Kant in *DSS*. Since we dealt with it fully in Part I, there is no need to consider it any further here.

Another, more common alternative is for mystics to participate in an organized religion, seeking to conform their religious experience to a set of traditional beliefs and rituals. This is indeed so common that such mystically inclined participants in organized religion usually do not think of themselves as mystics. As I have argued in *KCR*, Part Three, and throughout *CCKR*, Kant's Copernican Perspective on religion allows for the potential validity of this second sense of mysticism, whereby a person's encounter with the eternal dimension is symbolically channeled through religious activities and beliefs. Kant's Critical religion condones such religious/mystical experiences, based on the judicial standpoint, *provided that* they promote a rational (moral) discipline by clothing a pure religious conviction (*Gesinnung*)[1] with good actions, thus rendering practitioners worthy of receiving God's grace. However, mystics (as well as many ordinary religious people who would not presume to adorn themselves with such a title) more often speak of mystical experience in a rather different way.

The term "mysticism" can be used to refer not to the reflective act of pleasing God through the overcoming of one's evil heart, as expressed in the moral actions of a group of believers banded together to form a church, but to a more direct form of individual spirituality, expressed either as communication with a personal God or as communion with a transpersonal ultimate Being. Mystical encounters of this type may well take place outside the bounds of organized religion. The suggestion that Kant admitted the validity of such *immediate* and *personal* religious experience, and even encouraged its promotion as an important aspect of his philosophical System, is rarely entertained by his interpreters; when considered, it is almost universally denied. Nevertheless, my purpose here in Part II is to demonstrate that such a mystical experience lies at the very heart of the Critical philosophy: it is as important to the System as birth and death are to an individual person, for it sets up the limits and in so doing establishes for the System its ultimate meaning.

C.C.J. Webb calls attention to the traditional view that philosophy is "the daughter of Religion, and starts upon her career with an outfit of questions suggested by religious experience" (1926, 14). The term "religious experience" here refers not to communication with disembodied spirits, nor to the experience of God in humanly organized religion; rather, it is an immediate personal encounter fitting the description of the third type of mysticism introduced above. Kant's Critical philosophy, I maintain, is an example of the tendency Webb describes. For as I demonstrated in *KCR*, Kant's entire philosophical System has a distinctively religious and theological orientation, despite the failure of many commentators to recognize its presence. The task of validating belief in the primarily theological ideas of God, freedom, and immortality unites the three *Critiques*; indeed, Kant claims that his approach to these and other topics of religious and theological interest, though entirely philosophical in its presentation, can provide the only legitimate *rational* basis for religion (see especially *KCR*, Chapters IV and VII). Furthermore, as we saw in Part I, the last book he wrote before setting out on the path of constructing his Critical System (i.e., *DSS*) sets before him the question of how the philosopher is to cope with the claims of mystics such as Swedenborg; and as we shall see in Part III, the uncompleted book intended to fill the final gap in his System (i.e., *OP*) provides ample evidence that the ultimate aim of the entire Critical enterprise is to replace the extreme mystical and anti-mystical attitudes with a balanced approach that can best be called "Critical mysticism"—an aim whose fulfillment in the three *Critiques* and *RBBR* I will summarize in the Conclusion. Before turning to *OP*, let us examine in the remainder of Part II the extent to which Kant's *other works* reveal such a balanced mystical spirit.

NOTE

1. Kant's term, *Gesinnung*, has traditionally been translated as "disposition"; in his translations of Kant's three *Critiques* and *RBBR*, Pluhar renders it "attitude." In SP–15a and *CCKR* I argue that "conviction" expresses Kant's intended (religious) meaning more adequately than either of these alternatives. The term normally translated as "conviction" by English translators of Kant, *Überzeugung*, I translate as "convincing."

Chapter Six

Kant's Critique of Delirious Mysticism

Conventional interpretations of Kant portray him as consistently denying, or at least ignoring, any "possibility of an encounter with the transcendent" (Smart 1969, 5.62) and assume that "he ... found the notion of an imminent God unfamiliar and uncongenial to his mind" (Webb 1926, 50). Baelz (1968, 41) expresses this view in its classic form:

> Kant, while recognizing the demands of the moral law inherent in man's own rational being, had no room for any immediate apprehension of God, belief in whom was a postulate and no more than a postulate, inferential rather than direct, mediated by reason rather than immediately given in experience.

Even those who recognize that Kant's view of religion in *RBBR* is "not radically unlike the traditional Christian view" (Ward 1972, 168) generally agree that "any sense of personal fellowship with God, revelation from God or redemption by God is entirely lacking in the Kantian scheme." With this assumption in hand, interpreters often treat any reference Kant makes to mysticism in general or to experience of God in particular as a condemnation, regardless of what he actually writes. Thus, for example, Temple (1994, 111) claims that in *Lectures on Ethics* (*LE* 27.250) Kant *rejects* Plato's idea of "communion with the highest being" as being "mystical" and "visionary"; yet a careful look at the text reveals that Kant does nothing but *describe* this notion. He neither argues against it nor passes judgment on it (see also A314n/B371n).

As I have demonstrated elsewhere, such assessments of Kant's position are too harsh: Kant is always careful to leave a space for God's activity in relation to humanity and for faith in relation to knowledge;[1] what he criticizes is only the attempt to grasp or control God in such a way as to *force* revelation or redemption to occur (in the way that, for example, Platonic idealism might seem to entail). Thus Wiebe (1980, 530–31), rejecting the standard interpretation, sees in Kant "the glimmer of a notion of faith as a 'direct interior persuasion' in matters of religious truth" (quoting Baillie 1939, 117; cf. 130–31, 161, 257). The recognition that Kant's Critical philosophy functions as a System of Perspectives can, I believe, transform this "glimmer" into an unmistakable ray of noonday sunlight. It may even enable us to defend the suggestion in Du Prel 1889 (1.xxvi) that "the Kantian 'Critique of Reason'" points directly to mysticism.

The belief that Kant disallows any direct encounter with God stems from two misunderstandings that occur when readers ignore his dependence on the principle of perspective. The first arises out of the failure to make the important distinction between *mediate* experience (i.e., empirical cognition), and *immediate* experience (see *KSP* §IV.1). The fact that Kant tends to distrust those who claim to see "glimpses" of "the infinity in the finite and the universality in the individual" (Wallace 1901, 218) is taken by most interpreters as evidence that he completely rejects any notion of an immediate, mystical encounter with something *beyond* cognition, when in fact Kant's expression of distrust in such "glimpses" always relates to their inadequacy when viewed from reason's *theoretical standpoint*, the standpoint that aims at and depends on empirical cognition. If, in reflecting on such glimpses, we view them for what they are—that is, *as* immediate experiences, and therefore not as the potential source of determinate knowledge—then there is no question of distrusting them, because we have not yet adopted any Critical standpoint that might arouse such distrust.

The second misunderstanding arises out of the failure to recognize that Kant does not regard the Copernican Perspective as one that must be adopted at all times. Only when a person chooses to *reflect rationally* on experience would Kant argue that the Copernican hypothesis should be adopted. By no means does such reflection entail a denial that people do have nonreflective (immediate) experience as well. Thus, when Kant makes statements such as that "the philosopher, as pure teacher of reason (teaching from bare a priori principles), must . . . abstract from all experience" (*RBBR* 6.12), he is not calling into question the reality or validity of such (immediate) experience, but only reminding us to distinguish between the a priori and the a posteriori. Likewise, his unwillingness to allow an immediate encounter with God to serve as a constitutive element anywhere in his philosophical System does not indicate that he views such an encounter as impossible, but only that he recognizes that it does not occur by means of philosophical reflection. Kant's strategy of explaining religious doctrines and activities in practical (moral) terms must not, therefore, be regarded as a denial of the legitimacy of an immediate experience of the nonsensible. His point, rather, is that, insofar as one wishes to *explain* or *interpret* such experiences, the practical standpoint always takes precedence over the theoretical standpoint.

Affirming that we have immediate (and hence nonreflective) experience is not problematic; but asserting that God is actually present in such experience does seem to go directly against Kant's own claims to the contrary. "A direct revelation from God," he says in 1798 (*CF* 7.47), "would be a supersensible experience, and this is impossible." For "a supernatural experience . . . is a contradiction in terms" (57); likewise, as he puts it in 1796, "to know [something] . . . by super-sensory experience . . . is a self-contradiction" (*RPTS* 8.401n). Before we jump to any conclusions concerning the implications of such negative statements, it is important to determine just what Kant means by the words "super-sensory [or "supernatural"] experience." Is he declaring that an immediate, nonreflective encounter between a human being and God is so absurd an idea as to be an impossible contradiction, or is he rejecting only the supposition that such an encounter can give rise to objective *knowledge* of God (i.e., from the standpoint of theoretical reason)? Because most interpreters fail to distinguish between immediate experience and experience in Kant's special, mediate sense, this question is rarely even asked. Once we make this distinction, however, it seems clear that Kant is referring to experience *as empirical cognition* whenever he rejects the possibility of supersensible experience. Immediate experience just *is*; words like "contradiction" do not really even apply to it, for if we *could* have knowledge of the thing in itself (see Introduction), all things would be known as One. Moreover, Kant himself, as we have seen in Chapter 2, was actually open to the *possibility* of mystical visions in *DSS*; and as we shall see in Chapter 10 he even affirms an immediate experience of God in *OP*. He would therefore be blatantly contradicting himself if he were to claim elsewhere that such ineffable experiences are, as such, *self-contradictory*. By contrast, a claim to theoretical *knowledge* of the transcendent (i.e., supernatural) ground of the empirical world clearly *would* be contradictory, inasmuch as the presupposition of Kant's entire System is that the transcendent ground (the thing in itself) is *un*knowable (see *KSP* §V.2 and Appendix V.1–4).

That Kant intended his various denials of supersensible experience to relate solely to the theoretical standpoint (i.e., to the impossibility of using mystical encounters to construct scientific knowledge) is substantiated by examining the context of such comments. For he never denies altogether that such experiences *happen*, but only requires that we change the standpoint from which we view them when we go about interpreting what they are about. In *CF* 7.57–58, for example, Kant is considering whether the "claim that we *feel* as such the immediate influence of God" can be used as "an interpretation of certain sensations" in order to *prove* that "they are elements in cognition and so have real [theoretical] objects." Although he concludes that "we can never make anything rational out of" such an attempted theoretical proof, he admits that such subjective experiences do occur; his point is that they must remain mysterious. Far from denying their validity outright, he employs them to emphasize the subjective, mysterious aspects of the supersensible (58–59):

> there is something in us that we cannot cease to wonder at when we have once seen it. . . . This ascendancy of the *supersensible* human being in us over the *sensible*, such that (when it comes to a conflict between them) the sensible is *nothing* . . . is an object of the greatest *wonder*; and our wonder at this moral predisposition in us, inseparable from our humanity, only increases the longer we contemplate this true (not fabricated) ideal.

As he explains in *CF* 7.47, the experience of divine supernatural power "comes to the human being through his own reason"; it is therefore not a "direct revelation" in the sense of coming in the form of a sensible experience that is objectively verifiable. Otherwise, a person watching someone who is experiencing, for example, an apparition of the Blessed Virgin would also be able to see the object just as clearly.

Similarly, in 1796 Kant says of this same "inward predisposition [*Anlage*] in mankind, and . . . the impenetrability of the mystery that veils it" that: "We can never weary of giving attention to it, and admiring in itself a power that yields to no power in Nature" (*RPTS* 8.402–3, alt.). He then identifies "the unshakable moral law" as "the secret which can become *possible to feel* only after slow development of the concepts of the understanding" (403) and explains that this gives us practical access to the supersensible "not, say, by a *feeling*, which purports to be the basis of knowledge (the mystical), but by a clear *cognition* which acts upon feeling (the moral)." (I explore this hint further in Chapters 8 and 9, below.) "Inner [e.g., mystical] experience and feeling (which in itself is empirical . . .) are aroused only by the voice of reason"; yet such feeling does not by itself constitute "a particular practical rule for reason . . . , which is impossible" (402). Here again Kant is explicitly considering whether or not such a feeling suffices for a *proof*: if it could give rise to a "rule for reason" (thus constraining *everyone's* reason), then it would be objective and could qualify as a supersensible experience that produces knowledge (either practical or theoretical) and thus serves as a constitutive element in his philosophical System.

Kant's point is that all such feelings arising out of our immediate experience will remain subjective;[2] but the certainty resulting from them is not for this reason any less valid (see e.g., A829/B857). Thus, he says in *RPTS* 8.397n: "there is no theoretical belief in the super-sensible. In a practical (morally–practical) sense, however, a belief in the super-sensible is not only possible, but is actually inseparably bound up with that point of view [i.e., with the practical standpoint]." So when Kant says the "feeling of the immediate presence of the highest being and the *differentiation* of this feeling from any other, even from the moral feeling, would be a receptivity to an intuition for which there is no sense [i.e., no faculty] in human nature" (*RBBR* 6.175, emphasis added), he is not denying that such a feeling can legitimately be experienced, as Ward (1972, 157) claims, nor is he altogether ruling out "the mystic's intuition" as a way of experiencing, as Schrader (1951, 240) claims; rather, he is only insisting that such an experience cannot properly be interpreted through reason. Thus, when criticizing the *excesses* of the "philosophy of feeling" in its attempt to lead us "directly to the heart of the matter," without "ratiocination from concepts," Kant *concedes* that "[p]hilosophy has its secrets that *can be felt*" (*RPTS* 8.395, Kant's emphasis). The mistake is to think that such feelings can be interpreted in such a way as to *replace* reason. This accords well with the recognition of most mystics that what is apprehended in a mystical encounter remains ultimately *mysterious*—i.e., it is something whose true nature *cannot* be apprehended sensibly (a point that Swedenborg himself often emphasized). Indeed, this very fact—that we cannot have a *sensible* experience of the transcendent as it is in itself (i.e., one that produces *theoretical* knowledge)—is what requires us to portray *immediate* experience as not fitting properly into any Critical perspective.

Unfortunately, Kant's own use of the term "mysticism" is rather narrow. He equates "mystical" with "magical" in 1793 (*RBBR* 6.120) and goes on to deride the "mystical delirium in the life of hermits and monks" (130), apparently assuming that *all* hermits and monks are delirious in their approach to mysticism. He refers to the "mystical cloak" (83) as covering up reason's light, indicating that for him "mysticism" implies confusion or lack of clarity. Thus he claims in 1796 that mystics seek to establish "an overleap (*salto mortale*) from concepts to the unthinkable" by means of "a power of seizing upon that which no concept attains to" (*RPTS* 8.398). Such efforts usually indicate "a turning of heads towards delirium" (398, alt.): because such mystical operations are "transcendent . . . and can lead to no true *knowledge* of the object, they must necessarily promise a surrogate thereof, supernatural information (mystical illumination): which is then the death of all philosophy." And in 1794 Kant argues that "the person who broods on this will fall into *mysticism* . . . , where reason does not understand either itself or what it wants, but prefers to indulge in delirium"—a situation that is not "fitting for an intellectual inhabitant of a sensible world."[3] Mystical encounters as such can hardly be called *speculation* in Kant's theoretical sense, yet he believes they are subject to the same criticism, because the pantheism on which he believes such practices are typically based "is a concept in which the understanding is simultaneously exhausted and all thinking itself has an end."[4]

As the foregoing passages clearly indicate, Kant's actual criticism of mysticism is that it errs insofar as it gives rise to *delirium*—i.e., insofar as its practitioners believe that their attempts at "interaction with God" can "accomplish anything in regard to justification before God."[5] However, mystics do not *necessarily* commit such an error—indeed, many do not. Kant's claim that mystics mistakenly convert what can serve "only as a *symbol* into a *schema*" (*CPrR* 5.70–71) implies that there may be a *proper* (symbolic, noncognitive) interpretation of mystical experiences. In *CF* 7.46 Kant explains that mysticism in the form of a delirious fantasy that "inevitably gets lost in the transcendent" can be avoided by establishing for it an *ethical* grounding, just as Schweitzer later recommended (see Chapter 5, above): philosophers should "be on the lookout for a moral meaning in scriptural texts and even . . . impose it on them," because "unless the supersensible (the thought of which is essential to anything called religion) is anchored to determinate concepts of reason, such as those of morality, . . . there is no longer any public touchstone of truth." So "mysticism, with its lamp of private revelations" (65) is not illegitimate in itself, but only when it fails to subject itself to the objective principles of practical reason, as expressed, for example, in time-honored religious texts such as the Bible.[6]

Like everything Kant subjects to his Critical method, mysticism is rejected only in its extreme form (i.e., as "delirium"), but remains viable in a moderate (i.e., "Critical") form. Kant implies as much when he laments in *Observations on the Feeling of the Beautiful and the Sublime* (1764) that some of Plato's tendencies "may be somewhat *too* mystical" (*OFBS* 2.240, emphasis added). He expresses his support for such a middle way even more explicitly in *CF* 7.59:

> And so, between *orthodoxy* which has no soul and [delirious] *mysticism* which kills reason, there is the teaching of the Bible, a faith which our reason can develop out of itself. This teaching is the true religious doctrine, based on the *criticism* of practical reason, that works with divine power on the hearts of all human beings . . .

The three words Kant emphasizes in this passage suggest that his real aim is to defend, in accordance with the real aim of the biblical message, not only a kind of *Critical orthodoxy*,[7] but also a balanced, *Critical mysticism*. Thus, although Kant criticizes the belief that we can "be aware of a supersensible object" in experience, he readily admits that "in the mind there sometimes occur movements working toward what is moral" (*RBBR* 6.174). As a *support* for the moral life, Kant not only condones the attention a mystic pays to such "movements," but, as we shall see, he actively nurtured them in his own life. Indeed, whereas delirious mysticism leads to "the moral death of reason" (175), Kant's Critical mysticism begins as a simple acknowledgment of the immediate experiences that engender the moral *birth* of reason.

Mystics, in fact, often regard the revitalization of everyday life as an inevitable result of an authentic mystical journey (see e.g., Copleston 1974, 82). For mystical experiences are not generally characterized by confusion or irrational delusion, as is so often wrongly assumed (see e.g., note 6.6), but by immediate clarity and enhanced balance. We shall see in Part III that Kant's own attitude toward God in *OP* attests to this same sense of immediacy and balance. Moreover, just as mystics (contrary to Kant's opinion) typically do not try to *grasp* God (or even their own "nothingness" in many cases; see note 6.3) but instead open themselves up to be *grasped by* the transcendent Ground of Being, so also Kant portrays the voice of God, speaking through the moral law within, not as a way of controlling God, but as a way of immediately recognizing and receiving God's guiding Word—which he names "the Become! [*das Werde!*]" in *RBBR* 6.60—and thereby being empowered to apply it to one's everyday actions (see *CCKR* §4.2 for details). We shall explore Kant's references to the voice of God more fully in the next chapter.

That Kant was intrigued by the possibility that his position might be consistent with a certain way of being a mystic is suggested by the fact that in 1798 he toys with a "mystical chronology" (*CF* 7.62–63n) in which "sacred numbers" can be "calculated a priori," using 4s and 7s in various combinations to construct an a priori history of the world. Taken at face value, this and other passages (e.g., *APP* 7.194–96) portray Kant as having a clear interest in and an open-minded attitude even toward such nonmoral speculations—though he was always reluctant to "join the bandwagon," so to speak—much like his attitude toward Swedenborg in the mid-1760s (if we put aside his occasional digressions into ridicule in *DSS*). Some interpreters insist on reading between the lines. Commenting on *CF* 7.103n, for example, Roger White says mysticism "obviously fills [Kant] with horror" (1990, 53, 56): Kant "scarcely disguises his hostility towards 'the sects' whose teaching he is here attacking." Yet Kant's footnote contains no explicit hostility; rather, it is a reasoned criticism of those Pietists who proudly claim to be God's elect, yet show little if any evidence of it in their conduct. Likewise, while he admittedly regards mystical chronology as religiously dangerous (*CF* 7.62), Kant's attention to it probably stems from his serious view that mathematics arises out of pure intuition in the same way that metaphysics arises out of pure reason. Thus, *CF* 7.28 depicts "pure mathematics and pure philosophy" as the two sciences of "pure rational cognition," and Kant later notes the similar benefits of "tak[ing] an *immediate* interest in mathematics" and in philosophy: perhaps because they represent the sciences of pure intuition and pure reason, respectively, he claims that both can enhance one's *power*, especially in old age.[8]

Kant confirms even more explicitly that he is not entirely antipathetic toward mysticism by appending to his discussion of theology and religion in *CF* a lengthy letter wherein Carl Wilmans, a young doctoral student, summarizes the content of the Critical philosophy and then claims that he knows a group of mystics who follow the principles of Kantian philosophy to a tee. Kant warns that "I do not mean to guarantee that my views coincide entirely with his" (7.69n); but the title Kant gives to this Appendix, "On a Pure

Mysticism in Religion" (69), suggests that his main reason for including this letter is to *encourage* the reader to flirt with the enticing claim Wilmans makes at the end, that at least one approach to mysticism is entirely consistent with, and perhaps even entailed by, the Critical philosophy.[9] Moreover, if Kant had objected to Wilmans' claim and merely wanted to show appreciation for the letter because it begins with an extensive (and fairly accurate) summary of the Critical System, as some interpreters have claimed (see note 6.9), he could easily have omitted the last portion of the letter, where that System is portrayed as a form of mysticism, and quoted only the earlier, uncontroversial portion. Significantly, Wilmans' own argument begins at the very point in the letter where he concludes his summary and first addresses Kant (74–75, alt.); it is worth quoting at length:

> I had reached this point in my study of your writings . . . when I became acquainted with a group of people, called separatists but calling themselves *mystics*, among whom I found your teachings put into practice almost verbatim. It was indeed difficult to recognize your teachings, at first, in their mystical terms, but after persistent probing I succeeded. It struck me as strange that these people . . . repudiate all "divine service" that does not consist in fulfilling one's duties: that they consider themselves religious people and indeed Christians, though they take as their code not the Bible, but only the precepts of an inward Christianity dwelling in us from eternity. —I inquired into their conduct and found in them (except for the mangy sheep that, from self-interest, get into every flock) pure moral convictions [*Gesinnungen*] . . . I examined their teachings and principles and recognized the essentials of your entire moral and religious doctrine . . . they consider the inner law, as they call it, an inward revelation and so regard God as definitely its author. It is true that they regard the Bible as a book which in some way or other—they do not discuss it further—is of divine origin; but, . . . they infer the divine origin of the Bible from the consistency of the doctrine it contains with their inner law. For if one asks their reason, they reply: The Bible is validated in my heart, as you will find it in yours if you obey the precepts of your inner law or the teachings of the Bible. For the same reason they do not regard the Bible as their code of laws but only as a historical confirmation in which they recognize what is originally grounded in themselves. In a word, if these people were philosophers they would be (pardon the term!) true Kantians. . . . Among the educated members I have never encountered delirium, but rather free, unprejudiced reasoning and judgment in religious matters.

If one of Kant's long term (though private) goals in constructing his philosophical System was to promote just such a Critical mysticism, then his (otherwise very strange) willingness to devote an Appendix to the quotation of this lengthy letter makes perfect sense. But in that case we would also expect to find some other evidence of a mystical tendency, both in his life and in his philosophical writings. Although it is rarely taken at face value, ample evidence of such a tendency actually exists in both areas. In *CPrR*

5.71, for example, Kant openly favors mysticism in comparison to empiricism: "*mysticism* is still compatible with the purity and sublimity of the moral law," even though it all too often improperly "strays into the transcendent" because its practitioners believe they have a capacity for "supersensible intuitions." Nevertheless, empiricism "is much more dangerous than any delirium" (71, alt.), for it "destroys at its roots the morality in convictions [*in Gesinnungen*]." With this tantalizing foretaste, let us therefore consider in the next two chapters some of the evidence that can be used to support Wilmans' intriguing suggestion that Critique itself is an experience that leads naturally to a type of mysticism.

NOTES

1. See *KCR*, Part Three, and *CCKR*; see also *KSP*, Chapter V. Given that he views God as outside of space and time, Kant suggests at one point (*LPDR* 28.1098) that it makes most sense to regard God's mode of relation to the world as consisting of "only one action"—an act that encompasses the *entirety* of what we know of as space–time. This can be regarded as a mystical notion of God's relation to the world.

2. Along these lines he argues in 1793 that "just as one cannot from some feeling infer and ascertain any [particular] cognition of laws, and that these are moral, no more and even less can one through a feeling infer and ascertain the secure mark of an immediate divine influence. . . . Feeling . . . is something that each person has only on his own and cannot expect of others" (*RBBR* 6.114).

3. *EAT* 8.335, alt. The example he cites in this passage (335) is that "Chinese philosophers, sitting in dark rooms with their eyes closed, exert themselves to think and sense their own nothingness." For a set of more well-informed assessments of the relation between Kant and Chinese philosophy, see the papers collected in SP–10a, especially Parts X–XII.

4. *EAT* 8.335–36. Interestingly, as Regina Dell'Oro reports (1994, 134n), Pierre Labèrge (in *La Théologie Kantienne Précritique*, 65) sees in *UNH* a "verification of Kant's pantheistic conception of God." Dell'Oro rejects this suggestion on the grounds of an alleged "contradiction," whereby Labèrge portrays Kant as attributing both necessity and contingency to "the things of nature." But if we treat this instead as an intentional paradox, then we can accept it as Kant's implicit acknowledgment of the analytic a posteriori, which, as I shall argue in Chapter 11, is (albeit, only implicitly) a key component of his Critical mysticism.

5. *RBBR* 6.174; see also *CF* 7.54–57. On the importance of Kant's use of "*Schwärmerei*," see p.4, above.

6. It is relevant to note here that Kant's theory in *RBBR* of a *moral* interpretation of Scripture has a close parallel in some medieval theologians, who referred to this type of interpretation as revealing the "*sensus mysticus* of a scriptural passage" (Cassirer 1918, 389). Unfortunately, Cassirer falls into the common trap of dismissing such interpretations as leading "into a mere mystical darkness" (390), rather than as providing extreme clarity, as mystics claim they do.

7. I implicitly defend this way of reading Kant's theory of religion in Part Three of *KCR* and throughout *CCKR*. See especially *KCR* 135, 239–42. The point is not that Kant was an orthodox Christian, but that his theory of religion attempts to provide a philosophcal grounding that can transform Christianity into a rational system that is more viable, more worthy of assent than orthodox interpretations of Christianity often tend to be.

8. *CF* 7.102; see also 113–14. For an analysis of the role of pure intuition in Kant's theory of mathematics, see SP–87d.

9. After mentioning Kant's quotation of Wilmans' letter, Hare (1996, 48) surmises: "Perhaps Kant was a 'pure mystic!'" Adamantly opposed to this obvious implication of Kant's Appendix, Wood (1996, 331) claims (without argument) that it was "absurd" for Wilmans to

have suggested "that there might be an affinity between Kantian moral religion and any form of religious mysticism." But Kant was sufficiently interested in such a possibility that he sent Wilmans' doctoral dissertation on Kantian mysticism (Wilmans 1797) to his friend Jachmann (a Lutheran pastor) and asked for an assessment. Jachmann 1804 is, admittedly, a scathing refutation of Wilmans' claims. But Kant's Preface to that work (*PJE*, the last published work that Kant himself ever wrote) carefully avoids an explicit endorsement of Jachmann's conclusions. For details, see my forthcoming article on *PJE* in the *Cambridge Kant Lexicon*. For further reasons to reject Wood's hasty dismissal, see de Vries 2002, 82–83n. Peter Byrne is another contemporary Kant interpreter who acknowledges a mystical "strand" (2007, 55) or "streak" (171) in Kant's philosophy. For a detailed discussion of the implication of Wilmans's position for a proper understanding of Kant's view of mysticism, see Kvist 2008, 115–20.

Chapter Seven

Immediate Experience of the Moral

Kant's Critical philosophy bases belief in God not on theoretical proof, but on an existential *"conviction* that dawns most spontaneously in all minds."[1] We are now in a position to consider to what extent this conviction exhibits the sort of immediate experience of the transcendent that mystics often claim to have. As Norburn (1973, 432) puts it: "Kant himself never doubted the existence of a Supreme Being. . . . He claimed that our awareness of God came by another route, a route not open (like logic) to the clever devil." Indeed, Kant sometimes uses phrases that imply some sort of communicative relationship between God and human beings,[2] as does his definition of religion in terms of regarding "all human duties as divine commands" (*RBBR* 6.84, 110; see also 153). In *LE* Kant speaks of ethical laws as being determined by the mutual participation of God and human beings in practical reason, the power that establishes the moral law in each individual.[3] And in *Lectures on the Philosophical Doctrine of Religion* (*LPDR*) Kant describes this mutual participation in terms that sometimes border on the mystical, as when he claims that, in order for religious belief to be meaningful, one must believe in a God who *acts* upon human beings, but that the only way to conceive of a timeless God doing so would be to think of God's interaction with us as taking place in "one action" that extends simultaneously throughout all time (28.1096). Thus it should come as no surprise when Kant says in *Metaphysics of Morals* (*MM* 6.491): "The question of what sort of moral relation holds between God and the human being goes completely beyond the bounds of ethics and is altogether incomprehensible for us." Ward (1972, 158) somehow construes this to mean that God and human beings *are not related*. Yet Kant's point surely is that a *relation holds* between God and mankind, even though the nature of such a relation is "incomprehensible" when viewed from the theoretical standpoint; it must be *experienced* in order to be believed.

Kant's favorite idiom for expressing the relation between human beings and God, an idiom he employs on numerous occasions in his later writings, is that the "voice of God" speaks to human beings through their common participation in practical reason. The question as to how this "voice" is experienced—i.e., as an inner feeling, as an audible voice, or even as accompanying an apparition—is not important, as long as the person who experiences it recognizes that it comes not as a theoretically *knowable* communication, but through an immediate encounter with our "morally legislative reason" (see e.g., A819/B847). To let our activity be guided by this mysterious, inwardly impelling force or spirit (i.e., by practical reason) *is* to let ourselves be guided by God.

The claim that God's voice comes to us immediately, through practical reason, provides us with a negative principle for assessing alleged mystical experiences. Kant makes this point briefly in *RBBR* 6.187, where he warns against listening to a presumed apparition of God if it recommends a course of action that bears "the risk of violating a human duty." He explains the point at greater length in *CF* 7.63:

> For if God should really speak to a human being, the latter could still never *know* that it was God speaking. It is quite impossible for a human being to apprehend the infinite by his senses, distinguish it from sensible beings, and *be acquainted with* it as such. — But in some cases the human being can be sure that the voice he hears is *not* God's; for if the voice commands him to do something contrary to the moral law, then no matter how majestic the apparition may be, and no matter how it may seem to surpass the whole of nature, he must consider it an illusion.

Kant's approach to visions of God draws attention away from the theoretical and toward the practical, as usual, in order to guard against delirium and its cousin, religious delusion.[4] But his references to this "voice" are by no means *entirely* negative. On the contrary, he associates it with a specific judicial faculty of the human mind, called "conscience."

Kant describes conscience in *LPed* 9.495 as "the representative of God, who has erected a sublime seat above us but also a judge's seat within us." That it belongs to the *judicial* wing of Kant's System, functioning as "a tribunal" to which everyone can appeal, is evident from the fact that Kant describes it as "an instinct" (and thus not "a free faculty") that mediates between the faculty of understanding in its role of "judging whether a thing is right or wrong," and "the moral feeling" in its role as "a faculty of liking and disliking, to judge concerning ourselves, no less than others, what is pleasing or displeasing" (*LE* 27.296–97). "The *consciousness*, therefore, that an action *which I want to undertake* is right is an unconditional duty. . . . One could define conscience also as follows: it is *moral self-judgmental discernment* [die sich selbst richtende moralische Urtheilskraft]" (*RBBR* 6.185–86). Through this "consciousness of an *internal court* in the human being" (*MM* 6.438, 560), God is revealed to be both transcendent ("above us") and immanent ("in us").[5] Kant does not *identify* conscience with God; rather "conscience must be thought of as the subjective principle of being accountable to God for all one's deeds" (439), for "I, the prosecutor and yet the accused as well, am the same *human being*" (439n). God, when regarded as the third person in the Trinity (*RBBR* 6.145n), is "the actual judge of human beings (before their conscience)." For "the judge of human beings as presented in his divinity (the Holy Spirit) . . . speaks to our conscience in terms of the holy law recognized by us" (140n). "The inner tribunal is correct; it looks at the action for itself, and without regard to human frailty, if only we are willing to hear and feel its voice" (*LE* 27.295); for conscience commands on God's behalf in accordance with the moral law.

This experience of the voice of God can always be trusted as a person's "guideline" (*RBBR* 6.185); the problem is to be certain that the voice one appeals to for guidance really has its source in conscience: "an erring conscience is an absurdity . . . I can indeed err in the judgment *in which I believe* to be right, for this belongs to the understanding which alone judges objectively (rightly or wrongly); but in the judgment *whether I in fact believe* to be right (or merely pretend it) I absolutely cannot be mistaken" (*MPT* 8.268). It is potentially misleading, however, to interpret Kant as saying that "God's will cannot be . . . ascertained otherwise than through our conscience" (Webb 1926, 86); for Kant does not mean that we cannot learn of God's will in any other way, but only that whatever the outward form (e.g., a passage from Scripture, a sermon, or even an apparition), the *validation* that it is from God occurs when we can recognize the message as sourced in an immediate encounter with conscience. If a message touches the depths of our being (i.e., if it speaks to our practical reason, via conscience), we are justified in treating it as coming from God. In proposing this view, Kant is not freeing individuals to follow the whims of their desires so long as they convince themselves not to feel guilty. That would be to *ignore* the voice of conscience, which is essentially a voice that requires us to subject our actions and choices to the *corpus mysticum*, the idea of all human beings as members of a universal body, wherein they mutually seek to promote the highest good.[6] Rather, the ultimate goal of all reflection—and so also of doing philosophy—is to learn how to distinguish properly the voice of God from the impure incentives that speak against the moral law. Along these lines Kant says in *EAT* 8.336 that "*Wisdom*, that is, practical reason using means commensurate to the final end of all things—the highest good—in full accord with the corresponding rules of measure, dwells in God alone; and the only thing which could perhaps be called human wisdom is acting in a way which is not visibly contrary to the idea of that [divine] wisdom."

Kant's theory of conscience as God's means of judging individuals is entirely consistent with Jesus' teaching about judgment in the Sermon on the Mount. Both insist "it is impossible for us, with certainty, to infer from another person's actions the degree of that person's virtuous conviction. He who sees into the inmost chambers of the heart has reserved for Himself alone the right to pass judgement on others."[7] Along these lines Kant criticizes the tendency of some clergy to impose non-universalizable rules onto the laity's conscience (*RBBR* 6.133n): this tendency (unlike the rules imposed by a purely political authority figure) can "prohibit even thought, and really also prevent it," especially when it assumes that doubting theoretical doctrines "would be tantamount to lending an ear to the evil spirit." For a person can become aware of "the judgment of the future judge (conscience awakening within himself, along with the empirical self-cognition [he has] summoned)" not by examining the correctness of various theoretical beliefs, but only by discerning "the lifestyle that he has really led" (77). This implies that God judges us on the basis of the judgment of conscience, a view that seems also to be implied by Jesus' proclamation that "in the way you judge [yourself and others], you will be judged [by God]; and by your standard of measure, it shall be measured to you" (Matt. 7:2). In any case, Kant's understanding of the role of conscience provides significant evidence that his concern is not only with "the rational 'form' for the decision-making procedure that a Christian would follow, anyway, . . . if he acted fully in accordance with Jesus' teachings" (Thomas 1970, 195)—a description that does accurately describe a key aspect of Kant's strategy in constructing his practical philosophy—but also with the existential experience of the divine–human encounter.

Further evidence of Kant's concern for understanding the experience of a human encounter with the divine can be gleaned from his discussion of "devotion," understood as "the mediate relation of the heart to God"—"not an act, but a method of making oneself ready for actions" (*LE* 27.315). I discussed this theme at length in *KCR* §VIII.3.B and Appendix VII.4 (see also *CCKR*, §12.2). Here it will suffice to recall Kant's view of devotion as an effective way of preparing oneself to act, rather than as a way of manipulating God. (Kant's special term for the latter tendency is "*Andächtelei*," which I translate as "devotionality"—i.e., an attempt to curry favor from God through acts of "sincere" devotion, but without changing the moral basis of one's choices and actions.) This is precisely the emphasis mystics often put on spiritual exercises such as meditation, prayer, and fasting. Most mystics use such disciplines not to *grasp* God, nor to render themselves well-pleasing to God, but to open themselves up to the immediate presence of God, so that the ordinary actions of their everyday life become imbued with what in some religious traditions is called divine energy. Kant's advocacy of such Critical mysticism comes to the fore when, as I argued more fully in *KCR* Appendix VIII, he portrays true prayer as arising only for those who first recognize that "God is manifestly aware of our needs, and the nature of our convictions [*Gesinnungen*]" (*LE* 27.323, alt.): "The setting forth of our convictions in words is equally useless, since God sees what is innermost in us." If Kant were demonizing all mysticism, as if there were no grain of truth in it, then his account of prayer would end here. But it does not; instead, he goes on to develop a theory of the subjective usefulness of prayer for those who have experienced the power of Critique. For as a discipline that can form a legitimate part of a rational religion, prayer as well as other forms of devotional exercises can "kindle morality in the innermost heart" (323).

The traditional view, that "a private relation to God . . . is in Kant's eyes incompatible with sound morality and sane reason" (Webb 1926, 155–56), is based on a seriously flawed interpretation of Kant's Critique of mysticism. Kant's position actually *encourages* a *personal* (i.e., practically verifiable) relation between God and human individuals, through our mutual participation in morality; he objects only to the supposition of a *public* (i.e., scientifically verifiable) relation, based on a supposed empirical intuition of God. Thus, he begins the General Comment to the Third Piece of *RBBR* (6.137) by claiming that anyone who probes into the "inward make-up" of a historical faith that has genuine (moral) religion at its core "inevitably comes upon a *mystery*, i.e., upon something *holy*, [in other words,] something which can indeed be *known* by each individual, but which nonetheless cannot be publicly *familiar*, i.e., communicated universally." This is not only inevitable but quite acceptable, philosophically, as long as we understand that this experience of the "*holy* . . . must be a moral object" and is therefore "to be sufficiently cognized inwardly for practical use, yet as something *mysterious*, not for theoretical use, because then it would have to be also communicable to everyone and thus also able to become familiar outwardly and publicly." Thus, when he criticizes "the tendency of prayer to turn God, the proper object of faith, into an object of intuition" (Ward 1972, 63; referring to *LE* 27.338), Kant is not arguing that *any* attempt at "fellowship with [God]" is "imaginary" (Ward 1972, 62; see also Webb 1926, 155), but that a religious person's encounter in such fellowship (which in itself is neither practical nor theoretical, but *immediate*) can be adequately explained only if we interpret it as being *rooted* in practical reason. Far from denying the validity of a fellowship based on practical faith, Kant actually *defends* its sufficiency: "We know God, not by intuition, but through faith. . . . To be sure, faith is just as strong as intuition" (*LE* 27.337–38; see also *RBBR* 6.52).

Kant comes close to allowing us to have an actual intuition of God when he explains the nature of physico–theological proofs for God's existence "by connecting speculation with intuition" (A637/B665). But he is careful to warn that this does not provide us with objectively valid theoretical knowledge, but only "a preparation of the understanding for theological cognition," if used as a supplement to "other proofs" (e.g., the moral argument of *CPrR*). This suggests that we may be able to *intuit* God, even though it is impossible to verify that the object of our intuition really is God. After citing this passage, Hicks (1974, 385, 397n) quotes from *LPDR* 28.1048, where Kant explains that the teleological conception of God is based on "the experience which . . . is the simplest experience there could be, namely, the knowledge of our self."

In a helpful clarification of the implications of Kant's theory of intuition for mystical experience, Robert Oakes argues that when a person experiences God as present in some sensible object (1973, 37)—as, for example, in the sound of church bells ringing—the person is "having a *sensible* experience of God, i.e., in Kantian terms, God must be understood as the object of her 'sensible intuition.'" In such a case, "the experience of God *supervenes* upon the experience of the bells. . . . That is, in so far as the experience of the bells is *at the same time* an experience of God, the woman would thereby be having a *sensible* experience of God." Oakes is right to regard both the hearing of the bells and the experience of God as "mediated" experiences. But his view of "God as a possible object of sensible intuition" (37) is mistaken inasmuch as it fails to take into account the perspectival difference between these two types of mediated experiences. Bells can mediate in our experience of God by pointing indirectly to something *nonsensible* beyond them: they remain symbols of a transcendent ideal that can never become an object of empirical cognition. Yet the mediate element in our experience of the bells *as bells*—i.e., the sensible intuition of the bells ringing—points *literally* to a real sensible object, which gives rise to our empirical cognition. From the Perspective of immediate (nonreflective) experience, both of these are equally valid. The fundamental difference between them is revealed as soon as we reflect upon them theoretically: our sensible intuition of the bells points "forward" to a publicly verifiable empirical cognition that can be viewed theoretically, whereas our awareness of God's presence in such an experience points "backward" to a transcendent and therefore theoretically unverifiable ground of all empirical cognition.

This clarification of the implications of Kant's position provides an effective response to the criticism that is so frequently leveled against Kant, that his epistemology bars human beings from *any* experience of God. This common assumption is well-expressed by Rudolph Otto: "It is one thing merely to believe in a reality beyond the senses and another to have experience of it also; it is one thing to have ideas of 'the holy' and another to become consciously aware of it as an operative reality, intervening actively in the phenomenal world."[8] As we have already seen, Webb (1926, 22) reads Kant as defending the former option in each pair: "With Science and with Morality one feels that Kant was completely at home. . . . With Aesthetics, and with Religion . . .the case is otherwise. The circumstances of his life denied Kant any extensive experience of visible beauty, whether natural or wrought by art." He adds that, in spite of his "congenital incapacity for much that is most characteristically religious," Kant's philosophy of religion "is epoch-making in theology" (24; see also 60). Similarly, Hedge (1849, 58) portrays Kant as a man without much personal experience of life when he remarks: "no sage ever lived" who was "more purely secluded within himself."

Such judgments appear to be supported by the well-known biographical details of Kant's life: the fact that he never traveled more than ten or twenty miles from his birthplace in Königsberg;[9] his rigidly structured daily schedule, so "mechanically regular" (Hedge 1849, 58) that his neighbors supposedly set their clocks by his daily comings and goings;[10] and his lack of church attendance (see e.g., Klinke 1952, 38,43; see also note 7.11, below). Yet none of these traits makes Kant a "philistine," as Heine (1959, 111, 270; cf. *CJ* 5.229) claims. On the contrary, many mystics would say travel only makes it more difficult to maintain the mystical center of one's experience (i.e., one's spiritual "home"). Surely one does not have to view natural wonders such as the Grand Canyon or Mount Everest in order to appreciate God's presence in a blade of grass: the most ordinary landscape is quite capable of evoking a deep (mystical) response from a person who is intimately familiar with it. And it is typically not the philistine but the mystic who lives in a highly disciplined, seemingly self-enclosed way; for a self-disciplined life provides the proper context for discerning the voice of God in the midst of the ambient noise of one's own inclinations. Moreover, it seems extraordinarily odd to assume that someone who is capable of expounding the rational heart of the Christian message, as Kant did so profoundly in *RBBR* (see *KCR*, Chapters VIII and IX), was himself uninterested in—to say nothing of congenitally *incapable* of!—religious experience as such. Instead, we should read Kant along the lines suggested by Gene Fendt, who describes the *Critiques* (1990, 85) "as a kind of spiritual exercises, for their aim is to discipline Reason." Indeed, it is highly significant that the first chapter of *CPR*'s Transcendental Doctrine of Method is entitled "The *Discipline* of Pure Reason," for the most highly self-disciplined forms of religious practice are typically *mystical* in character. The problem is that undisciplined religious *dreamers* are also often called "mystics." *Critical* mysticism is Kant's way of *disciplining* a lazy reason's dreams.

If we ignore the well-known caricatures of Kant, mentioned above, and consider the facts carefully and with an open mind, there turns out to be ample evidence that he not only *believed* in the reality of the transcendent God represented by reason's theoretical idea, manifested in our practical reason (speaking through conscience), and communing with us in prayer, but also *encountered* this reality in his daily life. Even Webb admits "there is no doubt that Kant could . . . have given in all sincerity an affirmative reply to the question": "Whether he feared God from his heart" (1926, 28). Manolesco 1969 portrays Kant as "a religious man" who "knew the voice of God in the depth of his conscience" (28; see also Despland 1973, 18, 111–12, 267). Similarly, Loades (1981, 299) says Kant's "life's work [was] completed in homage to the deity." And Gabriele Rabel supports this view with a moving story:

> Kant was a profoundly religious man. . . . When Kant had discovered that in a bad summer swallows threw some of their own young out of the nest in order to keep the others alive, he said: "My intelligence stood still. There was nothing to do but to fall on one's knees and worship."[11]

To a nonmystical person, out of touch with the voice of God in conscience, the voice of the *corpus mysticum* that calls us to see every event as an aspect of the unified whole that encompasses everything, the observation that swallows had sacrificed their own young would be more likely to evoke confusion or disgust with the senseless misfortunes of nature than an attitude of worship. Yet for Kant, who believed we should always try "to discover the good in evil" (*LPed* 9.495), it evoked an overwhelming sense of divine Providence (see *KCR*, Appendix VI.1, and *HPE* 1.431). Notably, it evoked this response of reverential fear precisely because *he was unable to understand it*: reason rests in the face of immediate experience; yet we encounter this rest as much in death as in birth, for every death *is* a new birth, when reason remains open to a vision of wholeness. This is the Perspective affirmed by Kant's Critical mysticism.

Kant expresses the twofold aspect of his mystical worldview most clearly with his famous exclamation in *CPrR* 5.162 (emphases added to second sentence; cf. *CJ* 5.482n):

> Two things fill the mind with ever new and increasing admiration and reverence, the more often and more steadily one reflects on them: *the starry heavens above me and the moral law within me*. I do not need to search for them and merely *conjecture* them as though they were veiled in obscurity or in the transcendent region beyond my horizon; I *see* them before me and connect them *immediately* with the consciousness of my existence.

A statement of such depth could be made only by a person who had spent long hours contemplating the hand of God in nature and the voice of God in conscience. Kant most likely intends the starry heavens and the moral law to symbolize the unknowable mysteries (or noumenal Mystery) that undergird(s) his theoretical and practical systems, respectively. As we have already examined the way conscience functions as the purveyor of the moral law, let us turn now to the first *Critique* for evidence of mysteries that may have similarly sparked his "admiration and reverence."

In *CPR* Kant depicts several a priori elements or functions of the mind as ultimately mysterious. In A141/B180–81, for example, he describes "schematism of our understanding" as "a hidden art in the depths of the human soul, whose true operations we can divine from nature and lay unveiled before our eyes only with difficulty." Along these lines, Heidegger 1929 identifies imagination as the key mystery underlying all the machinations of Kant's theory of knowledge and thus giving rise to Kant's self-confessed admiration. An even more plausible option, however, can be found by taking note of the sections of *CPR* that most captured Kant's own attention in an "ever new and increasing" way—namely, "The Deduction of the Pure Concepts of Understanding" and the "Paralogisms of Pure Reason," because (other than the Preface and the Introduction) these are the only major sections of *CPR* that Kant almost completely rewrote for the second edition. The common factor between these two sections is that in both Kant devotes considerable attention to discussing the implications of what he calls "the radical faculty of all our cognition, namely, transcendental apperception" (A114). This clue suggests that his sense of "I," as the subjective source of the categories, is the "brute fact" that constitutes the ultimate limit of his theoretical system, and is therefore the best theoretical counterpart to the moral law: the "I" generates the reverence we feel when we observe the starry heavens, just as it does when we encounter the moral law.

Kant's treatment of what he calls the "unity of apperception" does indeed have a certain mystical flavor. For the concept refers not simply to the ordinary person's empirical sense of "I," but to a deeper, *transcendental* limit of all human experience—a limit that comes into view only as we gradually *forget* about (i.e., hold in abeyance) the empirical diversity of our ordinary experiences. And this, like Kant's overall a priori approach, is remarkably similar to the claim of many mystics, that in order to encounter God (cf. answer philosophical questions) we must first go through an experience of *unknowing*. Meister Eckhart, for instance, says (Walshe 1982, 7):

> the more completely you are able to draw in your powers to a unity and *forget* all those things and their images which you have absorbed . . . the nearer you are to this [encounter] and the readier to receive it. To achieve an interior act, a man must collect all his powers into a corner of his soul . . . *hiding away* from all images and forms. . . . Here, he must come to a *forgetting* and an *un*knowing.

Forman 1988 examines this process of forgetting in some detail, noting that it eventually serves to *revitalize* the very details of life that had been "forgotten" (263). (More recently, Fischer 2017 has thoroughly examined the close relation between Kant and Eckhart. See also Moskopp 2019, who focuses on the mystical implications of Kant's theory of apperception.) In the same way, the "I think" is for Kant the thought-less core or starting point of all thought; apperception is the perceptionless perception of a unitary "I" that enables us to become aware of all our perceptions. As such, it *establishes* the (Transcendental) Perspective that empowers us to view the empirical details of human cognition in a self-conscious, enlightened way.

The role of transcendental apperception as an element in Kant's description of his experience of "admiration and reverence" is actually implicit in the text quoted above from *CPrR* 5.161–62. For he says "the starry heavens above *me* and the moral law within *me*" give rise to this mystical encounter; I, too, will experience them with reverence only if (and because) "I . . . connect them *immediately* with the consciousness of my existence"—that is, only if I encounter them as "at one" with the deepest layer of my self-identity, the functioning of transcendental apperception within me. That this encounter is *immediate* is confirmed in the fragment on inner sense, where Kant describes apperception as follows: "I am immediately and originally conscious of myself as an entity in the world" (*IS* 257). But because this aspect of Kant's mystical reverence remains merely implicit, I shall devote the next chapter to a closer look at two objects of Critical meditation that Kant acknowledges more explicitly.

The foregoing account of Kant's two sources of admiration and awe seems to fit best with his own explanation in *CPrR*. However, there is another alternative. For what fills the mind with reverence is neither empirical cognition of the stars nor moral activity as such, but rather a meditative observation of how these wonders operate in our immediate experience. And that relates more to *CJ* than to *CPR*. If "the starry heavens" correlates not to the limits of the *theoretical* standpoint, but rather to the limits of the *judicial* standpoint (i.e., not to *CPR* but to *CJ* [see e.g., Walsh 1963, 265]), then the problem becomes one of discovering something in the *latter* system that Kant views with "ever new and increasing admiration and reverence." But even if we grant that Kant was most likely associating the starry heavens with our theoretical cognition of nature, we can still ask: Is there a third object of meditation corresponding to Kant's judicial system? This is a debatable question. A negative answer is suggested by the fact that his judicial system is concerned not with knowledge, but with *feelings*. "Feelings are not cognitions and therefore also do not designate a mystery" (*RBBR* 6.138). Kant's explanations in *CJ* of purposiveness in nature and of beauty as the "symbol of morality" (see *CJ* 5.351–54 and *KSP* §§IX.2–3) could therefore be regarded as attempts to justify, from the judicial standpoint, the *feelings* of reverence that arise out of meditation on the *mysteries* of his theoretical and practical systems. For if Kant can be said to have had any mystical experiences himself, they arose through his lifelong habit of baring all in reason's light, revealing the bare necessities of conscience and nature to his Critical gaze, not through blind acceptance of the clothing of religious tradition. This observation can explain why he initially chose aesthetics and teleology, rather than more traditional forms of religion, as two of the main topics of *CJ*, the *Critique* that should be the closest to answering the essentially *religious* question, "What may I hope?" (see *KSP* §XI.1). Indeed, Kant seems to confirm the common assumption that beauty and natural purposiveness are really the *main* topics when he states in *CJ* 5.482n (see also *MM* 6.483): "The admiration of the beauty as well as the emotion aroused by the so diverse ends of nature . . . have something similar to a *religious* feeling about them." But surely this is not the whole story, for *CJ* itself does convey a candidate for a third object of Critical meditation that also has distinctly religious features.

This third aspect, being tucked away at the center of *CJ*, is often ignored in discussions of Kant's theology or philosophy of religion: it is his theory of the *sublime*.[12] William Hund makes up for this neglect, though he regards the appeal to morality as "a distortion of the experience of the sublime" necessitated solely by "Kant's architectonic" (1983, 68). This criticism collapses when, as I have argued in *KSP* and *KCR*, we regard Kant's appeal to reason's architectonic unity as a positive rather than a negative bias; moreover, Kant's position can be strengthened by recognizing that it does not require a person who experiences the sublime to have a conscious *awareness* of being morally good; the point instead is that it is a transcendental condition of the possibility of experiencing the sublime for it to be *possible* for us to be morally good, for the "supersensible" substrate of our existence that we encounter through such experiences is the very aspect of our nature that enables us to be moral. Without defending his negative claim to the contrary, Hund opines that the assumption of a formless (mystical) "Presence in nature" (68–69) could readily *replace* Kant's appeal to the moral law to explain our experience of the sublime. But once we regard this "Presence" (being, in my view, the very reality Kant calls "the supersensible") as also the source of our practical reason, shining its light on every aspect of our experience of the world, there is no longer a need to choose one or the other.

In an earlier passage, Hund (1983, 43) observes that none of the (then) major commentators on *CJ* had "once mentioned the idea of God in Kant's theory of the sublime." In *OFBS* even Kant himself did not "mention the idea of God in the experience of the sublime" (Hund 1983, 46). Nevertheless, "the idea of infinity . . . is essential for the experience of the sublime" (56) and "the infinite itself is thought of as the supersensible substrate of nature. In other words, we have passed over to the Ideal of Pure Reason where the Infinite Being is the common substratum of Nature" (56–57). This supports the claim that Kant's account of the sublime is one of his key examples of how we *encounter* the hand of God in nature. After all, as Hund again notes, "Kant did explicitly mention God as manifesting His wrath and sublimity in natural events"—i.e., in the dynamically sublime, but not in the "mathematically sublime" (57).

Kant's theory of the sublime is thus closely associated with what is traditionally referred to as the fear of God—a type of fear that is very different from ordinary fear. As Hund (1983, 62n) notes, Kant's first connection of God with the sublime comes as early as *CJ* 5.263, where both God and the sublime are depicted as "a source of fear" (Hund 1983, 59); in both cases, if "our own position is secure," the experience makes the object "all the more attractive," yet "[t]o be actually afraid would exclude the experience of sublimity." For, as Hund speculates (60), the Kantian source of our security in the face of an experience of the sublime is our immortality, though he admits Kant does not explicitly state this. Through such experiences, "objects in nature reveal to us a supersensible faculty" (60). "In the . . . dynamically sublime," Hund adds (62), "the infinite power in nature is considered to be God." Hund makes the significant point (63) that we only need to be afraid of the sublime's power if we have not lived a morally good life, because then the prospects of a final judgment are daunting. This is the source of the sublime's deep relation to the practical standpoint. As such, Kant regards "a morally upright conviction [*Gesinnung*]" as being "a second necessary condition for the experience of the sublime (the first was physical safety)" (63, alt.). Against Kant, Hund argues "that God in nature appears as a non-moral force" because the thought of being judged "by God after death is certainly extraneous to the experience" of both types of sublimity (67). Hund may well be correct here. But Kant might counter that such a morally charged thought *ought* to be present in anyone who wishes to appreciate the sublime *and* interpret the experience rationally, in terms of the wholeness of the *corpus mysticum*.

Adopting an explicitly Kantian (Transcendental) Perspective, Otto (1950, 45,112–14) expounds in more detail the implications of this view of religious feeling. Otto's claim that our deep religious (or other mystical) experiences have an essentially *mysterious* (i.e., nonrational and even nonmoral) factor might seem to be a direct rejection of Kant's emphasis on *reason* as the source of both natural and moral knowledge. But in fact they are almost entirely consistent. Otto's account of Kant's statements regarding the impact of conscience and nature on his philosophical feeling would be something like this. Kant experiences reverence when confronted with the moral law and starry skies because he recognizes these as symbols of a transcendent, mysterious source of the two sides of human existence. They represent the two "brute facts" against which we "bump our heads," so to speak, in our efforts to encounter the one ultimate Reason that gives rise to human reason. This Reason *creates* nature and *creates* morality, but is it itself rational and moral? The fundamental tenet of Kant's theoretical philosophy is that *we cannot know the answer* to such a question. And that is precisely why our *experience* of these two limits, in the process of doing Critique, arouses such "admiration and reverence"! (This paradoxical situation often arises, incidentally, when a fundamental principle is tested for self-referential consistency: the principle itself cannot be coherently submitted to the criteria it imposes.) Once the perspectival character of Kant's thinking is taken into account, it becomes clear that he would have no trouble accepting such an explanation of his deepest experiences. "Reason" is Kant's name for the ultimately unknowable mystery that generates all our human capacities for knowledge and goodness.[13] To be mystical in a *Critical* sense, therefore, is to allow our reason to strip away the clothing of bias and private interest that tends to masquerade as knowledge and goodness, in order to bathe oneself in the pure light of wholeness that shines forth from this distinctly human faculty. With this overarching clothing metaphor in mind, let us now look at some of the other metaphors that guide Kant's Critical mysticism.

NOTES

1. Peccorini 1972, 64. For a detailed explanation and defense of Kant's approach to proving God's existence, see *KCR* §IV.4 and Appendix IV.1–3.

2. Kant's students, for example, recorded him as using phrases such as "God says..." (*LE* 27.322) on numerous occasions (see also *CF* 7.67). In a letter he wrote to the censor, in response to the accusation that his writings (especially *RBBR*) cast religion in general and especially Christianity in a bad light, which he then published in the Preface to his next religiously oriented book (*CF* 7.9–10), Kant shares that he thinks of a divine judge as looking over his shoulder, as a way of empowering conscience: "When composing my writings, I have always pictured this judge as standing at my side to keep me not only from error that corrupts the soul, but even from any careless expression that might give offense; for which reason now, in my seventy-first year, when I can hardly help thinking that I may well have to answer for this very soon to a judge of the world who scrutinizes men's hearts, I can frankly present this account of my teachings . . . as composed with the utmost *conscientiousness*." Several similar expressions of his concern for attending to matters of conscience, in the form of a divine judge residing within us to empower our moral conviction by making us self-judgmental, occur in *RBBR* (e.g., 6.70n, 74, 116, 145–46n, 186); see also *CCKR* 525–26.

3. Kant declares that the laws of ethics (as opposed to political laws) "have no relation at all to other people, but only to God and oneself" (*LE* 27.280).

4. In the Fourth Piece of *RBBR* Kant devotes much of his attention to the task of exposing the danger of religious delusion. Whereas "delirium" refers to a false way of *feeling* when engaged in a religious experience, "delusion" refers to a false way of *thinking* about religion and/or religious experience.

5. This dual aspect of the relation between God and human beings is the key to understanding Kant's theory of religious symbolism—a point I argue in further detail in *KCR* §V.1–2.

6. Kant's first formulation of the categorical imperative, the precept that we must always act in such a way that the maxim guiding our action could become a universal law, is often maligned as being the source of an unacceptable "formalism" in Kant's ethics. However, once we recognize its grounding in Kant's theory of conscience, it becomes clear that the formula of universalizability is a crucial application of Kant's Critical mysticism: if we see ourselves as members of a *mystical body* of human beings who share a common destiny, then we *will* limit our moral choices to those that any member of the body could adopt. To make oneself an exception in moral situations is to withdraw oneself from the *corpus mysticum* of conscience. To highlight this feature of Kant's theory of conscience, my translation of *RBBR* takes Kant's

use of *"Gewissen"* (which he normally uses with the definite article; literally "the conscience") as an abstract noun. That is, whereas other translators often render the definite article loosely, as "his" or "our," I normally omit the article altogether in order to show that Kant is referring not to an individual's unique conscience—if such were possible!—but to the "transpersonal moral reality" of conscience–in–general (see *CCKR* 187n).

7. *ICNM* 2.200, alt.; cf. Matt. 6:1, 16 and 7:1–5. For a more thorough discussion of the relation between the moral precepts of Kant and Jesus, see *KCR*, Appendix V.2–4.

8. Otto 1950, 143; see also note 10.15. Chapman (1992, 502) defends Otto's approach as not being guilty of "the pathological response of mysticism whereby the individual was granted a direct *knowledge* of God." However, neither was Kant, and for essentially the same reasons; the whole point of Kant's *Critical* mysticism is that an encounter with God at some level is possible *without* involving empirical cognition.

9. The exact distance varies from one account to another. Hedge 1849 puts the distance at just "seven miles from his native city" (57–58).

10. See *KCR*, note IV.1. Bax (1891, xxxvi) says the period of Kant's highly regular lifestyle was mainly from 1783 to 1802. But Kuehn (2001, xi, 154–57, 219–23, 240–41) links the regularity of Kant's daily walks to his intimate friendship with the English merchant, Joseph Green, which lasted from around 1765 to Green's death in 1786.

11. Rabel 1963, vii; cf. Wisnefske 1990, 95. Wallace relates the same story in more detail in Wallace 1901, 53, adding that Kant once said "he had held a swallow in his hand, and gazed into its eyes; 'and as I gazed, it was as if I had seen into heaven.'" There are, of course, many who question the genuineness of Kant's faith, but these doubts are usually based on the interpreter *not* taking Kant's own words at face value, but instead judging him on the basis of conventional standards of religiosity. Bax, for example, observes (not entirely accurately): "He never . . . practised the rites of any *cultus*, public or private. He never attended church. . . . It must always remain a delicate question in how far Kant really believed in the necessity, nay, even the possibility, of a theology based solely on practical considerations" (Bax 1891, lxviii–lxix). Concerning Kant's moral proof, he further speculates that there may be "a Mephistopholic smile lurking somewhere between the lines." Having already responded in full to such claims in *KCR* §IV.1 and Appendix IV.3 (see also notes VIII.4, 34, and 49), I shall not comment further on them here.

12. For interesting interpretations of the sublime, see Tsang 1998 (who uses Kant as a springboard for his own analysis) and Clewis 2009. However, neither of these interpreters stakes a claim regarding the specifically *mystical* implications of Kant's theory.

13. See *KCR*, Appendix IV.4; *GMM* 4.461–62; Kroner 1956, 32; and Wisnefske 1990, 128.

Chapter Eight

Key Metaphors Guiding Kant's Critical Mysticism

We have already considered in some detail how, as Webb puts it (1926, 58), "Kant's attitude towards the moral law is always profoundly *religious*, full of . . . what Professor Otto . . . taught us to call *das Numinoses*" (see note 7.8). In *RBBR*, for example, Kant says the human soul regards "with the highest amazement" and with exalted "admiration . . . the original moral predisposition in us" (6.49), for "the ungraspableness of this predisposition" announces "a divine descent" (50). An autobiographical remark toward the end of his life shows that Kant put into practice the theory of conscience that, as we saw in the previous chapter, he develops in *RBBR* and elsewhere:

> . . . when composing my writings, I have always pictured this judge as standing at my side to keep me not only from error that corrupts the soul, but even from any careless expression that might give offence; for . . . now, in my seventy-first year, ... I can hardly help thinking that I may well have to answer for this very soon to a judge of the world who scrutinizes men's hearts (*CF* 7.9–10; see note 7.2, above).

This meditative attitude toward the moral law can be adequately summarized as an attempt not to know God, but to acknowledge and accept God's proper role as "a knower of hearts"—a designation Kant uses for God on numerous occasions.[1]

While Kant's religious interpretation of human morality is widely acknowledged (though often underplayed and treated with dismay or incredulity), commentators are usually not so aware of Kant's profoundly religious attitude toward nature. Webb (1926, 177), for instance, laments "that Kant did not more clearly perceive in his own attitude in the presence of the starry heavens a proof that Religion has other roots than the experience of moral obligation." However, the fact that Kant refuses to accept any theoretical proof as adequate to demonstrate the existence of God, and therefore insists that religion can claim a rational basis only in morality, does not mean he fails to appreciate the religious significance of our encounter with the substrate of nature. On the contrary, as I argued in *KSP* §IX.3 (see also *KCR*, §IV.3, and Appendix IV, note 14), Kant *admits* the force of the teleological argument for God's existence, as long as it is viewed as providing good *empirical reasons* for belief, rather than as an absolutely certain, theoretical proof. Surely, this indicates just as clear an appreciation for the presence of God in the experience of nature as in "the experience of moral obligation"— though in neither case is our feeling of such a presence a sufficient basis for theoretical proof. Indeed, evidence of Kant's meditative attitude toward nature can be found both in the details of his life and in the contents of his writings.

Kant's mother, whom he greatly respected, taught him at an early age to appreciate his natural surroundings.[2] As he once told his friend and first biographer, Jachmann: "she planted and tended the first seeds of good in me. She opened my heart to the impressions of nature; she awakened and widened my ideas, and her teachings have had an enduring, healing influence on my life" (Jachmann 1804, 99–100; trans. Klinke 1952, 16). This educational emphasis was no doubt an aspect of her Pietism, which "laid great stress on radical inwardness" and involved "intensity of emotion" (Crosby 1994, 122), though "the education of the will" was typically just as important. In his early adulthood (between 1746 and 1755) Kant worked as a live-in tutor for several wealthy families who lived on country estates near Königsberg.[3] During these seven or eight years, he must have had ample opportunity to tune his heart to "the impressions of nature," as his mother had taught him. As Kant was a theology student at Königsberg University—a fact strangely denied by McCarthy (1986, 59)—it should come as no surprise to find that he also preached sermons occasionally in the nearby village churches.[4] Along these lines, Manolesco 1969 says that before writing *DSS* "Kant had still maintained some mystic remnants from his youth" (14) and that by 1770, the year traditionally regarded as the starting-point of his Critical period (because, as we saw in Chapters 1 and 3, this is when he first applied what he later called his "Copernican" hypothesis), "he managed to rid himself completely of his mystic baggage" (20)—by which he is referring mainly to Kant's "painful" childhood years at a religious school (24–25). I argued in Part I that in writing *DSS* Kant's youthful "baggage" was not destroyed completely, but was *transformed*. As such, his Critical philosophy can be regarded as a *defense* of his mother's genuine faith *against* the domineering tendencies of his early teachers. McCarthy (1986, 58) expresses a similar notion: "Even as he was neither a deist nor an atheist, Kant was finally neither a pietist nor a mystic." But in place of "neither" I would say "not *merely*," for in a *Critical* sense, he was in each case paradoxically both: just as there are aspects of Kant's theism that strike many as closer to either deism or even atheism, so also there are aspects of his view of immediate experience that are closer to Pietism or mysticism than to the irreverent elitism that is often read into Kant's texts.[5]

Even after becoming a professor at the age of forty–six, Kant disciplined himself to break away from the lively conversation at his dinner table at 4pm in order to enjoy an hour or more of peaceful walking.[6] These daily walks he usually took in solitude, either along the river Pregel (on what is now called the "Philosophers' Embankment") or to the north–west of town along various garden paths (Wallace 1901, 40–41; Klinke 1952, 48). (He also enjoyed "going for excursions into the country surrounding his native town," especially to the "idyllic" forest just a mile to the northeast, where in 1764 he composed *OFBS*, his pre-Copernican essay on aesthetic feeling [Klinke 1952, 27–28].) As he walked, he was careful to keep his mouth closed and breathe through his nose, because he believed this could help prevent disease—but perhaps also as an excuse for walking alone in silence (49). (Kant describes his attitude toward the proper relation between thinking, walking, and eating in *CF* 7.109–10, adding an interesting footnote about "*drinking air*" through the nose (110–11n).) Such an interest in disciplined breathing, practiced during periods of silence and solitude, is likely to give rise to a religious experience of some sort, even if one is not consciously fostering a mystical bent, as these are all typical examples of the type of discipline practiced by mystics. Furthermore, Kant usually fasted on "nothing but water" in between the one meal he ate each day.[7] That Kant may have been more conscious of the spiritual benefit of his disciplined lifestyle than is generally recognized is suggested by the fact that, upon returning home from his walks, he would spend the next few hours doing what could well be called *contemplation*: "As darkness began to fall, he would take his seat at the stove, and with his eye fixed on the tower of Loebenicht church would ponder on the problems which exercised his mind."[8]

The impact of Kant's contemplative mind-set on his attitude toward nature is clearly reflected in his writings on natural philosophy. For example, he says in *HPE* 1.431: "Man, to whom the husbandry of the Earth's surface has been entrusted, has the capacity [for contemplation and admiration of nature] and the desire to familiarize himself with them, and praises the Creator through his insights." The book that contains Kant's most important empirical insights into nature (i.e., *UNH*), proposing a revolutionary new nebular hypothesis of the universe (often called the Kant–Laplace theory), has at times an "almost mystical tone."[9] In the "Opening Discourse" Kant explicitly links his reflections to his own *experience* of the presence of God (*UNH* 1.221–22): "when I saw that with every step the mists dispersed . . . , the glory of the highest being shone forth with the most vivid brilliance." With such near-visionary experiences in his background, Kant's reputation as an inspiring orator should come as no surprise. Jachmann (1804, 79), for example, relates a story that the merchant Motherby told him, about a conversation he once heard between his business partner, Green, and Kant, who were discussing current political events: "in this speech Kant seemed to [Motherby] and to all present to be inspired by a heavenly power, which bound their hearts to him forever." This character trait of being or at least seeming to be inspired can be seen even in his early writings, for as Alison Laywine (1993, 124) observes, referring to Kant's treatment of issues relating to the mind–body problem, "the early Kant might have claimed to touch the intangible." While I have previously cast some doubt on certain aspects of Laywine's interpretation of Kant's early work (see *KCR*, Appendix II.2), she accurately testifies at this point to what I regard as Kant's inherently mystical tendencies. He exhibits this tendency as he draws his discussion in *UNH* to a close, exclaiming at one point that "the divinity . . . paints [*malt*] itself in all creatures" (1.360, alt.), thus hinting at the view he develops in *CJ* of nature as the artwork of God.[10] And in the final paragraph of *UNH* he makes one of his most profound statements relating to the mystical experience of the hand of God in nature (367, alt.): "In the universal stillness of nature and the calmness of the senses the immortal spirit's hidden faculty of cognition speaks an ineffable language and provides [us] undeveloped concepts that can certainly be felt but not described."

This attitude toward nature is by no means limited to Kant's early writings. In *ID* 2.410, when he had already applied the Copernican hypothesis to intuition, he nevertheless affirms that "we intuit all things in God"—an allusion to Baruch Spinoza repeated several times in *OP* as well (see Chapter 11). Far from giving up this view in his later life, Kant regarded his entire philosophical System as an explanation of its implications (see e.g., *MM* 6.482). Thus, in his lengthy discussion of prayer in the General Comment to *RBBR*'s Fourth Piece, we find a passage that is reminiscent of the foregoing quote from the end of *UNH*; toward the end of his life, he affirms (*RBBR* 6.197, emphasis added):

> Thus the contemplation of the profound wisdom of divine creation in the smallest things and of its majesty on the large scale . . . is such a power, not only to transfer the mind into that sinking mood, annihilating, as it were, the human being in his own eyes, the mood called *worship*, but also, in consideration of his own moral predetermination therein, a soul-elevating power, that words by comparison . . . would have to vanish like empty sound, because the feeling [arising] from such an *intuition of the hand of God* is ineffable.

The main difference between this and his earlier endorsements of the mystical contemplation of nature is that Kant now distinguishes between the delirious tendency to allow oneself to be *annihilated* by the mystical "vision" and the *Critical* mysticism whereby one accepts the inexpressible but immediate presence of God as a personal confirmation of the moral postulate of God's existence.

Adina Davidovich emphasizes the centrality of contemplation in Kant's Critical philosophy, claiming that *CJ*'s "purpose is to establish a perspective" that enables us to make sense of "purposiveness" (1993a, 25–26). "The solution is to be found in a type of contemplation that participates equally in" theoretical knowing and practical acting (26). This means (29) *CJ*'s "task is neither theoretical nor practical, but contemplative." For example (31), "in contemplating beautiful objects in nature we gain an awareness of something beyond it." Making frequent use of perspectival terminology (much like that used in *KSP*), Davidovich stresses that the key perspective in *CJ* is not God's, but humanity's (33): "this perspective is the status of the rational agent as an end in itself." From *CJ*'s standpoint (38), "reflective faith in grace . . . is . . . a belief that nature is ultimately conducive to the realization of moral ends. . . . [This] is not a practical ability; it becomes possible through the faculty of judgment." Hund 1983 likewise says (48): "the sublime" and "the beautiful" have in common that "both please" through "a contemplative kind of pleasure which is not a means to something else." When we take into consideration the fact that Kant's judicial system takes up the standpoint of Critique itself and is therefore the most fundamental of Kant's three standpoints (see *KSP* §IX.1), this view of the judicial standpoint as essentially contemplative fits right in with the notion that one of the main purposes of Kant's System is to pave the way for Critical mysticism.

If we now recall Schweitzer's definition of the mystic as the person who feels a connection with the eternal even "amid the earthly and temporal," and who encounters situations wherein this very division is somehow transcended (see Chapter 5), then we can safely conclude that Kant's deep awareness of the "beyond," toward which nature and conscience point us, qualifies him as being a mystic. A further confirmation of this conclusion comes in *MPT* 8.264, when the philosopher whose "bent" in life was supposedly "remote" from any emotional experience of God's presence[11] declares that, in the end, the only solution to the problem of evil is a full appreciation of God's presence in one's contemplative experience of nature ("the world") and conscience ("practical reason"):

> As a work of God, the world can also be considered by us as a divine publication of his will's *purposes*. . . . For through our reason [i.e., in the "*authentic theodicy*" provided by our moral encounter with God] God then becomes himself the interpreter of his will as announced through creation; . . . that is not the interpretation of a *ratiocinating* (speculative) reason, but of an efficacious practical reason which . . . can be considered as the unmediated definition and voice of God through which he gives meaning to the letter of his creation.

The final confirmation of the mystical character of Kant's worldview will require a thoroughgoing examination of *OP*, for in that work Kant attempts to realize his long-standing dream (cf. Part I) of establishing a Critical mysticism on the basis of his Critical metaphysics. When examining this work in Part III, we shall see that it treats the hand of God in nature and the voice of God in conscience as two sides of one mystical reality. At this point we can observe that the limitations placed on mysticism in *DSS* provided Kant with a context for developing a fully Critical mysticism in his writings prior to *OP*. Although Kant lacked a name for his new view of how human beings experience God, he did not lack a clear understanding of how it works, nor did he fail to practice it in his own life. Moreover, as I have argued in *KCR* (especially Appendix II.1), Kant has influenced mystics of many types, leading them down a Critical path that protects them from the pitfalls of delirious forms of mysticism. What remains to be seen is how *OP* confirms and/or further clarifies the role of Critical mysticism in Kant's System of Perspectives.

A helpful way to conclude our inquiry here in Part II will be to relate Kant's dual emphasis on experiencing the voice of God in conscience and the hand of God in nature to his metaphor of the Critical philosopher as standing on the shoreline between the sea and the land. As Beck observes: "Kant speaks of hugging the shore of experience and staying far away from the high and stormy seas of metaphysical speculation. Yet that may have been where his heart was."[12] Indeed, we can picture Kant standing on the wet sand at the beach near Königsberg, with the gentle waves of the Baltic Sea periodically splashing over his feet, contemplating the moral law as he watches the sun setting below the horizon and the stars gradually appearing overhead. This imagery may be somewhat fanciful, yet it is suggested by Kant's own favorite metaphors and can be regarded as highly appropriate in light of the architectonic structure of his System of Perspectives. For the Critical philosopher stands at the *crossroads of immediate experience* (cf. *KCR*, Figure III.4), casting a reflective gaze over the earth of theoretical knowledge on one side and the sea of moral faith on the other, and recognizes that only on the *boundary* between these two can a person fully appreciate the awesome presence of God as it manifests itself through the voice of conscience in one's heart and through a vision of the starry heavens in nature.

None of these perspectives on its own suffices to define human nature, yet together they suggest the picture of Kant's mystical worldview shown in Figure 8.1. These four metaphors correspond directly to the main divisions in Kant's System.[13] The sea (as viewed from the shoreline) represents transcendental Critique, the source of the theoretical knowledge examined in *CPR*; conscience (the heart) gives us immediate awareness of our freedom, as informed by the moral law, and is therefore the existential source of the practical knowledge examined in *CPrR*; the earth represents experience, the

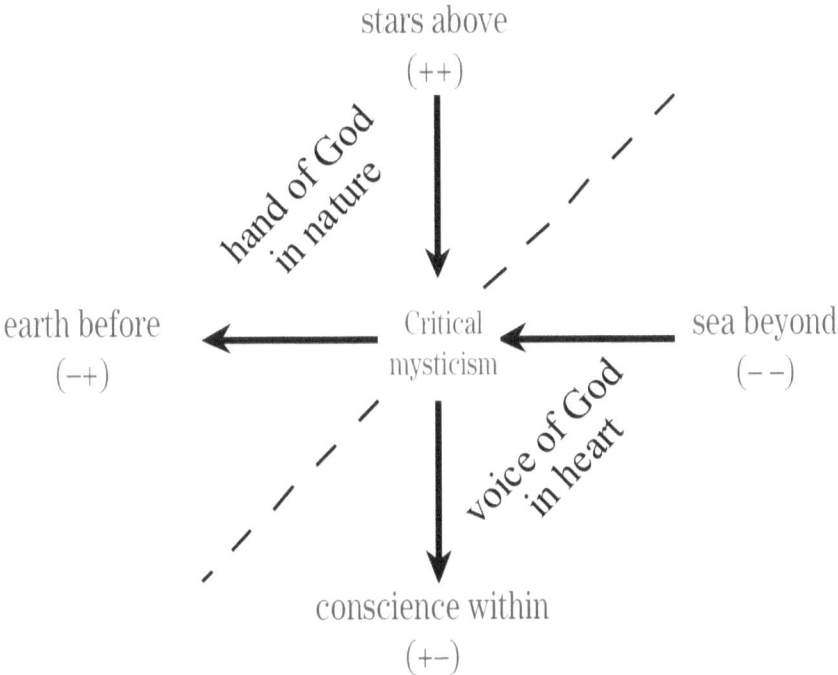

Figure 8.1. **Four Basic Metaphors of Critical Mysticism.**

source of the judicial knowledge of beauty and purpose examined in *CJ*; and the starry heavens here represent metaphysical reality, the ultimate (yet empirically unreachable)[14] object of Kant's philosophical love, and so also (following the analogy of dreams in *DSS*) of his Critical mysticism, which itself corresponds to the "I" of apperception that stands at the crossroads between all human perspectives.

Kant is not called the "sage of Königsberg" for nothing. As a true sage, he makes his home quietly on the borderlands, denying all extremes, including extreme mysticism. Thus, his worldview does not really fit into any of the three types of mysticism mentioned in Chapter 5, but establishes a fourth type instead. Kuehn (1985, 168) rightly identifies this fourth approach when he insists that "Kant makes . . . very clear that he is on the side of the common man or common sense." "For Kant," unlike many of his Enlightenment contemporaries, "the 'crowd' is not an object of contempt." In *DSS*, when the key features of his mature philosophy were just beginning to dawn on him, Kant openly acknowledges the dependence of our judgment "on the *universal human understanding*" (*DSS* 2.334). As he puts it earlier (325): "Sound common sense often apprehends a truth before it understands the reasons by means of which it can prove or explain that truth." It is important to emphasize, however, that the philosopher's task is to *explicate* common sense; as Kant points out in A783–784/B811–12 (see also *PFM* 4.259), it is therefore unjustifiable for the philosopher "obstinately to appeal to healthy human understanding (a refuge, which always proves that the cause of reason is in despair) rather than to attempt new dogmatic proofs."

Unfortunately, because Kant puts in the place of such specious methods a complex tangle of abstract terminology and argumentation, interpreters often ignore or do not take seriously his belief that his System of Perspectives upholds the view of the common person (see e.g., A831/B859). Yet the overall purpose of his System is certain to be misunderstood if its aim in this respect is ignored. For the whole of Kant's philosophical project can be seen as an attempt to place limitations on the various extremes that threaten to sway ordinary people away from the beliefs and actions toward which their reason naturally points the way (see e.g., Bxxxif). Thus Velkley (1985, 101) is right to portray Kant's "transcendental turn" as implying that "theoretical philosophy can have no higher theme than 'ordinary experience.'" Indeed, this emphasis carries over into Kant's personal attitudes as well. Thus, he confesses that "before a humble common man in whom I perceive uprightness of character in a higher degree than I am aware of in myself *my spirit bows*, whether I want it or whether I do not" (*CPrR*, 76–77). What Kant offers on behalf of the common person is a vision of life—a Critical mysticism—that can be enjoyed by any and every person who is willing to submit to the God of the shoreline, the God who always escapes our theoretical grasp, yet speaks to each of us in our universal encounter with nature and conscience.

NOTES

1. In *RBBR* alone, Kant uses the term *Herzenskündiger* four times (see *CCKR* 508); see also *MPT* 8.269 and *OP* 21.147.

2. Bax 1891, xiv–xvi; Wallace 1901, 12, 53.

3. See Wallace 1901, 19–21, and Klinke 1952, 22–23. For further details on this period of Kant's life, see Kuehn 2001, xv, 95–99.

4. See Bax 1903, xviii; Cassirer 1981, 32.

5. For example, Wood 1991 claims Kant is a deist rather than a theist, and di Giovanni 2012 claims his position boils down to atheism. For a response to such claims, see *KCR*, Appendix IV.4. Firestone and Jacobs (2008, 202) think Kant's position in the Third and Fourth Pieces of *RBBR* can be read as having "an elitist tendency"—a claim I dispute in *CCKR* 302n.

6. See Wallace 1901, 34. For an excellent summary of the quasi-mystical attention Kant gave to detail in his arrangement of his regular afternoon dinner parties (which took place from 2pm to 4pm, his only meal of the day), see Cohen 2008.

7. Klinke 1952, 49. Jachmann (1804, 82) reports this rather differently: Kant "wholly renounced supper" only after Green's death, for it was a "time, once sacred to his most intimate friendship, he wished to pass in silence, as a sacrifice to his deceased friend" (quoted in Bax 1903, xxvi). This, too, would suggest that his decision to eat only once a day was a genuine discipline of fasting, performed for what many would regard as a spiritual purpose.

8. Wallace 1901, 41. Kant also "sat in meditation" from about five until six each morning, a habit he valued so highly that he once remarked: "This is the happiest time of the day for me" (quoted in Klinke 1952, 48).

9. Wallace 1901, 108. Stanley Jaki's translation of *UNH* is unfortunately overliteral, and his introduction and notes are grossly unfair to Kant's true position. I criticize Jaki's approach in detail in SP–87b.

10. That Kant's artist–God might have a sense of humor is suggested by his remarks on sex in a 1795 letter to Schiller (*C* 12.11): in reflecting on "[t]he organization of nature" Kant admits that he sometimes inadvertently finds "running through" his head something that "has always struck me as amazing and as a sort of chasm of thought; I mean, the idea that fertilization . . . always needs two sexes in order for the species to be propagated." However, Kant shies away from imputing to "providence" the motive of choosing "this arrangement, almost playfully, for the sake of variety." Instead, it "opens up a prospect on what lies beyond the field of vision" if instead we "believe that propagation is not possible in any other way."

11. Webb 1926, 60. Such a stoic view of Kant's personality is flatly contradicted by the accounts of the man given by those who knew him personally. One of his closest friends, Jachmann, describes him as "a spirited orator, sweeping the heart and emotions along with him, as well as satisfying the intelligence" (Jachmann 1804, 30–31; trans. Klinke 1952, 34), and adds that in social gatherings he was unsurpassed: "All his friends were unanimously of the opinion that they had never known a more interesting companion" (Jachmann, 140–41; Klinke, 45). Moreover, Kant openly described himself as having a "very easily affected, but otherwise carefree spirit" (quoted in Klinke 1952, 32). What Kant objected to was not emotion as such, but "emotional thinking" (52). With this in mind, W.H. Walsh's claim that for Kant "the path to God starts from the moral emotions" (1963, 287) might seem rather odd. But it makes sense if "emotions" here refers not to emotions in the traditional sense but to our immediate experience of what Kant calls "the feeling of pleasure and displeasure," which gives rise either to judgments of beauty and sublimity (via our experience of nature) or to the feeling of respect (via our experience of the moral law).

12. Beck 1986, 11. The key passages where Kant expresses this sentiment in terms of the earth–sea metaphor include *PFM* 4.262, *ENPM* 1.475, and *OPA* 2.65–66. The best known passage of this sort is A235–36/B294–95, where Kant describes the domain of "pure understanding" as "an island," with "unalterable boundaries [set] by nature itself. It is the land of truth (a charming name), surrounded by a broad and stormy ocean, the true seat of illusion, where many a fog bank and rapidly melting iceberg pretend to be new lands and, ceaselessly deceiving with empty hopes the voyager looking around for new discoveries, entwine him in adventures from which [like dreams!] he can never escape and yet also never bring to an end." Similarly, Kant's use of the concept of a "horizon" (a word that occurs 10 times in *CPR* (16 in Norman Kemp Smith's translation; see SP-87a:171) is closely related to his analogy of the shoreline. Thus, for instance, in A297/B353–54 Kant compares the illusion created by the antinomies to the fact that the sea appears to be "higher in the middle than at the shore."

13. Figure 8.1 is a corrected and improved version of the diagram first published in *Philosophy & Theology* 4.1, 89, where it was distorted almost beyond recognition by the editor's apparent overconfidence in computerized text-transfer technology and published without any proofs having been sent to me for correction. The metaphors in this revised version correspond directly both to *KSP* Figure III.8 and to *KCR* Figure III.4.

14. Kant expounds his Critically enlightened metaphysics in *MFNS*, *MM*, and *OP*. But as we shall see in Part III, he was never quite able to realize the starry-eyed goals of *OP*.

III

The *Opus Postumum* as an Experiment in Critical Mysticism

> The love of wisdom is the least that one can possess; wisdom (for man), the highest; and therefore, boundless. — Transcendental philosophy [is] the progression from the latter to the former — The final purpose of all knowledge is to cognize oneself in the highest practical reason.—*OP* 21.155–56

Chapter Nine

Can the Original (Threefold) Synthesis Be Consciously *Experienced*?

Kant's *Opus Postumum* (*OP*) is much more than just a series of jumbled footnotes to or revisions of a transitional argument Kant had insufficiently developed in his earlier works, as Eckart Förster claims.[1] While its many repetitions and incomplete arguments offer plenty of evidence that Kant was suffering from the onset of dementia as he struggled to write the book—this, surely, is why he worked on it for so long without being able to publish it during his lifetime—*OP* can nevertheless be regarded as Kant's valiant attempt to complete the architectonic structure of his System. The only way he can do this is to reveal as clearly as possible "the idea of the whole" (Bxliv) as a transition that itself consists of *multiple* transitions.[2] As we shall see here in Part III, Kant discusses at least three distinct types of transition in *OP*. Each in its own way brings us to a point that marks the *end*—both in the sense of "purpose" or "aim" and in the sense of "finishing point"—of philosophy as such. By requiring us to accept a brute fact in silent recognition of its transcendent presence, each transition relates to an immediate experience that serves as the highest expression of Critical mysticism.

After this introductory chapter, Part III's account of the content of *OP* begins where I believe Kant himself was planning to begin his final book: Chapter 10 discusses the idea of God as rooted in the categorical imperative, considered as philosophy's *moral* end.[3] Chapter 11 then deals with the idea of the world as rooted in the universal presence of an underlying, unknowable substance, identified by Kant as "ether" or "caloric." This is followed by a discussion in Chapter 12 of what I believe was Kant's main goal in *OP*: to show how the presence of human beings in the world serves to unify the otherwise opposing ideas of God and the world. That chapter concludes Part III with some reflections on how philosophers can cope with the "end" of philosophy as so announced. It also serves as a conclusive statement of Kant's most developed defense of his Critical mysticism.

Kant's critics in the last two decades of his life presented him with what is still often regarded as the most difficult problem raised by his theory of knowledge in *CPR*: is the object that affects us in the experience of sense–perception an empirical object or is it the thing in itself? Kant interpreters then and ever since have tended to divide themselves into three camps based on their responses to this issue:[4] (1) the phenomenalism or idealism of contemporaries such as Salomon Maimon, J.G. Fichte, and J.S. Beck, later defended by the Marburg School, regarded only phenomenal affection as valid; (2) the noumenalism of contemporaries such as J. Schulze, later defended by the Heidelberg School, regarded only noumenal affection as valid; and (3) later interpreters such as Hans Vaihinger and Erich Adickes regarded both as valid, and therefore devised the infamous theory of "double affection" as an interpretation of Kant's view.[5]

What is rarely appreciated is that Kant himself was developing his own answer in *OP*, an answer that follows a fourth way: considered from the perspective of our immediate experience, *neither* the thing in itself *nor* the empirical object is identical to the sense–object that affects us, for the latter distinction itself arises only out of *reflection on* that immediate experience of being affected. Kant's final answer to the question, in other words, is that in immediate experience *reality* (under whatever name the subject/object assumes, whether Self, God, Sense–Object, Reason, etc.) *affects itself*. "The first act of reason is *consciousness*" (*OP* 21.105), and out of this initial act all reflective perspectives eventually arise. When adopting the transcendental perspective philosophers must posit the thing in itself as the source of the material of perception; when adopting the empirical perspective empirical objects must be so regarded; but in our pre-perspectival immediate experience, neither explanation holds. *OP* can be interpreted properly only if we recognize Kant's intention to counter the various diverging interpretive tendencies with a truly Critical (i.e., perspectival) answer to this question. That he is no longer starting with the transcendental object (i.e., with the abstract concept of experience generally), but is showing how even this abstraction arises *out of* the subject's immediate experience, is clear when he says: "The first act of thinking contains a principle of . . . the self-affecting subject in a system of ideas which contain merely the formal [factors] of the advance [from immediate experience of particulars] to experience overall [*überhaupt*]."[6]

OP's single, all-encompassing principle, serving as a vortex that everything else flows into, is expressed in a variety of ways—e.g., as "Self," "God," "Nature" (the "Sense–Object"), or "Morally–Practical Reason"—but its most fundamental characteristic is always the same: *self-creativity*. This "one principle" of Zoroaster, repeatedly mentioned in *OP*, is sometimes associated with Spinoza's "principle of intuiting all things in God." As we saw in Chapter 8, Kant showed interest in this principle as early as 1770 (*ID* 2.410); now he continues to toy with it, reformulating it as "the capacity of thought as inner intuition to develop *out of itself*" (Adickes 1920, 730; trans. in Kemp Smith 1923, 640; see also *OP* 21.15)—i.e., as the capacity for the kind of self-transcendence that alone gives rise to knowledge.[7] Kant explains in *OP* 21.152 that God should be represented "not as a being in the world but [as] the pure idea of self-constitution, similar to the pure intelligence of the subject itself.— The highest intelligence."[8] Similarly, he says "I am an object of myself and of my representations. That there is something else outside me is my own product. I make myself. . . . We make everything ourselves."[9] When Kant talks in this way about self-creativity, we must keep in mind that he is no longer assuming a reflective perspective of any sort, but is attempting to speak about the unspeakable (i.e., immediate experience) and its relation to the standpoints and perspectives adopted throughout his entire System. From this new, hypothetical "standpoint," no distinctions can be made at all: *everything is One*. Even the distinction between reality and appearance breaks down. The Self's encounter with itself is all there is. As mystical writers are often well aware, the only way to speak about the unspeakable is to use the logic of paradox (e.g., in the form A = -A), as Kant does when he virtually identifies the object with the subject (e.g., 22.414–15) or claims a proposition can be "Synthetic and analytic" (22.88; cf. SP–00, 78–85, and SP–16a).

The common assumption that Kant thought this spontaneous and "self-creative character" belongs to "the noumenal self" (Kemp Smith 1923, 627; see also Ward 1972, 163) can now be seen to be based on a subtle conflation of perspectives. The noumenal self is a construction arising out of our human consciousness as a "world–being," or "being–in–the–world" (*Weltwessen*), and only the latter can be said to be self-creative. For Kant, immediate experience is therefore not a mystical intuition (at least, not one that itself constitutes empirical cognition), not a noumenal "act," not an action subjected to moral laws, and not a subjective feeling; it is what *gives rise* to all of these—the nonreflective, undetermined, raw material we *use* to construct various types of reflective experience. It is the "birth" of reason itself, through which the essential self-creative nature of God is expressed: "The concept of [God] is not that of substance—that is, of a being which exists independent of my thought—but the idea (one's own creation . . .) of a reason which constitutes itself into a thought–object [an "ideal"]" (*OP* 21.27). This self-creative core of human nature can be regarded as the mystical source of all perspectives and of every element in the entirety of Kant's System of Perspectives (see above, pp. 2, 15, 25, and 54).

Kant's distinction in *OP* 22.113 between four types of "being" helps to clarify what he means by the term "world–being": "1) A sense–being; 2) a reason–being; 3) a rational being, of which there can be several [types]; 4) a highest Being in the highest sphere—God—who establishes all rational beings in the unity of moral relations, through the categorical imperative." As shown in Figure 9.1, these types obviously correspond to animals, spirits (i.e., purely rational beings such as angels or disembodied souls), humans (i.e., sensible beings who are also rational), and God, and can be mapped onto what I elsewhere (SP–00, §5.1) call the 2LAR cross (i.e., a cross diagram whose poles stand in a "second-level analytic relation"), assuming first-level distinctions between sensible (-) and rational (+) and between lower (-) and highest (+). Out of these four types, humans alone count as "world–beings" because we are the only ones that combine rationality with sensibility.

The sharp distinction in Kant's theoretical system between a knowable object's transcendent material (i.e., the unknowable thing in itself) and the formal unity imposed by the *transcendental* (not noumenal) subject (i.e., by the "I" of apperception) is valid only from the theoretical standpoint. But if we take our starting point not from rational faith in the thing in itself, as posited by transcendental reflection, but from our own undifferentiated immediate experience (of the human person as a *world–being*), then the former distinctions must be regarded as derivative. From this standpoint of immediacy Kant is therefore able to say that the self *posits* both itself and its object, and in so doing provides the means for avoiding solipsism: arising out of the nonreflective ignorance of immediate experience—what some medieval

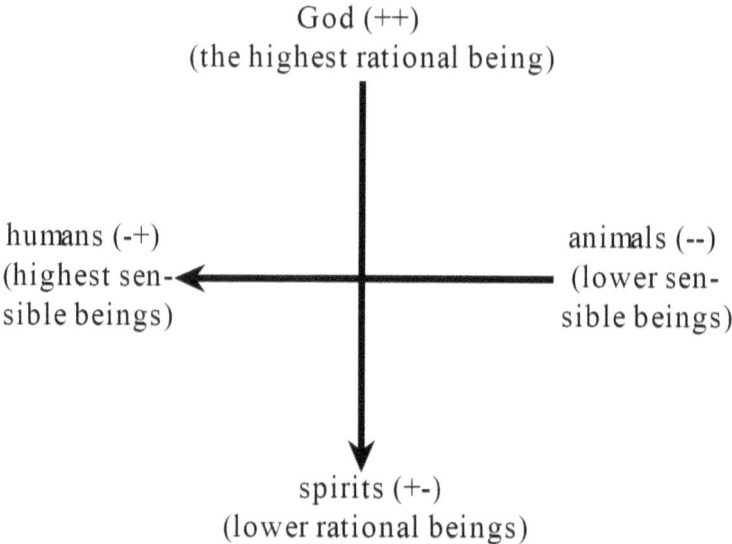

Figure 9.1. Kant's Distinction between Four Types of Being.

mystics called *docta ignorantia* or *knowing* ignorance—such self-positing first establishes the potential for reflective perspectives. This is done by dividing the sense–object into subjective and objective components: "The thing in itself is not another object, but another mode of making oneself into an object" (*OP* 22.415). But in immediate experience the thing in itself and the subject are not yet distinguished, for "the thing in itself is the subject which I make into the object" (see also 22.43–44).

Such comments do not imply that Kant has abandoned the unknowable "transcendental absolute" in favor of "the absolute of autonomous thought," as Vleeschauwer (1962, 189) suggests, but only that he recognizes that the former gives way to the latter when transcendental Critique transforms itself into metaphysics, where autonomous thought is recognized as absolute precisely *because* the transcendental absolute is *immanent in* immediate experience. That Kant has not abandoned the thing in itself to Fichte and the German idealists, but has merely changed his standpoint, is evident from the fact that he affirms the key Critical doctrines at numerous points in *OP*.[10] When he says "transcendental philosophy is an idealism: namely that the subject constitutes itself" (21.85), he is not denying the objective reality of the phenomenal world, as established in his theoretical system and as presupposed throughout all the nontheological sections of *OP*;[11] rather, he is attempting to describe the *pre*reflective source of the very distinction between phenomenon and noumenon. This is why he says in *OP* 21.552 that "idealism . . . belongs to another branch of philosophy, with which we are not here concerned"—i.e., legitimate idealism (of the transcendental type) belongs to Critique, whereas *OP* belongs to metaphysics (see *KSP* §III.4). Ultimately, however, *OP* belongs to the judicial wing of Kant's system of metaphysics, which is precisely why it turns out that "the distinction between transcendental and metaphysical finally collapses" (Förster 1989, 298) in this work.

This original act of self-creative and self-legislative reason is what first produces the Kantian ideas of reason: God, the world (including our freedom from it), and humanity (including our destiny as immortal souls). This is a source of great confusion among interpreters, who wrongly interpret Kant's statements in *OP* as evidence that Kant wishes to *identify* God with human reason (see e.g., Insole 2013; but cf. *KCR*, Appendix IV.4). Friedman (1986, 507), by contrast, points out that "Kant does not call freedom, God, and immortality facts of reason. They are not immediately present to me." On this view, only our awareness of the moral law is immediately present; the ideas have to be inferred from this. *As ideas*, this is no doubt accurate. However, the reality behind the ideas is immediately present to us, even though the impact of our encounter with that reality is necessarily beyond the reach of our (always mediate) empirical cognition—this being a core insight of Kant's Critical mysticism. Thus, Kant affirms as early as 1756 that "God . . . is immediately present to all things, albeit *internally* present"

(*ENPM*, 483)—a view that corresponds closely to numerous passages in *OP*, as when he calls ideas "pure intuitions" (21.79).

Our immediate awareness of *human duties* gives rise to the idea of God; our immediate consciousness of *sense–objects* gives rise to the idea of the world; and our immediate experience of *our own self*, as a self-creative sense–object, gives rise to the idea of the human person as an immortal "being–in–the–world." Similarly, in *PM* 20.295 (alt.) Kant explains the relation between the three "transcendent ideas" as representing "the supersensible *in us* [freedom], *above us* [God], and *after us* [immortality]." This initial synthetic act thus establishes the framework for the standpoints that pattern Kant's philosophical System: the world (-) is opposed to God (+) just as Kant's theoretical system is to his practical system; and the former pair is synthesized by the human person (x), just as the judicial system synthesizes the latter pair.[12] We can now present the relationship between *OP*'s three ideas, the ideas as introduced in *CPR* (shown in Figure 9.2 using brackets inside the triangle), and their origin in different types of immediate experience (cf. *KCR*, Figure VI.1), as shown in Figure 9.2.

Within the framework established by these ideas, Kant hopes in *OP* to construct a "complete system of the possibility of the absolute whole of experience," the "grounding" of which "by means of the *a priori* principle of the possibility of experience overall [*überhaupt*]" was the purpose of the "theoretical" wing of his philosophical System (*OP* 21.104, my translation). As I argued in *KSP* (see especially §IV.3 and §VII.2), Kant's use of the term

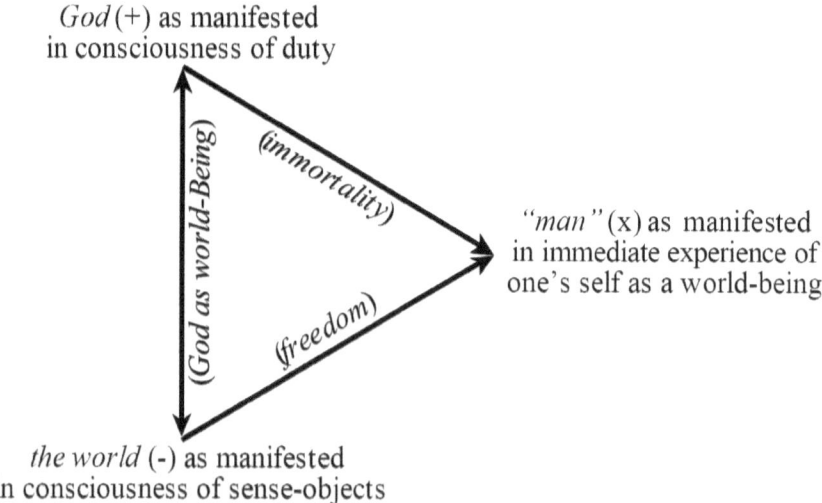

Figure 9.2. The Original Synthesis of Ideas in Immediate Experience.

"possibility of experience" is closely connected with his notion of "immediate experience": the former just *is* the latter, viewed as something that *might* give rise to empirical cognition. If we keep this in mind, then Vleeschauwer's assessment of Kant's unpublished essay on progress in metaphysics (i.e., *PM*) takes on added significance. Vleeschauwer (1962, 156) observes that in *PM* "the possibility of experience . . . is often represented as the highest task of transcendental philosophy." Indeed, *PM* was one of the first things Kant wrote (c.1791) after completing *CJ*. Significantly, the essay reveals a crucial change of standpoint, displaying for the first time the heightened emphasis on the role of the subject that comes to the fore in *OP* (and was taken even further by Fichte and Schelling). In *PM* "the whole discussion [revolves] around the living kernel of the synthetic activity of the subject (Vleeschauwer 1962, 154). Moreover, as Vleeschauwer goes on to explain (165): "The Critical whole in its three parts is raised to the level of philosophy instead of occupying . . . the modest place of a preliminary study." Here we see Kant dealing with "metaphysics as the most powerful spring of the human personality" (154), the proper treatment of immediate experience being its "highest task."

The properly metaphysical wing of Kant's philosophical System having already been elaborated in its applications to natural science (*MFNS*) and morality (*MM*), all that remains for *OP* is the "task" of unifying these in a final metaphysical system of immediate experience—the mystical core that ties together Kant's entire life's work.[13] In the theoretical system, as well as in the other two Critical systems, the ideas function primarily as regulative concepts, but here in *OP* they "are not mere concepts but laws of thought which the subject prescribes to itself" (21.93). They "give the material [*der Stoff*] to synthetic *a priori* laws from concepts, and so do not merely emerge from metaphysics but found transcendental philosophy" (21.20).

This sharp opposition between the ideas of God and the world (or nature) is presupposed throughout all of Kant's writings. Yet the two ideas are often used ambiguously, making it unclear "whether Kant, in phrases like 'the intelligible substratum' is talking about God or about the world in itself" (Buchdahl 1982, 91n). Thus Dister 1972 argues that Kant confuses the cosmological and theological ideas in *CPR* by portraying both as "the source of purposiveness in the world" (269n; see e.g., A699/B727). Kant seems, however, to have viewed God and nature as two sides of the same coin (the coin of "totality"): "God is a kind of mirror image of the 'intelligible substratum' of the world" (Buchdahl 1982, 91; cf. Goldmann 1971, 66–67). Kant often talks about nature's "will" in much the same way as he talks about *God's* will (e.g., *PP* 8.365, 367). Michel Despland discusses the close relationship between God and nature in Kant's understanding of "Providence" (1973, 7; see also 57, 73, 90–95, 274): especially in his writings on the philosophy of history, Kant develops the notion of "a Nature which is Providence, the mother of mankind, the mainspring of progress, and the guarantee of order." "Kant attributed no moral indifference to this Nature. Its purposes are normally wise and they are good for us men" (47). Despland goes on (48) to quote George Vlachos' apt comment (trans. from Vlachos 1962, 180) that for Kant "freedom does not rise over against nature but is born in nature." Although the interpenetration of God and nature is not always clear in Kant's theoretical and practical works, his intention to establish such a position becomes more clear in those works that adopt the judicial standpoint. In *OP* more than anywhere else, Kant attempts to work out the details of this interpenetration.

At an early stage in *OP*[14] Kant distinguishes between three types of transition that will occupy his attention in this final installment of his philosophical System. Specifying the book(s) in Kant's System that correspond to each type, we can summarize them as follows: from *MFNS* to physics; from physics to *CPR* (assuming that by "transcendental philosophy" Kant is referring to its foundation in the first *Critique*, not to the three *Critiques* as a whole); and from *CPR* to both *MFNS* and *MM* ("the system of nature and freedom"). These three transitions, taken together, give rise to what Kant calls "cosmotheology": "the universal connection of the living forces of all things in reciprocal relation: God and the world." In the latter case Kant is taking "God and the world" as *one idea* (*OP* 21.19), whose unity constitutes "[t]he highest standpoint of transcendental philosophy" (21.23). That Kant regards his investigation of these transitions as a part of his third, *judicial* system, with its more teleological and empirical orientation, is evident from comments such as that his goal will be to construct "a world–system (according to *purposes*)" (22.193, emphasis added), based on a "schematism of *discernment* [*Urtheilskraft*] for the moving forces of matter" (21.291, my translation; emphasis added) that enables us to anticipate "the *empirical* investigation of Nature."[15] If *OP* were meant to be part of the theoretical wing of Kant's System, and hence to adopt the standpoint of *CPR* and *MFNS* rather than that of *CJ* and *RBBR*, then its world–system would surely be mechanical, not purpose driven.

In the remaining chapters I shall demonstrate how the paradoxes referred to as "transitions" in *OP* can each be resolved and/or explained most clearly by interpreting their epistemological status in terms of what I call *analytic a posteriority*.[16] This will serve not only to provide us with the elusive "idea of the whole" for interpreting *OP*, but also to confirm the conjecture made in *KSP* §III.4, that *OP* constitutes the final, synthetic step in Kant's third ("judicial") system and as such occupies a "doctrinal" position corresponding to the analytic a posteriori (cf. *KSP*, Figures III.9(c) and IV.2). As Kant puts it in *OP* 21.478, "the transition from metaphysics to physics" moves "from ... the concept of a matter in general," which as a pure concept would properly be regarded as analytic, "to the system of moving forces," including various "empirical principles" (21.482; see also 22.141) that can be known only *a posteriori*. As we shall see, Kant's analysis of the resulting "system of the universal doctrine of forces"—like that of the doctrinal systems proposed in *MFNS* and *MM*—would have been much more clear had he identified the doctrine's status as analytic *a posteriori*.

NOTES

1. Förster 1987 argues that Kant intended *OP* to fill a minor gap that he had noticed in the argument of *CPR*. For a detailed refutation of this claim, see *KCR*, Chapter XI, where I argue that Förster is right to recognize the importance of transitional arguments in *OP*, but wrong to limit them to one type and identify them with the book's overall purpose.

2. See e.g., *OP* 21.61; 22.86; 22.97. In one of his most suggestive uses of the quoted phrase (22.193), Kant says "the transition . . . is a product of the idea of the whole, in the thoroughgoing, self-determining intuition of oneself." As we shall see in Chapter 12, this "idea" is intimately connected with self-awareness as an *experienced reality* (i.e., an "intuition of oneself").

3. Kant placed most of his notes on this subject in the first of *OP*'s twelve fascicles. In their translation of *OP* for the Cambridge Edition of Kant's Works, Förster and Rosen ignore the order of Kant's fascicles and arrange the notes by topic instead. Förster justifies this on the grounds that the order of the fascicles represents nothing more than the approximate *reverse chronological order* Kant wrote them in. Thus, the translators unfortunately place Kant's discussion of God last in their translation, rather than first. By giving the impression that the discussion of God was a mere afterthought or appendix, they conveniently lend credence to Förster's own theory (see note 9.1, above) that *OP* is mainly about Kant's recognition of the need to write a transition between *MFNS* and physics.

4. See Kemp Smith 1923, 627–36. In a 1794 letter to Kant (*C* 11.510) Beck complains that "even the friends of the *Critique* . . . don't know where they ought to locate the object that produces sensation." I argue in *KSP* Chapter VI that this confusion is due to Kant's perspectival methodology, whereby transcendentally the "object" is the thing in itself, while empirically it is the phenomenon. The problem is further compounded by the fact that Kant uses two terms that are both normally translated as "object": *Objekt* and *Gegenstand*. See Introduction, note 9.

5. See Adickes 1920, 18; Kemp Smith 1923, 612–13. Over the past century these three schools have been represented by scholars such as P.F. Strawson (only phenomenal affection), Martin Heidegger (only noumenal affection), and Graham Bird and Henry Allison (double affection, reinterpreted as two aspects of one affection). More recently, Rae Langton and Lucy Allais have offered alternative moderate interpretations that also attempt to take account of both the phenomenal and the noumenal.

6. *OP* 21.99; see also 22.77. Elsewhere Kant treats this "intuition of oneself" (22.11) as *immediate*, inasmuch as it is totally pre-conceptual: "The first act of the faculty of representation . . . is the representation of oneself . . . through which the subject makes itself into an object . . . : that is, representation of an individual" (22.43; see also 22.77 and *LM* 28.592). Although Kant does not assign this function to one of the faculties of the mind, it would seem to fit the mysterious power of imagination more than any of the others—an option famously defended by Heidegger 1929. On my translation of Kant's *überhaupt* as "generally" (when it explicitly contrasts with something specific) or "overall" (when it does not), see *CCKR* 523–24.

7. As Kemp Smith (1923, 618) notes, the "fundamental problem" of the whole Critical System is "how the self-transcendence involved in knowledge . . . can be possible. The self can be a knower only if it be a creator." Thus, Kant suggests a symbolic (transcendental) reversal of Spinoza's principle: "we carry our concept of God *into* the objects of pure intuition" (*OP* 22.59, emphasis added; see also 21.22), not vice versa.

8. Like many others, Sullivan (1971, 114) regards this passage as evidence of Kant's "idealist" reduction of God to human practical reason. To do so, however, he has to mistrans-

late "*gleich*" ("similar to") as if it were "*zugleich*" ("at the same time"). On this issue, see *KCR*, Appendix IV.4.

9. *OP* 22.82. Later (22.353), Kant makes the same point more cautiously, seeming to make room for the possibility that we do not make the thing in itself, though we can have no insight into it: "we have insight into nothing except what we can make ourselves. First, however, we must make ourselves." As early as 1791 (the year he first met the young Fichte), he explains (*PM* 20.299) that "we make these objects [i.e., God, freedom, and immortality] for ourselves as we judge the idea of them to be helpful to the ultimate end of our pure reason." Such radical statements sound like concessions to the budding movement of German idealism; with this in mind, Walsh (1967, 323) suggests that it may be "fortunate for Kant that he was not able to get his final philosophical thoughts into publishable form." (But see note 9.10, below.) Webb (1926, 181) interprets Kant's references to self-creativity to be mainly about perfection. For this is the only sense in which God and human beings share this characteristic (184; cf. Adickes 1920, 774): "God . . . cannot . . . create holy beings; only so far as they are natural beings is he the creator of men; as moral beings they are their own creators."

10. See e.g., *OP* 22.24, 34, 36, 37 and *KCR*, note XI.5. That Kant's thinking in *OP* was influenced far more by Beck than (as Copleston claims) by Fichte is convincingly argued by Zweig 1967, 26–31 (see especially 31n; see also Despland 1973, 314, and Gilson 1937, 240–42). Indeed, Kant indicates in a 1798 letter that he had not even read Fichte up to that point (*C* 12.239)—and he may never have done so. Kant explicitly rejects Fichte's work "as a totally indefensible system," for it "is nothing more or less than mere logic" (396–97). Nevertheless, Kant does give the impression in *OP* that he is competing with the early idealists to close a gap that was widely recognized to exist in philosophy. Schleiermacher (1955, 5), for example, asks how "extremes are to be brought together, and the long series made into a closed ring, the symbol of eternity and completeness?" In opposition to what he saw as Kant's over-emphasis on morality, with its drawback of always being "manipulating" and "self-controlling" (29–30), Schleiermacher locates philosophy's ultimate standpoint in "piety"—i.e., in a religious *experience* characterized by "a surrender, a submission to be moved by the Whole that stands over against man." What I am aiming to demonstrate in the present book is that Kant's final position was not as far removed from Schleiermacher's as is often assumed. The difference is that Schleiermacher explicitly begins where Kant implicitly ends, by claiming that scientific knowledge and moral action arise out of our deeply felt, immediate experience. Assessing whether Schleiermacher—or for that matter, any of the key philosophers of the early nineteenth century—closes Kant's gap better than Kant himself did is beyond our present scope (see Barth 1972, 306; 655–56).

11. Kemp Smith (1923, 617) believes Kant is making such a denial. Copleston's view is more accurate: "We cannot suppose that the human intellect creates its objects by thinking them. Kant never accepted pure idealism in this sense" (1960, 205; see also 385).

12. Only in this sense of absolute opposition (as also depicted in *KCR*, Figure V.3) is Copleston correct to claim that in *OP* "the World is conceived as dependent on God" (1960, 387; see also 383). Kant would not support the claim that the details of our *knowledge* of the world are directly dependent on our *knowledge* of God. Rather, Kant's version of a theocentric orientation treats God as a mystical center around which everything revolves (see *KSP*, Figure IX.2), making all knowledge possible, yet without allowing itself to be known. In this sense, Collins (1960, 198; see also 433) is also correct to say "Kant sought to prevent the identification of God's own being with the natural world." However, as we shall see in Chapter 12, he does regard them as reaching a higher synthesis in human personhood. As Despland (1973, 73) puts it, nature and Providence are "two teleological systems which pursue distinct though related ends." Nature's purpose is humanity, whose purpose is freely to choose the purpose of Providence (cf. *CJ* 5.436); for "God pursues two sets of ends, those pursued through Nature's plan . . . and those pursued through his moral Providence" (Despland 1973, 73).

13. Before he ever conceived of the notion of Critique as a propaedeutic to metaphysics, Kant had planned to compose a system of metaphysics with separate theoretical and moral wings. His discovery of the Copernican hypothesis merely delayed the realization of that dream until the final two decades of his active career. That, as early as the mid-1760s, he was already planning the works that eventually became *MFSN*, *GMM*, and *MM* is evident from his Decem-

ber 31, 1765, letter to Lambert (*C* 10.56), where he announces his plan to "publish a few little essays, the contents of which I have already worked out. The first of these will be the 'Metaphysical Foundations of Natural Philosophy' and the 'Metaphysical Foundations of Practical Philosophy.'" Throughout his career he also repeatedly announces his plan to compose a full-fledged metaphysics of nature and morals (see e.g., *C* 10.97, 145, 406; 11.399, 434; 23.495; cf. Axxi, A841/B869, A850/B878), though of course *MFSN* was not the *full* realization of this aspect of his plan (see *C* 10.406).

14. The text in question, *OP* 21.17, appears in the first fascicle; unfortunately, Förster's translation obscures its early origin by placing it near the end of his topic-organized text.

15. Copleston 1960, 381, emphasis added. Since Kant, as usual, follows the pattern of the categories to work out the details of this schematism, Förster is correct in saying *OP*'s purpose is to explain "the *a priori* systematicity of physics" (Förster 1989, 296). A key problem with Förster's interpretation is that he writes as if this is the work's *only* (or at least, primary) task. One of my purposes here in Part III is to demonstrate how grossly inadequate such an assumption is. As we shall see, the details of Kant's systematic transition to physics are not central to our concern. Although Kant never settles on a single, consistent account of the "moving force" (Kemp Smith 1923, 612n), Kemp Smith suggests a plausible candidate (611): "In respect of *origin*, motion is either inherent . . . or communicated . . . ; in respect of *direction* either attractive or repulsive; in respect of *place* either progressive or oscillatory; and finally, in respect of *filling* of space, it must either . . . be coercible, or . . . incoercible." Kemp Smith agrees with Adickes (and many others) in finding such an a priori scheme "entirely worthless" (612) and "from the start doomed to failure" (611). Nevertheless, I have argued in a series of articles (SP–10b, SP–11, SP–13, and SP–15b) that Kant's philosophical system has had quite a significant impact on the development of modern physics. See also note 11.6, below.

16. Kant's only explicit reference to the notion of analytic a posteriority comes in the second edition Introduction to *CPR*, where he hastily dismisses its relevance as a meaningful epistemological classification: "it would be absurd to ground an analytic judgment on experience" (B11). For a full discussion of my position on the analytic a posteriori, see SP–12.

Chapter Ten

The Categorical Imperative as the Voice of God

The sections of *OP* dealing with the idea of God (i.e., with the moral aspect of the "transition from metaphysics to transcendental philosophy" [*OP* 22.129]) focus mainly on the philosophical implications of the moral law, as mediated through our encounter with the categorical imperative. Kant repeatedly stresses in these sections (see e.g., 22.104–5) the direct or immediate connection between the proposition "There is a God" and our awareness of the categorical imperative. Sometimes he goes far beyond a mere reference to the proposition, as when he says "our reason expresses [the moral law] *through* the divine" (22.104, emphasis added) and the idea of God "is the feeling of the presence of the divine in man" (22.18). Elsewhere (e.g., 22.123) he adds: "The idea of [the categorical imperative] is that of a substance which . . . is not subordinated to a classification of human reason." A few paragraphs later he comes right out and calls God "a personal substance" (22.125). God is "the idea of an omnipotent moral being" who "is both all-powerful with regard to nature" and "universally commanding for freedom;" we must regard God not merely as "a generic concept" but as "an individual (a thoroughly determined being)" (22.127–28)—perhaps even "a threefold person."[1]

Ward (1972, 166) expounds *OP* 22.118 to mean that "God is a Personality, not external to man as a separate substance, but within man." But he downplays the importance of such claims, interpreting Kant as referring merely to "the legislative capacity of originative reason, and not [to] the sort of subjectivity that belongs to human persons." Webb 1926, by contrast, highlights such claims as being among the most significant in *OP*. The language of "personality," he reminds us, was "rare . . . before the end of the eighteenth century" (181), yet in *OP* "Kant constantly . . . speaks of God as a

'Person' and of God's 'Personality.'"[2] Indeed, Kant repeats this notion on numerous occasions, such as in *OP* 21.19, where he appears to be hinting at a synthesis between his theoretical and practical systems: "The concept of God is that of a being as the highest cause of world–beings and as a person." And *OP* 21.48 (my translation) says: "The concept of God is that of a personality of a thought–being, an ideal Being which reason itself creates. Man is also a person, but [one] which still at the same time belongs to the world as sense–object." So a key difference between a divine person and a human person is that only the latter has a physical body (see Figure 9.2, above). Such comments are likely to mislead us unless we keep in mind that "reason" for Kant refers not to a *property* possessed by each individual, but to a transcendent reality that endows all human persons with a certain *capacity*, so that whoever participates in it (by activating that capacity) should thereby also *submit* to it. This seems to be what Webb (1926, 192) has in mind when he interprets such claims to mean that "[i]n recognizing the Law we find ourselves in God's presence; . . . for the Law itself *is* the revelation of his Personality." From this new standpoint, "the Moral Law" just *is* "the Presence of God . . . immediately revealed" (199), "a Presence [that is] 'closer to us than breathing and nearer than hands and feet'" (200)—just as mystics from many religious traditions have acknowledged.

In his introductory essay to his translation of Kant's *Religion*, T.M. Greene agrees that "Kant's thought tended always to conceive of God in terms of the basic concept of personality," rather than that of the (far more static) "Unconditioned" or "Absolute" (1934, lxviii). Yet F.E. England, after noting that in *OP* "Kant frequently describes God as a person," complains that "Kant . . . had a very imperfect notion of what was implied in the notion of personality" (1929, 192n)—the main problem being that Kant's view seems too "static." This is hardly fair to Kant, for he describes God dynamically as a "living" substance who, like human beings, "is capable of rights" (*OP* 22.48). Personality in the *human* sense (e.g., involving duties as well as rights) "cannot be attributed to the Deity;" for God's personality is "omnipotent," "omniscient," and "omnibenevolent" and therefore is not constrained by any duties. Kant's earlier claim (in *RBBR* 6.28) that "the moral law . . . is personality itself," so that a human being's "predisposition to *personality* is the receptivity to respect for the moral law" (27), need not be regarded as static, provided we associate the moral law with the living voice of conscience within us (cf. Kant's reference to the "holy Ghost" in *OP* 22.60), rather than taking it as a fixed logical principle.

The "personal" in itself is a *nonreflective* mode of being; it *is* the "I" that gives rise to all reflective perspectives. As such, we could regard the third stage of any judicial system as adopting the "personal perspective"—i.e., the perspective whose task is to determine the necessary conditions (or precepts [*Grundsätzen*]) that govern personal experience. Two such conditions would be that personality is inherently spiritual, yet manifested in a material form. Thus, "*God is a spirit*" (*OP* 22.58), and this divine person "is immanent in the human spirit" through the moral law,[3] yet also present in nature (22.61–62, emphasis added; see also 22.57):

> What is God? — He is the unique being, unconditionally commanding in the *moral*–practical relation (i.e., according to the categorical imperative), exercising all power over *nature*. This is already in its concept a unique [being]: . . . the very thought of him is at the same time belief in him and in his *personality*.

Here Kant expresses the profound *immediacy* of what many ordinary religious people would call *knowing God*. While he dare not use the term "knowledge" to describe this "moral–practical relation," for fear that this would encourage delirious delusion regarding what such religious experience can accomplish, Kant is here bearing witness to the same basic experience of a direct (unmediated) encounter with a personal being.

Kant goes so far as to depict the moral imperative as the voice of God in the human soul:[4] "The categorical imperative . . . leads directly to God, yes, serves as a pledge of His reality"; "the virtuous individual experiences directly, in the categorical imperative, the voice of God and . . . apprehends Him, with the certainty of a personal faith, as a transcendental reality"; for "in morally–practical reason and in the categorical imperative God reveals himself."[5] Schrader (1951, 239–40) appeals to the perspectival character of Kant's System in order to explain why this does not contradict the practical system's view of the moral law as independent from all external determination (including God's): "It is from the standpoint of religion that the moral law is to be regarded as the 'voice of God.' The passages from [*OP*] in which Kant makes such assertions are perfectly consistent with his critical position."

Interestingly, Kant refers to "instinct" in *CBHH* 8.111 as "that *voice of God* which all animals obey." He goes on (112) to suggest that the story of Adam and Eve is the account of how human beings first came to "cavil with the voice of nature"—here corresponding to the "voice of God" in instinct—through "the first attempt at a free choice" (cf. Despland 1973, 60). Along these lines Despland points out (45; cf. *IUH* 9.18–19) that for Kant nature "does not contain the destiny of man. Nature's role is first of all limited to the task of bringing man to the point where he can and must assert his independence from her." This is what I call the "birth" of reason. "The plan of Nature," Despland adds, "is to make man a self-governing being." This could also be called *God's* plan: to nurture human reason toward maturity. My contention is that Kant hoped *OP* would bring together and clarify this "big picture" that guided his thinking: the God who gives us both nature and reason expects us to use the latter to separate ourselves from the former (and so also, from the instinctual form of God's voice) in order to hear the *moral* aspect of God's voice. Thus *OP* was to culminate Kant's philosophy of history by showing how our ultimate *hope* is in the union of both extremes. In our own experience of self-governing, we come to see the self-governing of God in nature, and ultimately, we see the unity of both in immediate experience—though we can never hope to *explain* it, since reason dies at this point. Despland (1973, 46) is therefore only partially correct to say: "A rational man is a man divorced from nature." This divorce is finalized in Kant's practical system; what Despland's comment neglects is the happy remarriage that takes place in Kant's judicial system, where nature offers us symbols directing us back to the supersensible. In any case, the account of reason's "birth" in *CBHH* suggests that our free reason is the very thing that puts up a barrier between us and God, which in turn implies reason must in some sense "die" or come to its final resting point before God's voice becomes fully audible to us again. We shall return to this provocative suggestion in Chapter 12.

Kant's definitions and descriptions of God in *OP* consistently link God to practical reason. The claim that "[m]oral–practical reason . . . leads to the concept of God" (22.116) seems quite consistent with the moral argument for God's existence that plays an integral part in *CPrR*. Likewise, the notion that God is "a being which has only rights and no duties" (22.120; see also 21.9–11; 22.48–49), who is "obligating" but "never obligated" (22.127; see also 22.124), holds no surprises for readers of *RBBR* (see 6.153–54n). That God "has unrestricted power over nature and freedom under laws of reason" does seem, however, to be going further.[6] Clearly Kant sees God as an *active force* in the world. But what kind of force? Whatever else this force may be (see Chapter 11), it is *personal*, for as we have seen, Kant repeatedly insists on viewing God as a "person" (e.g., *OP* 22.119–20). Sometimes he borrows biblical imagery to describe this relationship: "In . . . the idea of God as a moral being, we live, and move and have our being" (22.118; see also 22.55; cf. Acts 17:28). But at its most extreme, Kant's tendency to associate God with practical reason leads him to *identify* the two: "The concept of God . . . is not a hypothetical thing but pure practical reason itself in its personality" (22.118). "There is a God for there is a categorical imperative" (22.106 [Sullivan 1971, 120]; cf. 104–5).

Some interpreters have taken such claims at face value, concluding that Kant's God, especially in *OP*, is indeed *identical* to reason. Such an interpretation has an element of truth in it: the foregoing quotes demonstrate that Kant does regard God as *immanent in* the web of a priori conditions that reason uses to bring true knowledge, good action, and beautiful purposes within the grasp of human beings. Sometimes he refers to "the categorical imperative in me" in close proximity to statements that allude to the meaning of his own first name: "*Est deus in nobis*" (Latin for "God is in us," reminiscent of "Immanuel," meaning "God is with us" in Hebrew) (*OP* 22.129–30; see also 22.54). When Kant himself raises the issue of whether there is anything *real* that corresponds to our concept of God (22.117)—that is, anything that would *distinguish* God from human reason or extend *beyond* the categorical imperative—he usually avoids any direct answer, calling this issue "problematic"; but he clarifies elsewhere that this being "is different from me" even though I become aware of it only "in me" (21.25). In some sense, we participate in God whenever we use our rational capacities properly. Yet, to regard this intimate participation as a complete identification is to ignore Kant's equally important emphasis on God's *transcendence* (see *KCR* §V.1). For, although Kant always insists that God abides by the moral law, he does not therefore believe God is subordinate to it; rather, "the categorical imperative is a command *of* God."[7]

God may be present *in* our reason, but our reason is not coextensive with God's nature. For God must also have some reality over and above the whole System of reason's perspectives. Despland (1973, 146) accurately portrays these two aspects when he says "Kant's moral theism secures a subjective interior approach to our thinking about God and secures a transcendent, religiously available God." Just as Copernicus derived his theory concerning the movements of the planets from the hypothesis that a motionless sun lies at the center of the planetary system, so also Kant derives his theory concerning the meaning of human perspectives on truth, goodness, and beauty from the hypothesis that a real, transcendent God—the ultimate thing in itself, residing "outside myself" (*OP* 21.15; 21.22)—emits the pure (but unknowable) "Light" of Truth, Goodness, and Beauty from the suprarational, perspectiveless center of the philosophical System (see e.g., *CF* 7.47). We human beings tend to obscure that Light by expecting to find truth, goodness, and beauty in sources other than reason. Kant's prerequisite for trusting the imperfect light of human reason is that we deabsolutize the ideas of reason through the experience of Critique, by baring all our human perspectives to the transcendent Light at this mystical core of the System. That Kant regards this whole process as happening "within us" (i.e., in our immediate experience) prompts Weber (1896, 472) to claim that "the three *Critiques* culminate in absolute spiritualism."

In *KSP* §§V.1–4, I demonstrated that Kant's philosophical System *begins* with a special sort of "theoretical faith" in the existence (or perhaps more accurately, the "reality") of the thing in itself. We can now see that the System *ends* where it began, only now with a deep awareness that this faith can be validated only through what is usually called *religious experience*.[8] A mystical encounter with what Kant calls "the transcendental" is the ultimate way of validating the initial, theoretical faith required to enter the System; without such an experience, all theological reflection is groundless. Whereas in his practical system Kant had argued that morality provides us with *rea-*

sons for belief in God, "he now . . . suggests that the moral experience *itself* may legitimately be regarded as an experience of the Divine."⁹ Or as Norburn (1973, 439) puts it, *OP* tries to show "that our awareness of God goes *along with*, not is merely postulated by, our awareness of the moral law."

This expression of the consciousness of moral obligation as an immediate consciousness of God is sometimes interpreted as *OP*'s new way of proving God's existence. Along these lines, Copleston (1960, 390) portrays Kant as developing "a moral equivalent of or analogue to the ontological argument." As an example he quotes a statement Kant makes in *OP* 22.109: "the mere Idea (*Idee*) of God is at the same time a postulate of His existence. To think of Him and to believe in Him is an identical proposition." Copleston says this means "that within and for the moral consciousness itself the idea of the law as the voice of a divine legislator is equivalent to belief in God's existence." While there is indeed an interesting similarity here, associating this view with the ontological argument is highly misleading, for the latter is a theoretical argument, whereas Kant's claims in *OP* are judicial and doctrinal (in Kant's special sense), relating solely to our existential awareness of the moral law, not to logical proof.

William Sullivan (1971, 129), arguing against a similar view defended by S.J. Poncelet, agrees that in the context of *OP* such assertions are "not an ontological argument at all." Against Copleston's version of this position, Sullivan claims (121) that the qualifications Kant places on his affirmations of God in *OP* indicate that he is not attempting to prove "the existence of God in any traditional sense . . . , i.e., 'God as an objective reality.'" Sullivan supports his argument with numerous quotations from *OP*, but unfortunately edits his selections in such a way as to give the impression that Kant's text supports extreme subjectivism more than it actually does.¹⁰ Sullivan (131) agrees, however, that *OP*'s treatment of God "is radically different" from that of the moral argument in *CPrR*: whereas the latter points to an *objectively* existing God, the former points only "to the knowing and willing subject." He interprets Kant as moving away from an emphasis on "a utilitarian God" and toward an "emphasis on the categorical imperative rather than on God" (123): "God's existence or non-existence—in the traditional sense of an independent, supreme substance—is not critical as long as the imperative character of the moral life is preserved."

This interpretation, however, is as misleading as Copleston's, for it ignores that *OP* takes Kant's Copernican hypothesis to its proper perspectival conclusion. True, Kant does not affirm God's existence in any traditional sense that would qualify as *knowledge* in the context of his theoretical system, and his reconfirmation of his own practical postulates is ambiguous at best; but what Sullivan misses is that Kant is *building* on these and thus affirming the *experienced reality* of God, when he interprets the moral imperative as God's immediate voice. There is no reason to suppose that in affirming an existential *encounter* with God through the moral law Kant must be *denying* the validity of his former arguments. The objective arguments of Kant's theoretical system can never establish anything but the *hypothesis* that an external God is possible; the moral argument of his practical system can postulate God only as a belief that reason *needs* an actual God; this new argument in *OP* establishes God's presence as necessary through an immediate encounter with the fact that we are moral–rational beings. An "objective referent" is indeed missing, as Sullivan (1971, 131–32) points out; but this is because, as so many mystics have affirmed (see note 11.7), object and subject are indistinguishable in the mystical unity of an immediate experience (see *KSP* §IV.1).

Adickes 1920 adopts a position even more extreme than Sullivan's, interpreting Kant's new arguments in *OP* as an outright repudiation of the moral proof given in the Dialectic of *CPrR*—a view often echoed uncritically.[11] Although Kemp Smith 1923 agrees with Adickes, stating that in *OP* Kant "acknowledges the inadequacy of his professedly practical, but really theoretical, proof of God's existence, advocating in its place a proof of a more consistently moral character" (610), he later admits that Kant "nowhere, in explicit terms, avows this change of standpoint" (638; cf. Wood 1970, 10–13). The former comment not only reads theoretical motives into Kant's moral argument that simply are not there;[12] it also fails to take account of the fact that the argument in *OP* functions not essentially as moral Critique, but as judicial, if not *existential*, metaphysics. As Schrader (1951, 235) explains, Adickes supports his position with three points: "(1) that Kant failed to restate ['the moral argument in the *Opus Postumum*']; (2) that he declared that no proof of God's existence can be offered; (3) that he stated that God is directly and immediately revealed in the categorical imperative." Given the immense and still pervasive influence of Adickes' interpretation nearly a century later, let us take a closer look at each of these points in turn.

The first point is merely negative and could just as well indicate "that Kant was quite satisfied with the formulations of the argument which he already had" (Ward 1972, 161). This alternative is supported by the otherwise grossly inconsistent fact that Kant continues to support the general idea of a moral proof (see e.g., *OP* 22.60; 22.121), regarding "the knowledge of all human duties *as* divine commands" as having "the same force as if a real world–judge were assumed" (22.125). That he does not restate the *details* of the proof does not mean he no longer accepts it,[13] but only that what is appropriate for practical Critique may be irrelevant for the judicial metaphysics of *OP*. The second point is likewise easily rebutted by anyone who is sensitive to Kant's use of the principle of perspective: *OP*'s rejection of theological proofs "is entirely consonant with Kant's Critical position, wherein he does not regard the moral argument as a theoretical proof" (Ward 1972, 161; see also Schrader 1951, 236–40). Kant apparently assumes the reader is familiar enough with his System of Perspectives to know he is referring only to the inadequacy of all *theoretical* proofs. When the first two points are accounted for perspectively, the third point loses its problematic character: an immediate encounter with God is not a problem as long as we remember that it is valid only from the standpoint of judicial metaphysics and therefore does not justify a claim to have established empirical cognition (see Chapter 7).

Against Adickes' third point, Schrader argues that certain passages in *OP* "would seem to make it impossible to conclude that Kant had come to accept a personal subjective faith in God based upon a direct revelation in the categorical imperative" (Schrader 1951, 237). The passage he quotes, however, states that the ideas of freedom and God "cannot be exhibited and proven *directly* (immediately) but only *indirectly* through a mediating principle: ... namely, in the human, moral/practical reason" (*OP* 21.30, Schrader's translation). This simply means that the immediate experience of God through practical reason cannot serve on its own as a direct *proof*; Kant is not here denying or contradicting his claims elsewhere in *OP* that our consciousness of God *is* direct and immediate.[14] Thus Adickes' third point is valid, but provides no evidence that Kant intends to repudiate *CPrR*'s moral argument. Because of their lack of attention to the principle of perspective, the positions represented by Adickes and Schrader both fail to take account of the crucial fact that the argument in *CPrR* is significantly different from that in *OP*: the former argues for the need to postulate God in order to make sense out of our morality; the latter argues that God is, at a more basic level, *present in* our immediate experience. There is therefore no good reason to regard the two arguments as mutually exclusive; both can be accepted, provided we distinguish clearly between their respective standpoints.

The distinctive character of Kant's argument in *OP* can be brought out still further by examining its epistemological status. I shall do this in more detail in Chapter 11, when considering Kant's claims regarding the mysterious substance that underlies and unifies our immediate experience of nature. At this point a few brief suggestions will suffice. Copleston borrows Otto's phrase, "religious *a priori*," to describe "the idea that man is by nature oriented to God or open to the Transcendent."[15] As Chapman (1992, 476) points out, Otto 1950 credits Schleiermacher with the insight of adding to Kant's first two questions a third, "What do we experience in the soul?" I would respond, however, by pointing out that Kant already intends his own *fourth* question, "What is man?" (*JL* 9.25; *C* 11.429), to cover such issues concerning our inner experience. Otto bases much of his thinking on Hans Fries' attempt to improve Kant's philosophy by allowing "direct access to things–in–themselves" (496). Otto believes that in so doing Fries provides "a philosophical refinement of Schleiermacher" (494).

Davidovich (1993b, 182–83; see also 185) calls Otto's religious category "an *immediate awareness of reason*." As such, it has an obvious affinity with Kant's portrayal in *OP* of our immediate awareness of the moral law; the difference is that Kant would never refer to such awareness as a "category," because it is not a cognitive power of the human mind. In response to those such as Otto, who posit a "'category' of blind and irrational feeling," Wood (1970, 204) points out, quite rightly, that Kant does not *ignore* such irrational elements in religion, but rather (202) "attempt[s] to make a *rational* assessment of them." Wood (204) quotes Kant's assertion (see *RBBR* 6.175) that this "inversion" is "the death of reason"—a claim we shall examine further in Chapter 12.

Noting that in Kant's writings the "characteristic nature of the religious sentiment is never treated as rendering it non-rational," Webb (1926, 204) claims: "Kant was . . . wrong in *identifying* the religious with the moral sentiment." But this accusation neglects the subtlety of what Kant was trying to accomplish in *OP*. For Kant, theology (knowledge of God) and religion (actions in response to God's commands) must always be rational; but the root experience that gives rise to these thoughts and practices lies beyond reason; it is perspectiveless. This is why Kant continually struggles with the *paradoxical* character of any attempt to describe this experience. Otto himself recognized that only the *base experience* out of which religion develops is supra-rational; what arises out of that experience must conform to rational norms. Thus I agree with Webb's claim (1926, 205) that "Kant's . . . own sentiment towards the sublimities and ingenuities of nature really implies the existence of something other than what is distinctively ethical, which is yet capable of arousing the religious sentiment." What I disagree with is the notion that Kant was unaware of this point. Kant's emphasis on the God-relation as being ethical-for-us does not require him to deny the possibility that God's hidden nature may be supra-ethical.

Neglecting Kant's openness to the transcendent in *OP* (and in a great many other texts), Kim (1988–89, 367) claims that "the rationality Kant champions is an 'immanent' rationality forever alienated from its transcendent object . . . ; the transcendent does not announce its presence within [the horizons of human subjectivity]." This may be true for Kant's theoretical system (though even there the presence of the ineffable "thing in itself" and its conceptual correlate, the "transcendental object" is all too evident), and perhaps even for his practical system (though, once again, the highest good is a transcendent object that informs the whole argument), but surely not for his judicial system; this is why, as I argued in *KCR* and *CCKR*, God is the ultimate (though unknowable) focal point for Kant's System and the judicial is its highest standpoint—especially as manifested in religion. Only here do we have access to the transcendent, and only here does Kant fully overcome the alienation Kim laments. Yet Kim concludes (367): "The whole philosophy of Kant emerges as a paradox," as "an intellectual panic" that comes close to Kierkegaard's "absurd." The problem with this conclusion is that Kim's argument focuses mainly on *CPrR* and *GMM*. His claim would be more feasible if it were not for the fact that Kant *balances* the judicial with other standpoints that are *not* merely existential leaps. Kim claims that Kant fails to meet the demand of "[r]eligious consciousness" for "an intelligible account of the openness of human subjectivity to the transcendent" (367). To some extent this may be true; at least, many of his readers have read Kant in this way. But I am arguing that he was at least *attempting* to meet precisely this demand in *OP*. Akhutin (1991, 78) expresses much the same point: "One can approach the meta-physical only as one would approach the meta-logical." Kant sees this in terms of "the noumenal darkness of the 'thing in itself'" (78) and thus regards "philosophizing" as "preserving the memory of that primordial perplexity which constitutes the root of human existence" (84). This tantalizing perplexity is just what Kant must have experienced as he struggled to write *OP*, in which he hoped to express the ultimate implications of Critique.

Kant would reject Otto's claim regarding a distinctively "religious *a priori*," not because he denies our theocentric orientation—he does not (see *KCR* §I.3)—but because it is not part of our nature in the same way the synthetic a priori conditions for knowledge are. Unlike space, time, and causality, as well as freedom and the moral law, we do not find "God" in our reason as a constituent element, epistemologically prior to all experience; rather, we *make* this idea a part of our nature, in response to and in proportion with our encounter with transcendent reality. That is, we are open to God "by nature" in a very different way: it is an *a posteriori response*,[16] whereby we impose the *concept* of the transcendent (analytically) onto our experience. The analyticity of this imposition explains why Kant says in *OP* 21.153 (my translation): "It is absurd to ask whether [there] is a God." To ask such a question, from *OP*'s existential standpoint, is tantamount to asking: "Do *I* exist?" For a basic "self-perceiving" (*Selbstanschauung*—i.e., "making oneself the object of one's own intuition") lies at the root of our immediate awareness of God. Describing its status as analytic yet *a posteriori* can help us appreciate why Kant speaks of it in such a paradoxical way (see *KCR*, Appendix IV.4). Although he does not express his position so clearly, he does hint at it on several occasions, as when he refers in *OP* 22.442 to our "self-intuition" as (paradoxically) both analytic and synthetic (see also 465).

Does Kant's appeal to a direct experience of God merely take us back to the pre-Kantian practice of philosophers calling on God to fill the "gaps" that they could not fill in with empirical evidence or rational proof? No. The difference between Kant's appeal to God and the typical "God of the gaps" approach is that the latter treats God as *an element in the system*, so that our theoretical cognition of God is regarded as absolutely certain, whereas Kant appeals to a person's *experience* of God, interpreted through an act of *practical faith*, as a paradoxical awareness of the presence of transcendence within the world—a purely subjective validation of a System that begins and ends with a recognition of our objective ignorance of the transcendent.[17] For some, this may be an inadequate, intellectually dissatisfying way to conclude such an impressive philosophical System. But according to Kant it is the only way to be philosophical without letting our philosophy rob us of what is most authentically human. As Norburn (1973, 442) puts it, "when we have acquired the humility to accept [the] truth [that "our situation" is "indefensibly human"], then all our thinking, says Kant, *centers our minds upon the idea of God. Can we ask for more?*" The core message of Kant's Critical mysticism is that anyone who experiences Critique, by allowing the light of reason to lay bare all of the dark recesses of human ignorance, will recognize that we cannot, and therefore should not, ask for more.

NOTES

1. *OP* 21.29. Kant analyzes the concept of the Trinity in the General Comment to the Third Piece of *RBBR*. Far from denying its legitimacy, he argues that, even though it remains an utter mystery when taken as a theoretical concept, we can form a clear practical concept of a divine Trinity in terms of God's three moral personalities: "holy lawgiver," "benevolent governor," and "just judge" (*RBBR* 6.139). For a detailed discussion of this treatment of the Trinity, see Appendix III of *CCKR*.

2. Personality is a key theme because it is the common factor that unites God and humanity, though in *OP* Kant often applies such terms "to the divine as distinguished from the human spirit" (Webb 1926, 183). To support his position Webb refers to Adickes 1920, 762–63, 766–68, 772–76, 778, 780, 819–24, 826–28.

3. Kemp Smith 1923, 639; see also Greene 1934, lxviii. Along these lines Kant says "the spirit of man" is "a being above the world" (*OP* 21.42). Looking at the same relationship from the opposite side, Collins (1967, 134–35, emphasis added) says: "A moral believer is one who is ready to accept the *personal spiritual reality* of God even though we cannot know God's existence theoretically."

4. See e.g., *OP* 22.64. On Kant's reference to the "voice of God," Schrader (1951a, 239n) lists *OP* 21.14, 17, 21, 56, 60, 113, 118, 143ff, 153, 157 and 22.55, 106, 109, 114, 124. Webb (1926, 82,175) associates this voice with both God's transcendence and God's immanence.

5. Greene (1934, lxvi) translates these *OP* passages from Adickes 1920, 801, 847, 806, respectively. An important point to note is that Kant says we encounter this voice as a transcendental, not a transcendent, reality. Even in *OP* we have no way of experiencing the transcendent as such.

6. *OP* 22.116–7. Kant's stress on God's "omnipotent" power (see also 22.122–23) reminds us that Kant's God is not merely a moral being. For God, "with respect to nature, is capable of everything" (22.127); as such God is also "the highest being in the physical respect." I downplayed this aspect of God's nature in *KCR* §§V.2–4 because the practical always has primacy for Kant.

7. *OP* 22.128, emphasis added. In *KCR* Appendix IV.4 I offer further evidence that Kant does not intend such comments as an absolute identification between God and practical reason.

8. In the Conclusion I discuss the implications of this position for the issue of the objective meaningfulness of religious experience, in dialogue with Antony Flew's position.

9. Greene 1934, lxvi. In the omitted text Greene adds "for the first time in his life"—a qualification that, as we saw in Chapters 7 and 8, is quite unjustified. Greene's failure to

recognize that this was not a new theme in Kant's mind, but only one whose proper standpoint had not yet been adopted, leads him to regard this as a radical reversal of Kant's former dependence on the moral proof. Ward (1972, 60), by contrast, sees in *LE* "a hint of [*OP*'s] doctrine that God and practical reason are to be identified." Quoting from *LE* 27.283, he says "God is required as the 'ground of obedience' to morality. That is, though the understanding can discern what the moral law is, it is God who 'imposes upon everyone the obligation of acting in accordance with' the law." A further hint can be drawn from *MM* 6.438–39, where God's presence in our conscience is portrayed as possibly "an actual person or a merely ideal person that reason creates for itself." Likewise, in *RPTS* 8.401n Kant says the "archetype" (see note 12.2, below) must be "made by ourselves" since it "appears personally to us." As emphasized above (see also *KCR*, Appendix IV.4), such comments should be interpreted with Kant's Copernican Perspective in mind, as not precluding the possibility that God also exists independently of our "production" of archetypal Presence.

10. That Sullivan 1971 was one of the main sources of *OP* passages in English translation for the last quarter of the twentieth century (until the Cambridge Edition of *OP* appeared, in 1993) contributed, no doubt, to a good deal of the confusion that still persists regarding Kant's position.

11. See e.g., Webb 1926, 66; Greene 1934, lxvi; Copleston 1988, 321. Some agree with Adickes while disagreeing with his reasoning. Beck (1960, 275), for instance, rejects Adickes' claim that Kant regards the moral argument as insufficiently subjective (see note 10.12, below); instead, he thinks Kant rejects it after realizing that it is actually a theoretical argument. Wood (1970, 171–76) effectively refutes Beck. By contrast, Ward (1972, 160) says that in *OP* "God becomes either a mere objectification of the moral law within, or the referent for a directly experienced personal being which makes itself felt immediately in the moral law. . . . Either view would constitute a radical change in Kant's doctrine of the relation of morality and religion." But this "change" turns out not to be so "radical" after all, once we see it as a change of standpoint. Failing to appreciate Kant's perspectival methodology, Ward goes on to reject this option, because for Kant "a direct revelation of God is metaphysically impossible and morally dangerous" (162; see also 165). What Ward fails to understand is that, as I have argued above, such worries are valid only if *theoretical* knowledge–claims are believed to follow directly from such an experience. As long as the experience remains what it is, immediate (i.e., as long as one's mysticism is understood Critically), such problems simply cannot arise.

12. Schrader (1951, 236–37) makes a similar point in his refutation of the position adopted by Adickes. He reports that "Adickes found Kant's moral argument [in *CPrR*] to be unsatisfactory on two counts: (1) that it failed to recognize the personal and subjective character of religious faith; (2) that it involved the introduction of a hedonistic element into Kant's ethics" (232; see also Silber 1960, cxl). He rightly denies the validity of both objections. The first ignores the perspectival difference between the practical and judicial standpoints: only the latter needs to take into account the "personal" element in religion. And the second is a misinterpretation of Kant's argument in *CPrR* (see *KSP* §VIII.3). Adickes' own dissatisfaction with the moral proof may explain why he was so intent on depicting Kant himself as rejecting it in *OP*.

13. Peters (1993, 98) makes the same point, but does not go on to relate it to a shift in standpoint.

14. Nor is he merely "stating his inner personal convictions for the first time"; as Schrader (1951, 237) rightly observes, this would be "trivial," since Kant makes it clear enough in many other writings that he is "convinced of the reality of God."

15. Copleston 1974, 7–8. The phrase "religious a priori" was popularized by Rudolph Otto 1950.

16. As Sullivan (1971, 132) says, Kant's argument for God in *OP* is concerned with "the *experience* of the moral life," not with its rational basis, as in *CPrR*. As such, it is a posteriori.

17. Akhutin (1991, 83) expresses a similar point when he says that with the metaphysical ideas, "[r]eason is not simply recognizing its own ignorance . . . : it perceives . . . that the metaphysical is something that sustains its world but is not part of it." This "perception" of the transcendent is the main focus of *OP*, though as Akhutin rightly says, we always remain ignorant of it in the process.

Chapter Eleven

Matter's Living Force as Immediate Experience of the World

The sections of *OP* dealing with the idea of the world (i.e., with the transitions between physics, *CPR*, and *MFNS*) focus mainly on the philosophical implications of the phenomenon we experience as *heat*. In keeping with a hypothesis commonly assumed by physicists of his day, Kant believed this and other phenomena are grounded on a hidden substance, called "caloric" or "ether"[1]—i.e., "a matter for which all bodies are permeable, but which is itself expansive" (*OP* 22.193). He regards "caloric" as the "presupposition" that "an *internally* moving matter" exists and fills "the whole of cosmic space."[2] This "inward" undulation or "vibration" does not expand the material object itself, but vibrates "in the space which it occupies" (22.142). Kant maintains that "the function of its activity is not [merely to generate] warmth"; instead, "heat may only be one particular effect of its moving forces" (21.228–29; see also 21.584–85, 21.602). The resulting "idea of the whole of moving forces ... is the basis of ... matter"; we experience it as "a sense–object" (21.582). Kant sees this universal and never-ending movement at the inner core of all matter as leading to "the concept of an *animated* matter" (21.184). That is, "the totality of our world," taken as itself "an organic body," can be thought of as being *alive*![3]

Although Kant unfortunately does not explicitly connect the basic energy of nature with his other concerns in *OP*, he does provide us with enough hints to develop a coherent reconstruction and to indicate that here, too, his concerns relate to what I am calling his Critical mysticism. For example, he poses the basic problem of this aspect of his final transition project as follows (*OP* 22.120): "There is a God in the soul of man. The question is whether he is also in nature." That Kant wants to encourage an affirmative answer to this question (but one based on rational faith, *not* knowledge) seems beyond reasonable doubt, given the weight of textual evidence. In this passage, after reminding us that "God and the world contain the *totality* of existence" (22.124), Kant draws an explicit analogy between God and "the ether": like ether, "God regarded as a natural being is a hypothetical being, assumed for the explanation of appearances" (22.126). Indeed, by taking such tantalizing hints seriously and regarding cosmotheology (God–in–the–world) as a key expression of *OP*'s aim (see 21.17), we can interpret Kant's long and hard focus on the topic of ether/caloric as an expression of his belief that this "living force" (e.g., 22.142) is an empirical manifestation of God's fiery presence in the natural world. Moreover, Kant's focus on understanding the significance of *living forces* in nature marks a return to the theme of his very first publication (*TELF*)—a neat bit of symmetry that is typically overlooked by commentators. For his doctoral dissertation (*SEMF*) consisted of reflections on *fire*, a topic that returns to center stage in *OP*. With respect to his early interest in natural philosophy, just as in the case of his early interest in philosophical theology, *OP* therefore brings Kant's philosophical life–work full circle with the ripened fruition of a Critical mysticism that has a physical as well as a spiritual side, aptly reflecting the dual interest of his youth.

Not just the matter that constitutes the bodies of plants and animals (*OP* 22.210), but *all* matter is, in this metaphorical sense, *alive*. Kant thus portrays the hidden, internal side of matter as endlessly vibrating in ways that do not expand the space it fills in the visible world, but which alone explains how *heat* can come about: "These pulsations constitute a living force" (21.310). Despite appearances to the contrary, this view does not require Kant to change or reject any of his Critical doctrines; rather, it merely indicates *OP*'s change of *standpoint*. For just as the thing in itself is unknowable in his theoretical system, so also we are "incapable of knowing [the ether] and its weight by any experience" (21.387–88); despite the crucial role they play in *OP*'s "transition" argument, both ether and caloric are "imponderable" (i.e., they lack density).

Kant shows special interest in the force of gravity because, unlike ordinary forces that act upon objects *externally* in order to propel them into motion (*OP* 21.308), gravity "acts upon the inside of matter *immediately*." Likewise, to account for our "sensation of warmth," Kant posits at one point a sixth sense, "an inward one," in contrast to the "five outer senses."[4] Given Kant's insistence that "a highest—namely, originally independent—understanding" underlies the "one universal [matter]" (21.183), we are justified in regarding such comments as yet further evidence of *OP*'s goal of highlighting God's immediate presence, not only in our moral experience but also in our experience of nature. Indeed, the foregoing quote is followed by a single word that ends a section: "*agitatio*." This seems to be Kant's shorthand way of indicating his intention to portray God as underlying the material world as its agitating force, a primal fire that shakes up and warms the entire universe.

As Sullivan (1971, 127) puts it, Kant regards "phlogiston, the principle of fire" as "[t]he most common example" of a phenomenon that requires us to posit God as "a hypothetical being" in order to explain its occurrence.

Physics, it seems, is revealing to us at its very root the same "Immanuel" ("God within us") we find at the foundation of true religion: "The *primum movens* [prime mover] is not locomotive but rather internal" (*OP* 22.200), for "this matter is . . . to be assumed as the prime mover . . . , subjectively" (21.553). Since "intention" cannot be a property of matter, Kant reasons, we must suppose an *immaterial* basis for the unifying force that makes organisms what they are—what some would call "a world–soul," though it can never be demonstrated to be such (22.548; cf. 22.100). Indeed, Kant warns on a number of occasions that he is not supporting the notion of a "world–soul" (e.g., 21.18–19; 21.92); rather, his view is that our "*Moral–practical reason is one of the moving forces of nature* and of all sense–objects." (22.105). That he has an analogical connection in mind here is suggested in *OP* 21.153: "To say absolutely that a God is . . . is analogous with the propositions that space is and time is. All these objects of knowledge are mere products of our own self-made representations (ideas) among which that of God is the uppermost." This analogy suggests that God is immanent (omnipresent) to our practical reasoning about our moral experience in the same way that space and time are to our theoretical reasoning about objects we experience in the phenomenal world (see *KCR*, Figure V.3). Kant sometimes expresses this so forcefully that he seems almost to be forgetting its analogical status (Adickes 1920, 827; trans. in Webb 1926, 199): "The idea of that which the human Reason itself makes of the universe is the active representation of God, not as the substance of a *separate* personality outside of me, but as the thought of a personality within me." Elsewhere Kant expresses even more explicitly what might be called his pan*en*theism: "*space is the phenomenon of the divine [omni]presence.*"[5]

Kant's reason for referring in a number of *OP* passages to Spinoza's "enormous idea of intuiting all things [*Sache*] . . . in God" (21.50; see also *ID* 2.410) is not easy to discern. These jottings may simply be reminders of a position he intends to refute later. Such an interpretation could find backing from Johann Georg Hamann's report (in his letter to Friedrich Heinrich Jacobi dated November 20, 1786) that "Kant confessed to me, that he had never properly studied Spinoza" (quoted in Bax 1903, xxxv) and that "Kant could never make anything of Spinoza, though he had many long conversations on the subject with his intimate friend Kraus." Yet I believe there is something substantive in Kant's references to Spinoza. For a refined version of Spinoza's formula expresses in a nutshell a view Kant himself elaborates throughout *OP* and thus serves as a significant means of expressing the culminating step of *OP*'s tantalizing task: to unite together the two most diverse human ideas, God and the world. For by "things" Kant is referring not to the abstract epistemological construct of the thing in itself (*Ding an sich*), but to the manifold phenomena (*Sache*) we actually experience in the *world*. Kant's point, then, seems to be that Spinoza provides us with a means of conceiving how the knowing subject unites God and the world in every act of intuition (see note 9.7, above).

Here again we have met the sort of paradox that typifies all the transitions (see e.g., *OP* 21.475), with their character as the synthesis of a pair of opposites: the living forces *of matter* are alive ("in God"), even though matter as we know it (as "all things") is *dead*. Let us therefore examine the epistemological status of Kant's claims regarding the mysterious substance that underlies and unifies the continuum we experience as space–time.[6] As I have argued in *KSP* §§IV.3–4 and elsewhere (see note 9.16), one of Kant's chief shortcomings was to limit his epistemological framework to three basic classifications instead of recognizing the role of the analytic a posteriori as the proper status of those elements in his System that are properly justified on the basis of rational faith rather than intuition-based empirical cognition. In an early draft for a Preface to his final work (21.524) Kant confesses his love of architectonic in terms that reveal why he remained blind to the power of the analytic a posteriori:

> As far as philosophy is concerned it is my plan—and lies . . . in my natural vocation—to remain within the boundaries of what is knowable *a priori*: to survey, where possible, its field, and to present it as a circle (*orbis*), simple and unitary, that is, as a system prescribed by pure reason, not one conceived arbitrarily.

Here Kant reveals his absolute bias for the a priori—a bias that may be regarded as the single most important reason Kant's goal remains, as I argued in *KCR*, Chapter XI, a tantalizing ideal that he is unable to grasp. For he has rightly identified the status of physics as an empirical science: its specific knowledge–claims must be synthetic and a posteriori. He has also rightly identified his own philosophical foundations for physics (established in *CPR* and *MFNS*) as providing synthetic a priori principles for science. He is even right to recognize that a gap still remains between the empirical status of physics and the foundations provided in *MFNS*. He goes wrong only by insisting that the gap he is searching for must be filled by something a priori.

Kant's treatment of this problem in *OP* shows he is aware of the paradoxical nature of his search: he is looking for something that could be a priori and yet empirical at the same time. As he writes at several points, "the transition is a descent" from a priori principles to the empirical (e.g., *OP* 21.476; see also 21.525). Kant seems well aware that he is on to something crucial to the unity and completeness of his philosophical System; but how to describe the *status* of this tantalizing transition repeatedly eludes his grasp.[7]

For the remainder of this chapter I shall argue that his search for an appropriate description for all the transitions, but especially for the vital role played by ether/caloric, can be satisfied by classifying them as *analytic a posteriori*.

Despite his repeated attempts to force it into his favorite, transcendental (synthetic a priori) mold, Kant elsewhere leaves no doubt as to the *analytic* status of his ether proof.[8] For example, he states in *OP* 21.226 that its principle—the principle of "full space," in contrast to the Newtonian concept of "empty space" (21.223–24)—is inferred "according to the principle of identity" from the impossibility of empty space (see also 21.228–29). Moreover, he comes right out and calls it analytic in passages such as *OP* 21.233: "the universally distributed caloric . . . is the basis for the system of moving forces which emerges analytically, from concepts—that is, according to the rule of identity—from the principle of agreement with the possibility of experience overall [*überhaupt*]." By referring to "the possibility of experience overall" he intends, no doubt, to suggest an a priori, transcendental origin for the ether principle. Yet he also wants to regard it as *empirical*—wherein, he admits, "appears to lie a contradiction" (e.g., 21.230; see also 21.244). Once again, he could have resolved (or at least, found a valid epistemological status to *clarify*) the paradoxical character of this ultimate principle by fully embracing its purely conceptual starting-point as analytic, but treating it as a regulative hypothesis that we impose onto our experience of the world, a posteriori. This would have given him a conceptual handle for describing how the concept of ether/caloric can at first be "a mere thought–object" (an analytic relation between concepts), yet can eventually come to be experienced as a real *sense*–object (an a posteriori relation between intuitions).[9]

The impasse in Kant's reasoning is caused by his unquestioned assumption that the concept of ether/caloric must be a priori in order to fulfill a significant philosophical function. Thus when he portrays the caloric essence of all matter "as an idea" that "emerge[s] *a priori* from reason" (*OP* 22.551–52), he *assumes* its rational origin makes it a priori, *even though* he is quick to point out the paradoxical fact that it is also "to be regarded altogether as an object of experience (*given*)." "Caloric is," as he puts it in *OP* 21.584, "a categorically given material." Once we recognize its emergence from reason as *analytic* (contained within the categories), we are set free to regard its material given-ness as an *a posteriori* characteristic. Along these lines Kant here admits that the concept of caloric can have a "hypothetical" use whenever we use it "to *explain* certain phenomena."[10] Although the ether proof makes use of the concept of "possible experience," as do all ordinary transcendental arguments, it exhibits an important difference that demands assigning it with a distinct epistemological status: the ether proofs are concerned not with the form (as "merely *thought*"), but with the *content* of possible experience (22.580)—a point again suggesting they are a posteriori. Kant says in *OP* 22.241 that the four principles of transition are "derived analytically from the mere concept of physics." Earlier in the same sentence he also says the transition is "*a priori*." But if the transition were *both* analytic and a priori, then it would be nothing but a merely logical operation. What Kant has in mind seems to be much more subtle—something *akin* to logic, but with deeper implications for the way we actually experience the world; unfortunately, he had disallowed the legitimacy of the term that would have enabled him to express such a quasi-logical status. The subtlety comes to the fore in the paradoxical statement that ends the same paragraph: "Regulative principles which are also constitutive." Being analytic enables a principle to regulate our knowledge conceptually; in order *also* to be constitutive of our experience, it would need to be a posteriori, not a priori.

Kant's treatment of the nature of organisms in *OP* provides yet another example of his inadvertent employment of the concept of analytic a posteriority. "The idea of organic bodies," he claims, can be established a priori, though only "indirectly," through "the concept of a real *whole*"; yet "[r]egarded directly," organisms "can be known only empirically" (*OP* 21.213; see also 22.356)—i.e., *a posteriori*. He goes on to explain that we learn what an organism is from our (a posteriori) consciousness of ourselves as organizing (rational, architectonic) beings, then we *classify* the objects we have organized according to the conceptual structures we impose upon our experience. He calls these structures *a priori*; but if the focus is on their *conceptual* status, he should have called them *analytic*.

The analytic a posteriori status of *OP*'s transitions is even more evident in an earlier passage, where Kant calls the four categorial forms of transition "*a priori* laws . . . drawn, not from the elements of physics [which would be synthetic] . . . but from *concepts* (to which we subordinate the elements of physics)" (21.183). To draw a law directly from concepts is an analytic procedure; to subordinate elements of physics to such a concept can have only a posteriori validity. This, as I have argued more fully in SP–87c, is essentially what takes place every time we *name* something. When Kant refers to his transition project as "the general–physiological" link with "*a priori* conceivability" (22.190; see also 22.191), we should read him as *naming a process* that *confers* an analytic a posteriori status on the transition—a status he merely assumes (without argument) to be a priori. Likewise, his claim that caloric "is determined *for* experience" (21.603) can now be regarded as epistemologically equivalent to the way naming an infant establishes a certain concept to determine a person's experience analytically, yet in an entirely a posteriori fashion. The difference is that this creative function is now expanded to cover the whole of our experience: "Caloric is actual, because the concept of it . . . makes possible the whole of experience" (22.554). As such, Kant's doctrine of caloric/ether functions as the analytic a posteriori equivalent of the synthetic a priori condition of experience that Kant elsewhere calls "substance."

Kant makes numerous direct comparisons between the God–hypothesis and the ether–hypothesis (see e.g., *OP* 22.128–29). Not only are both regarded as "substances" with a necessarily hypothetical status; both must also refer only to singular realities (one God and one world). We should not be surprised, therefore, to find that Kant has just as much difficulty in assigning an epistemological status to the former as to the latter. The assertion of God's existence, he tells us, "is neither an analytic nor a synthetic proposition" (22.128). The reason Kant is forced to make such vague and inconclusive statements, I believe, is that he never considers the possibility that the status of propositions such as "God exists" is actually paradoxical: *analytic a posteriori*. Identifying this status would also have gone a long way to clarifying the crucial role of the *third* idea that Kant focuses on in *OP*, the nature of the human being (or "man") as the (mystical!) synthesis of God and the world—to which we shall turn our attention in the next chapter.

NOTES

1. Kant sometimes identifies ether with heat or "caloric" (e.g., *OP* 21.214–15, 226), but he elsewhere makes a technical distinction between two kinds of ether: "light–material" and heat–material or caloric (22.214). On the identity of caloric and heat, see *OP* 22.141. Although he explicitly calls ether a "hypothesis" (22.193), Kant insists elsewhere that this underlying material—whatever it may be—is *not* "merely *hypothetical*" (21.226, 228).

2. *OP* 22.138–39. At one point (21.583) Kant describes this in terms of a "gap." Though we may be tempted to identify this with the "gap" Kant refers to in *C* 12.254 (see *KCR* §XI.1), the latter was a gap in the *Critical philosophy* itself, whereas here Kant is referring to a gap in our experience of the natural world.

3. *OP* 21.210–11. A few pages later he expresses this point by saying "our all-producing globe" is itself "an organic body" (21.213–14). Kant's emphasis on organisms (e.g., 22.546–48) provides further evidence supporting my claim in *KSP* §III.4 that *OP* belongs to Kant's judicial system, not to his theoretical system, given that organisms are one of the main topics dealt with in the second part of *CJ* (see *KSP* §IX.3.A). Likewise, Kant emphasizes that the "primitive moving forces of matter" being examined in *OP* are all "dynamic," inasmuch as "the mechanical are only derivative" (*OP* 22.239; see also 22.241)—a distinction that also suggests *OP*'s closer association with the dynamical explanations typical of *CJ*.

4. *OP* 22.343. Here Kant was echoing a view that he very likely learned as a child, from the popular schoolbook, *Orbis Pictus*, which identifies three manifestations of the sixth, "inward sense": "the Common Sense" (or *Sensus Communis* in the Latin version), "Phantasie," and "Memory" (Comenius 1887, Chapter XLII). Kant refers explicitly to the Latin version of this book (published in 1658) in *DSS* 2.325.

5. *LM* 28.214; see also Paulsen 1902, 262n, and *ID* 2.409–10. Whereas pantheism merely identifies God with the world, pan*en*theism views God as ever-present and participating *in* every aspect of the world, but ultimately transcending it (see e.g., *OP* 21.18). The importance of this distinction can be illustrated by noting Jaki's use of Kant's claim "I am God! [*Ich bin Gott!*]" as evidence of "Kant's gradual shifting into pantheism" (Jaki 1981, 33; 224). Jaki rejects Kant's starting point at the outset (8) and shows no awareness of the principle of perspective, so it is not surprising that he takes such a comment as a shift in Kant's position. (For a thorough critique of Jaki's treatment of Kant, see *SP*-87b.) In fact, as we have seen, the comment in question, and many others like it in *OP*, are simply Kant's way of expressing existential confidence in the *presence* of God in his own immediate experience and in his

encounter with all that is. For a detailed defense of the claim that Kant's philosophy amounts to a "moral panentheism," see SP–08.

6. Kant's tendency in *OP* to talk about space and time *together* (e.g., as "one space and one time" [21.227; see also 21.549, 22.416]) seems closer to Einstein than to Newton. I have examined the extent to which Kant's philosophy can serve as a foundation for the former as well as the latter in SP–10b and SP–11; this will also be a major theme of *Kant's Critical Science*, the planned third volume in the *Kant's System of Perspectives* series (Routledge, forthcoming).

7. The reason Kant's transition project takes on a paradoxical and even *mystical* character becomes evident when we consider the description of mystical perception in general advanced in MacKinnon 1978, 136: "It is by way of discarding the particular experience that the authentic incommunicable is communicated. If mystical experience is properly spoken of as one in which the opposition of subject and object is overcome, it must also be characterized as an experience in which the object is so totally transparent that one must speak of the subject as reduced to the near *locus* of its transparency." Learning to perceive the world with this kind of "simplicity," however, is a skill the mystic gains at "the end rather than [at] the beginning and very few achieve it." To this I would add that an unconscious participation in such immediate experience comes at the *beginning* of every human being's quest for knowledge; but the ability to become consciously aware of what I call the analytic a posteriori feature of human life is indeed an end product of the mystical path rather than its starting point.

8. In *OP* 21.581–82 Kant seems to support both positions. Although he states on the one hand that the ether proof is synthetic, he also says it derives "experience from concepts," which would make it a type of analyticity, whereby experience is somehow "contained in" the concept.

9. *OP* 21.604–5. Kant explains here that to regard caloric as "the object of a single possible experience" implies "that its assertion is an empirical proposition." Such passages are hopelessly incoherent, unless we recognize that he was attempting to explain something fundamentally paradoxical: the analytic a posteriori. The "pain like that of Tantalus" that Kant mentions in his September 1798 letter to Garve (*C* 12.254) was caused by Kant's insistence on binding himself to the chains of the a priori (see e.g., Forgie 1995, 99–100). For a full discussion of Kant's response to this pain, see *KCR*, Chapter XI.

10. This is particularly significant because, according to my reconstruction of Kant's System in *KSP*, his hypothetical perspective (the fourth and final stage in the architectonic structure of each of the three Critical systems) corresponds to (and therefore relies upon) the epistemological status of analytic aposteriority (see especially *KSP*, Figure III.4).

Chapter Twelve

The Highest Purpose of Philosophy as Exhibiting the God–Man

The foregoing chapters suggest that the mysterious quality of *OP* comes not so much from its disorderly, unfinished form—though this does add confusion to the mystery—as from the essentially mystical aim Kant has in view: to *describe* the One in the many. Along these lines, as Förster 1993 acknowledges at one point, some of Kant's theories are related, at least indirectly, to "cabalistic ideas" (277, n.105; see *OP* 22.421). Those who follow the common practice of portraying Kant as a philosopher who synthesized rationalism and empiricism (cf. *KSP* 355, 383) rarely take into consideration that such a synthesis can be effected only by subsuming both of these extremes under a *third term*. We are now in a position to suggest that the Critical mysticism that has been gradually emerging in the present study *is* this third "ism." For reason-based philosophy and experience-based philosophy can be held together at the most profound level only by an encounter (a *rational experience*), based on what Akhutin (1991, 73) calls a "believing reason"— i.e., a *Critical mysticism*. This is the spiritual legacy bequeathed to us by Kant.

The transcendent Fire of God–in–the–world eventually encompasses everything in Kant's System, forming a panentheism of the profoundest type. The "idea of the whole" that Kant hopes will unify this System in *OP*, complete with the three transitions suggested by Figure 9.2—God to humanity; humanity to the world; and (combining the first two) God–and–the–world to humanity—can be depicted in the form of the flow chart shown in Figure 12.1. The role Kant assigns to human beings ("man") in *OP* is a direct application of his view that philosophy is essentially concerned with four questions, the first three Critical questions (concerning knowledge, action, and hope) being summarized in the fourth ("What is man?").[1] Kant's

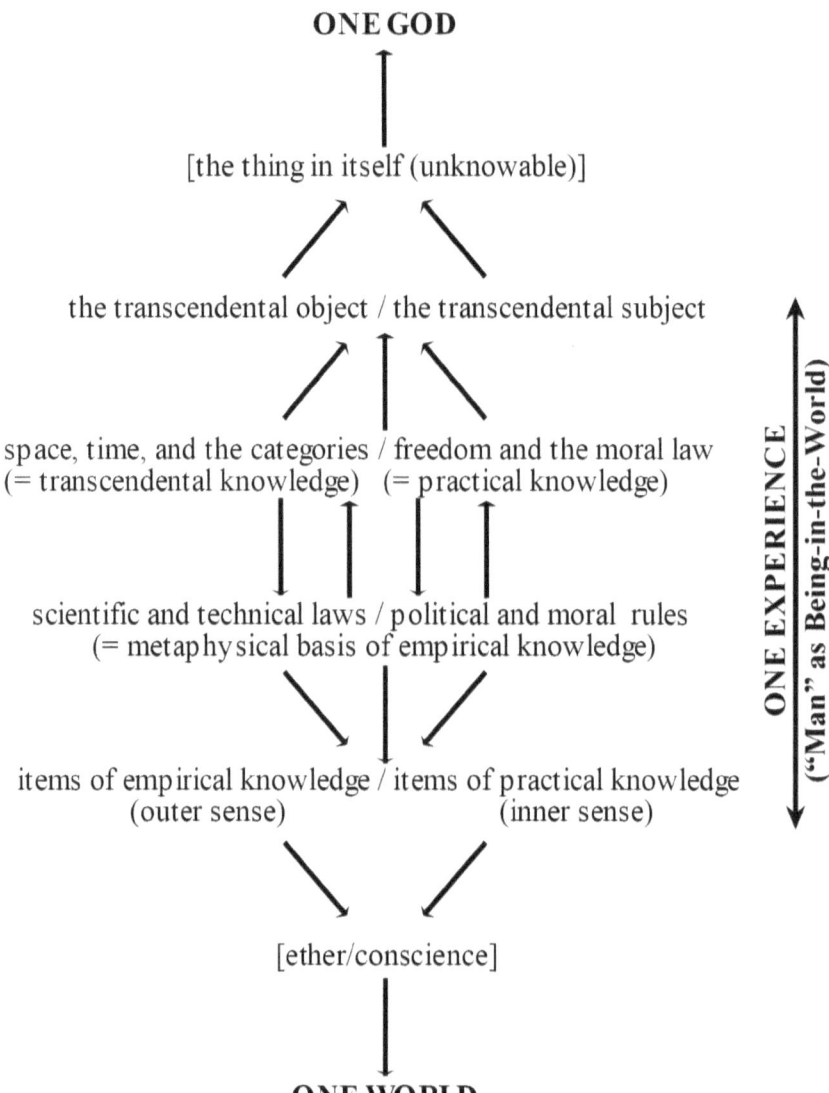

Figure 12.1. The Unity of Transcendental Philosophy in *OP*.

repeated references to "man" in *OP* should be read on one level as referring to the human individual in general, as understood in terms of the transcendental conditions set out in the three *Critiques* (i.e., to humanity); however, Kant also seems to have a more specific referent in mind—the ideal *God–man*.

Kant consistently emphasizes in *OP* that there can be but *one* God and *one* world: "it is as little the case that there are many Gods as that there are many worlds" (22.125). It should come as no surprise, therefore, that when he seeks to unite these two in humanity, he tends to focus his attention on *one man*. My central argument in this chapter is that this "man" can be identified with the idea that he elsewhere calls the "archetype" (*Urbild*)—i.e., the highest possible expression of human perfection, which in Christian tradition is instantiated in the historical person of Jesus. In other words, "the Christ" seems to be ever lurking at the back of Kant's mind (cf. Collins 1967, 177–78). The great merit of this conjecture is that it enables us to understand what Kant is doing when he makes odd statements with an almost postmodern ring, such as that God "judges me inwardly . . . ; and I, man, am this being myself—it is not some substance outside me" (*OP* 21.25). He is developing his own philosophical interpretation of the Christian view that all human beings are, at least potentially, "little Christs"—that is, sibling participants in the wholeness (i.e., perfection) that is initially represented by Christ Jesus, the God–man. This position is already suggested in *RBBR* 6.60, where Kant paraphrases John 1:2 in such a way that "humanity . . . in its complete moral perfection" is presented as being "in God from eternity" (see *CCKR*, 161–2). Since Kant proceeds to depict the archetype as the idea of a personal embodiment of this perfection, we can regard this passage as an attempt to present a symbolic interpretation of the Christian doctrine of Jesus Christ as the alpha and omega (cf. Rev. 1:8; 21:6; 22:13), the firstborn Son of God who in orthodox Christian theology makes it possible for every person to become a child of God (see e.g., Rom. 8:16–23).

If Kant's hidden intention is indeed to propose a philosophical interpretation of such notions, then it means Elizabeth Galbraith and others are quite mistaken when they charge "that Kant's theology does not have Christ at its centre."[2] Toward the end of her book (Galbraith 1996, 184), she affirms that in *OP* "Kant comes closest to realising that the philosophical system which has been the preoccupation of his life, has in fact been grounded in theism." She adds, however, that in *OP* Kant's prior "tendency to cling to Christianity is entirely absent." Insofar as "Christianity" refers to an organized historical faith consisting of specific doctrines and duties, the latter is certainly correct, as evidenced by Kant's many existential statements such as "[r]eligion is conscientiousness" (21.81); such historical "clothing" has fallen away in response to Kant's life-long discipline of Critique, as the experience of baring all in reason's light. Yet this does not mean he has lost his tendency to cling to a mystical experience of *the Christ*, affirmed as an existential ideal. Nor should we take this to mean that Kant was previously unaware of his System's theocentric orientation. For the notable absence of any doctrinal affirmations in *OP* does not imply that Kant has given up the beliefs he affirmed in *RBBR*; it only means he sees no more need to repeat those theories in this metaphysical context than he does to repeat the many doctrines of the theoretical and practical *Critiques* that are also absent from *OP*.

That Kant's entire philosophical System culminates in this "one man"—that is, in Kant himself, and potentially also in each of us, as representatives of the ideal God–man—can help us to understand an aspect of his philosophy that might otherwise cause undue confusion and/or concern. As Vincent Cooke observes (1988, 313), "Kant thinks about the self in a way very similar to the way he thinks about God." For example (315), the subject in itself, like God, "is not situated in time. . . . [I]t is a timeless acting uncaused cause." Kant thinks of God as well as the self (317) as "a simple, unchanging, timeless, spontaneous agent that produces effects in the spatio–temporal world without itself being influenced or determined by the spatio–temporal world." That "Kant can speak grandly of the self as lawgiver to nature" (320) is perhaps less surprising when its direct correspondence with God is taken into account. "Starting with a Godlike notion of the self can, over a period of time, lead to the idea that the self really is God." Here, Cooke (322) is thinking specifically of *OP* as Kant's attempt to bring his long-term tendency to its final culmination. We are now in a position to see this as quite accurate, though only from the specific standpoint of judicial metaphysics. Cooke regards such an implication as casting doubt on the religious significance of Kant's System. Yet this is only because he pays inadequate attention to the *paradoxical* nature of Kant's overall conception of the God–man relation. For as I argued in *KCR* §V.1, Kant's God is also transcendent and fundamentally different from us (see e.g., *KCR*, Figure V.3). Cooke does acknowledge (1988, 322) that God is "distinguished from human selves in so far as God is a *purely* rational agent, while human selves are also sensuous." But he fails to recognize the ultimate significance of this crucial difference; for this enables Kant to avoid a *complete* identification between God and humanity. Instead, humanity functions as the principle of *synthesis* between God and the world, once again illustrating that Kant's mystical tendencies do not make him into a *pan*theist, but into a pan*en*theist (see note 11.5).

If Kant is referring cryptically to the *ideal* God–man ("the Christ") on the numerous occasions when he refers in *OP* to "man" as the synthesis of God and the world, then to what extent is he also thinking of human beings overall, including ordinary human individuals? We can answer this question by comparing Kant's treatment of "man" to his treatment of "experience" in *OP*: "There is only one experience, and, if experiences are spoken of, . . . what are meant thereby are merely *perceptions*. . . ."[3] If this "one experience" corresponds to the perfection of humanity in the person of Christ, and if the thing being encountered in this ideal sense is the infamous "thing in itself," as I depicted it in the first paragraph of the Introduction, above, then each person who attempts to follow the Christ-archetype would correspond to the status of discrete perceptions in relation to the mystical wholeness that is the thing in itself. As I argued in *KCR*, §VII.2.B and §VIII.2.B, we should each therefore endeavor to make ourselves a living example of "this divine human being" who resides "in us" as a "standard for our actions" (A569/B597); and as long as faith in the historical Jesus *helps* us reach that goal, rather than hindering us—as it would for anyone who regards Jesus as the *only possible* instance of a human being who exhibits God's nature—such faith is quite compatible with Kant's System. Thus, he expresses his entire argument in a nutshell in *OP* 22.131: "I am a principle of synthetic self-determination to myself, not merely according to a law of the *receptivity of nature*, but also according to a principle of the *spontaneity of freedom*." Here again, the "I" refers to the ideal human as the synthesis of God and the world.

Kant says of the three metaphysical ideas that when we *idealize* God, the world, and humanity by regarding them as "archetypes" (i.e., noumenal objects of hypothetical knowledge), we must keep in mind that we can never know for certain if they actually exist (*OP* 21.51; see also 21.33; 22.128–29). This reference to the ideas as *archetypes* is reminiscent of the claim in Kant's religious system that the archetype is the "personified idea of the good principle" (*RBBR* 6.60; see DiCenso 2013) and again suggests that Kant's repeated use of the term "man" in *OP* should be read as being not merely equivalent to "the human race," but on a deeper level, as a reference to the *ideal* human person. For Christians, that person is Jesus. The Christian reader of *OP* can therefore safely read this text (as I believe Kant himself would have regarded it) as arguing not that every human individual is a real expression of the mystical union of God-and-the-World, but that this function is fulfilled by the most authentic man-in-the-world ever to live, the person who came to be called "the Christ." To be true to Kant (and perhaps also to the Bible) we must add, however, that *every true follower of Jesus' Way*, or of what the Chinese tradition calls the *Dao*, can also be regarded as a participant in (and so also, an example of) this mystical union, the mystical body of Christ or *corpus mysticum*, as Kant himself calls it (A808/B836; see note 12.15, below). The Christian reader, therefore, need not reject Kant's System on the grounds that it leaves insufficient room for Jesus to occupy a central role in human salvation. Being a *philosophical* System, it rightly leaves open the question of *which* individual(s) make(s) the archetype real. But it does not (as many have claimed) *dis*allow Christians from placing faith in Jesus as the archetypal Person in whom the metaphysical union of God and the world becomes a reality on earth. If anything, *OP encourages* such faith, by showing how it is metaphysically possible from the judicial standpoint.

This, then, is the ultimate philosophical transition, the transition from an abstract, reflective standpoint (either theoretical and world-oriented or practical and God-oriented) to a concrete, existential standpoint wherein one *encounters* (immediately experiences) God in the world and the world in God. Philosophy, as Plato pointed out so long ago, begins in wonder and thereby gives birth to reflection and logical reasoning; by contrast, its proper *end* lies not in a theoretical understanding of ideal "forms," but in a mystical experience of the oneness of all that is. This end, as we have seen, is the literal purpose (the *telos* or "goal") of human reason, even though it is also reason's symbolic death (its *termon* or "boundary").[4] Thus, what we might call "Kant's Socratism" must be viewed, following Velkley (1985, 102), as "an inversion of Plato's," for "the philosopher" in Kant's ideal (104) "shows us how little we need in the way of theory to attain our ends." In place of a mystical knowledge of transcendent forms, Kant (like Socrates) calls us to a mystical experience of our own humbling ignorance.

Immediate experience, as the end or goal of all philosophy, is indeed philosophy's death; for here we come face to face with what Kant calls "relations which are fundamental" (*DSS* 2.370), regarding which "the business of philosophy is at an end." Just as reason has its *birth* in the pre-rational womb of a subject's immediate confrontation with an unknowable thing in itself, so also must we now acknowledge that it *dies* in the supra-rational immediacy of a person's inward encounter with God and the world. That Kant was himself a closet mystic is therefore, despite its strangeness,[5] the inescapable conclusion of our study, for only in light of this awareness can his System be viewed as truly complete. The "death" of reason is lamentable only when the status of the unknowability of the thing in itself and of the mystical awareness of immediate experience are conflated: the rationalist, believing immediate knowledge of the thing in itself can be obtained, mistakenly regards the beginning of philosophy as its end; and the empiricist, believing experience can never be immediate, mistakenly regards the end as the beginning. Critical mysticism is the proper acknowledgment of our theoretical ignorance at philosophy's birth and of our judicial ignorance at its death, combined with the recognition that all our knowledge arises only *between* these two extremes. This places definite limits on the Enlightenment's naive trust in the all-sufficiency of reason, balancing its "sapere aude" motto with a corresponding "*non* sapere aude": "have the courage *not* to know,"[6] but to *experience*—i.e., to let reason die in the immediate encounter with God, in the hope that it will rise again, carrying with it the gifts of wisdom and holiness.

Hegel's critique of Kant assumes that such a limitation of reason is the mark of philosophy's *failure*; but as Friedman (1986, 521) rightly observes, "Kant sees [this "failure"] as wisdom." This is because "Kant speaks of a human and not an absolute standpoint. . . . While reminding me of the unseen[, reason] restricts my knowledge to the seen." In this respect, Friedman observes (522), "Kant's position is strangely Socratic." Both great philosophers affirm their ignorance while remaining faithful to their principles—though in the end "Socrates falls back on myth." The theological orientation and religious end of Kant's System suggest that Kant follows

Socrates in this respect as well; but Kant's defense of his Transcendental Perspective makes a significant advance on Socrates' highly suggestive but ultimately mythical approach (see SP–00, Lectures 5 and 8). In any case, Friedman's conclusion, that Kant's philosophy ends not in "hypocrisy," as Hegel claimed, but "in humility" (522), is surely valid. Indeed, Kant's Socratic ignorance is the key to Critical wisdom.

Kant mentions on several occasions the "*salto mortale* [or "deadly jump"] of human reason," referring to the tendency of many religious people to treat unjustified speculations about the transcendent realm as if they were certain truths.[7] Such a practice is philosophically disreputable when it is purely speculative; what Kant does not fully acknowledge is that, as Kierkegaard later argued, such a death leap may have a profound philosophical justification when taken instead on the basis of genuine existential awareness. This philosophical death of reason is not "the *euthanasia* (easy death)" that Kant says results from making happiness one's moral principle (*MM* 6.378); rather, it is the painfully self-conscious death of a suffering servant, as Kant argues explicitly in *RBBR* 6.61–66. As I showed in *KCR* §IX.2, the heart of the Christ–love that characterizes the Bible's depiction of the ideal human being is not pleasure and inclination, but suffering and (if necessary) death. Likewise, we can now see that Kant's entire System acknowledges a fundamentally tragic element in the human situation: like Tantalus in Greek mythology, we are constrained to seek after the unconditioned (e.g., as the highest good in Kant's practical system), in spite of the extreme unlikeliness of ever attaining it. Yet this is a tragedy not without significant rewards for those who are willing to endure it; for as Francisco Peccorini observes (1972, 65), "one feels prouder of being a man after having accompanied Kant through his painful, but most rewarding, critical journey." Lucien Goldmann concurs: "the critical philosophy [is] one of the great expressions of the tragic vision of the world, . . . a 'metaphysics of tragedy'."[8] Thus, when Kant makes statements such as that an appeal to the supernatural implies that "all use of reason ceases" (*RBBR* 6.53), we must not rush to assume he is disapproving entirely of reason's death (e.g., Galbraith 1996, 77; see *KCR*, Appendix VII.1). Kantian reason is an "organ," a living substance that has both a beginning and an end, which is precisely why Kant ends *CPR* with a chapter entitled "The History of Pure Reason" (A852f/B880f). An appeal to the supernatural is damaging, therefore, only when it comes too soon and would put philosophy to death *before its appointed time*.

The Critical System on its own (i.e., the three *Critiques*, apart from their corresponding metaphysical works) promotes a balanced view of religious life that is not so explicitly "tragic." Despland (1973, 269) aptly expresses this balance: "The mature form of Kant's understanding of religion emphasizes the finitude of our faculties [cf. *CPR*], the moral maturity of the religious man [cf. *CPrR*], and his confidence in a gracious Providence [cf. *CJ*]."

The tragic as an aspect of *this life* comes into full view only when we recognize that our immediate experience of God and the world cannot bring us the holiness and wisdom we desire, but rather condemn us to a never-ending struggle for knowledge and virtue. This contrast between the judicial and the theoretical–practical ways of understanding our encounter with God is neatly captured by John Smith's claim (1968, 19) that "God is in one perspective [the judicial, as in *OP*] a religious solution and a philosophical problem, and in another [the theoretical–practical, as in *CPrR*] a philosophical solution and a religious problem."

Philosophy's highest religious end is to pave the way for an experience of this mystical center. The promise it gives is that, out of reason's death will spring a new life, a new awareness of the proper way of relating our reasoning to the world we inhabit. In particular, wisdom and holiness manifest themselves as the twin ideals that can be realized only when this religious end has been experienced. Just as metaphysics is the fulfillment of Critique, so also wisdom, as the goal of the metaphysics of nature (see e.g., *OP* 21.156), is the spiritual fulfillment of *science* (i.e., *knowledge*), and holiness, as the goal of the metaphysics of morals, is the spiritual fulfillment of humanity's *political history* (i.e., *action*). But wisdom and holiness are not possible apart from a fundamental recognition that these ideals are ultimately rooted in a wholeness that transcends our grasp as humans, thereby belonging to God alone. As Kant affirms in *OP* 22.38: "Wisdom is the highest principle of reason.... Only the supreme being is wise."[9]

The humility that fills anyone who becomes fully aware of this "religious feeling" prepares us "to be educated by God, ... to obey and respect a higher moral authority than our own current insights and those of mankind."[10] Despland (1973, 267) argues that this step, far from entailing a merely agnostic admission that God's existence is *possible*, requires an active *worship* of God:

> ... this feeling becomes further characterized as a sense of the holiness of God. The God who is an educator of mankind is presented as a rational idea and as a necessary postulate. This should not obscure the fact that for Kant he is also—and he is primarily—the highest reality before which all knees bend.

Kant's claim in *CPrR* (5.11n) that wisdom and holiness are "identical in their ground and objectively" is obviously untrue, if interpreted from the standpoint of the three *Critiques* alone; it must rather be interpreted as a claim about the union of knowledge and action in immediate experience, where knowledge and action are *ultimately* unified in the God–man, the instantiation of both holiness and wisdom. This may well be what Kant has in mind in *RBBR* 6.83–84, when he enigmatically reverses the expected associations by referring to "the *holiest* teaching of reason" and the "wise" words of Jesus.

I argued in *KCR* §V.3 (see also *KSP* §IX.3.B and *R* 18.713–14, 485–86), that the God who is transcendent in Kant's theoretical system and immanent in his practical system is paradoxically *both* transcendent *and* immanent in his judicial system (and so also in his religious system). The mystery we now face is that at the center of Kant's entire System of Perspectives, God is in a sense *neither* transcendent *nor* immanent. Contrary to interpreters such as Ward (1972, 66), who claims that "God remains a remote and impassive being for Kant," the God of *OP* is the God of *immediate experience*—of an encounter where all distinctions (like language itself) ultimately break(s) down. Here God is no mere (transcendent) "idea," and even a more positive (immanent) term such as "postulate" does not do justice to the experience Kant describes. Rather, what Kant alludes to is a mystical feeling or intuition that somehow corresponds to the intellectual intuition of God's own nature (see *KCR* §V.1; cf. Greene 1934, lxi), yet avoids contradicting any Critical principles by virtue of the fact that it produces nothing tangible for us to cognize (either theoretically or practically). What it produces is the far more important (yet ineffable) *respect* for life (and by extension, for both oneself and one's fellow human beings), for nature (and by extension, for both the universe and the products of human culture), and for God that characterizes all of Kant's thinking, yet finds its ultimate expression only here. Anyone who reads *OP* as part of a mono-perspectival philosophy of *science* is bound to regard it as contradicting Critical principles in various places. But once we see it as developing from a new, distinctively metaphysical perspective, as a philosophy of *wisdom*, the problem of alleged inconsistency falls away. The conclusions of *OP* are not treated as truth claims ("κατ' ἀλήθειαν"), but as holistic claims worthy of analytic a posteriori belief by human beings ("κατ' ἄνθρωπον") (*PM* 20.306).

Kant's System can now be seen to revolve, like a hurricane, around a "dead center," a place of peaceful calm that has to be encountered in order to be believed—especially for anyone who is being tossed about on the stormy sea of philosophical speculation. The Critical philosophy provides a set of navigational tools that are designed to guide the thought–sailor safely into this harbor of rest. Here at the heart of the System, reason lies mysteriously dormant, resting from all the mighty endeavors that seemed so important just moments before. The philosophical "sailor" who is fortunate enough to locate this "end" of Kant's theocentric metaphysics will be empowered to venture back out into the spiraling storm of human reasoning, with a newfound appreciation of the moral order that makes nature, art, ethical norms, and even scientific knowledge itself worthwhile (cf. *CJ* 5.482).

Kant makes a similar point using a rather different metaphor in *MM* 6.441: "Only the descent into the hell of self-cognition can pave the way to godliness." (Tracing this vivid maxim to Hamann, Collins [1967, 140] says Kant regards self-knowledge "as the first condition for orienting myself and humanity toward God, in the religious relationship.") If reason dies when it reaches the latter and ascends to "heaven," if in so doing we have reached the still point at the mystical center of the Critical struggle, then what is there to look forward to when we venture back out into the storm of life? What we find is that the metaphysical ideas of the world (freedom) and the soul (immortality) bring us face to face with the same paradox that arises when examining the idea of God, but in new forms. Once we have fulfilled the religio–philosophical mandate of Socrates' "know thyself," we are prepared to meet the ultimate *historical* challenge by replacing the former with the maxim "cultivate thyself."[11]

Carl Friedrich expresses a similar point by saying (1949, vii–viii): "Kant's philosophy, existentially speaking, revolves around 'peace' and *not* around 'cognition.'" That this peace is an allusion to what the immortal soul can look forward to after the body's death is suggested by Kant's admission in *Perpetual Peace* that its title refers to a "satirical inscription on a certain Dutch innkeeper's signboard picturing a graveyard" (*PP* 8.343). Once we recognize that Kant's concern with politics and history extends beyond the grave, to the afterlife, the problem Yirmiyahu Yovel points out becomes all the more intense: "How can a bridge be built between the history of reason and empirical history?"[12] Yovel (1980, 20n) argues that, because the "supreme end round which [Kant's] system is organized is the supreme practical end," therefore "the historical ideal is placed not just within [Kant's] system, but in fact at its 'architectonic' center." Although this is something of an exaggeration (for history *as such* is not at the System's center, but rather the immediate experiences out of which all history is *woven*), it is accurate insofar as it accounts for the historical focus of many of Kant's later minor writings. Moreover, if we view history as God's way of educating humanity, "[t]he person of Christ," as Despland affirms, "becomes . . . the surest ground of hope."[13]

Etymologically, the word "transcendental"—the name Kant chose to denote the overall Perspective of his entire System (see *KSP* §II.4)—is closely related to the word "trance." Whereas "trance" means "pass away" (as in death, or loss of consciousness) and "transcendent" literally means "climb over" (e.g., a mountain), "transcendental" for Kant refers to the *boundary* that determines what is to pass away or to be overcome. The similarity between these words is more than accidental; for Kant's Transcendental Perspective, as we have seen, is the outworking of a new, waking "dream" to replace the old dream of speculative metaphysics and delirious mysticism. This new dream requires us to "climb across" (trans-cend) the "valleys" of our experience to reach the "mountains" of our metaphysical ideas, yet without losing our awareness of who we are in the world we inhabit—thus allowing us to travel only *up to* the boundary itself. This is possible because the Copernican "compass," as provided by the philosopher's use of architectonic logic (see *KSP*, ch. III) to orient reason's speculations, enables us to live in what we might call the "hypnogogic trance" of Critical mysticism—a state of mind that keeps us "awake" to the world of our experience without causing us to lose awareness of the mystery and meaning of the "dream" world, whose presence we can always encounter just beyond the reach of our cognitive fingertips.[14]

Is the death of all philosophy in the mystical awareness of the God–man dwelling within us a *mere* tragedy? Or is it also the realization of philosophy's true end? A decisive answer to this final question is suggested by comparing it with a parallel issue Kant addresses far more directly: the fate of church faith, the historical expression of organized religion. As I have argued in Part Three of both *KCR* and *CCKR*, Kant accepts that churchly structures serve a legitimate purpose as clothing to render the bare body of rational religion more presentable to the general public; but once their purpose (conveying moral–spiritual enlightenment to those who would otherwise have gone without it) has been served, and the rational meaning at their core has come to light, all such historical structures are best put aside. Their death is not something to be lamented, but is a natural developmental process we should accept as promoting the highest good.[15] In a similar fashion, philosophy too should be regarded not as an end in itself, to be kept alive at all costs, but as a means to the furtherance of human development toward our proper end. Lest this realization lead philosophy to a *premature* closure, however, we must also recall that Kant thinks this ideal end, where all church faiths (and so too, all philosophies) will become useless appendages thanks to a new level of human self-awareness, is still far off in humanity's distant future. Once we have attained the *insight* that is its goal, philosophy as such may be laid to rest. But until we can discern the political structure that will lead to this goal, we may affirm that philosophy, like all historical religious faiths, retains its value for the time being. We are still so far from the time when humanity can safely live continuously in the moment of immediate experience that we, as much as Kant, must be satisfied if we can catch a few tantalizing glimpses of our final destiny.

NOTES

1. For a further discussion of these questions and their relevance to Kant's System, see *KCR*, note III.5. Collins (1967, 93–94) claims that for Kant "the theme of man in the world . . . is not peripheral but the founding principle of philosophical inquiry itself."

2. Galbraith 1996, v; see also *KCR* §IX.4. Likewise, McCarthy (1986, 101) claims Kant's "reworking of this central Christian teaching [i.e., the Trinity] means the dismissal of Christocentricity as traditionally understood. Yet the example of Christ will be at the epicenter of moral–religious thought." McCarthy's subtle "yet" renders his otherwise inaccurate comment closer to being an acceptable rendering of Kant's position. For Kant does reject the traditional view—or to be more precise, he conspicuously avoids defending it. But he does not do away

with Christocentricity altogether. Rather, Christ remains as an ideal example (i.e., the "archetype" of all examples) here at the "dead center" of his entire System.

3. *OP* 22.661; see also 22.104. Note the striking similarity of form between the statement quoted here, repeated frequently throughout *OP*, and Kant's claim in *RBBR* 6.107 that "There is only one (true) religion; but there can be faiths of several kinds." This supports my claim that *OP* is an extension of the same standpoint adopted in *RBBR*, the judicial, only applied now to metaphysics.

4. This understanding of the "birth" and "death" of reason is filled with ironies. First, the Critical System was *born* out of the generating seed produced by Kant's analysis in *DSS* of Swedenborg's alleged communications with people who had *died* (i.e., departed spirits). Second, Kant was only able to witness the *birth* of (most of) his System when he was ever-mindful of his own impending *death* (i.e., he was entering old age). And third, Kant's own passing (into the realm of departed spirits, if such a realm exists) is what prevented him from completing his elaboration of the *death* of his own System.

5. This conclusion sounds strange not because there is a huge volume of literature providing evidence against it, but simply because the opposite conclusion is often repeated like a mantra—as if it were so obvious as to be beyond the need for support. Thus, when considering Kant's view of God in *OP*, Macquarrie (1990, 431n) calls attention to a similarity it has to a view expressed by mystical writers, then quickly and dogmatically adds: "But Kant was no mystic." Wood (1992, 414) likewise pronounces that Kant "had no patience at all for the mystical" and later calls any suggestion to the contrary "absurd" (Wood 1996, 331). But as Sewall (1900, 32) pointed out over a century ago: "It all depends on what is meant by the [term] *mystic*. Truly the whole idea of freedom is with Kant a mystic one." Kant's use of this term "mystic" is, of course, extremely one-sided (see e.g., A854/B882). The many undefended denials of Kant's mystical tendencies (see Chapters 6 and 8; cf. Butts 1984, 83 and Copleston 1960, 184) are therefore unjustified (but cf. Johnson, 1997, 31, and Greene 1934, lxxvii; see also Green 1978, 77).

6. Although the courage to know can be regarded as the *fruit* of Kant's Critical mysticism, this courage *not* to know (i.e., this awareness of one's ignorance) is its *root*. This is at least part of what I have in mind by coining the term "philopsychy" (literally, soul–loving): an approach to philosophical ignorance that regards psychological self-knowledge as its choicest fruit; and an approach to psychological self-knowledge that acknowledges philosophical ignorance as its root. For examples of these two approaches, see SP–00 and SP–08, wherein I develop two applications of Critical mysticism—though without using the term itself. For a synthesis of these two, see SP–03, the third book in the philopsychy trilogy.

7. *RBBR* 6.121; see also 174. The accompanying footnote (121n) illustrates the *proper* response to reason's death: Kant reinterprets the doctrine of predestination as a deep trust in the judgment of the timeless, "All-Seeing" One. This qualified affirmation of reason's "death leap" supports Ronald Green's claim that this is one of the several ways Kierkegaard develops themes first raised by Kant (Green 1989, 403–5). For a further discussion of the meaning and origin of this metaphor, see *CCKR* 317n.

8. Goldmann 1971, 170. Note the stark contrast between this view of Kant's practical system and the view that portrays it as an unsuccessful attempt to transcend the limits set by his theoretical system. In *CPrR*, as in *OP*, there would be no tragedy if Kant were not so careful to avoid making pretentious claims about having attained something that we humans can never succeed in attaining. As Tze-wan Kwan puts it (1984, 286), "matured morality is always tragic!" While this sense of the tragic, as a practical "process of self-ennoblement" (286), is a suitable description of the first three stages of Kant's practical system, the fourth stage (with its postulation of God and immortality) seems at first to remove the tragedy from living the moral life, but only if we mistake Kant's moral proofs for theoretical ones.

9. Along these lines, I demonstrated in *KCR* §V.4 that Kant consistently regards holiness as an attribute of the divine. I argue in *CCKR*, however, that in *RBBR* Kant portrays religion as a way of enabling human beings to participate in divine holiness.

10. Despland 1973, 267. In *RBBR* 6.113 Kant says religious feelings can result from "the effect of the moral law, the law that fills the human being with a profound respect and that also

deserves, on that account, to be regarded as divine command." This respect is directed toward the divine *commander*, "and the lawgiver is God" (*OP* 22.106).

11. This interesting suggestion comes from Raschke (1975, 227), who relates it primarily to Kant's philosophy of history. Unfortunately, Raschke writes as if history *replaces* God for Kant (225–27). This, as I plan to argue in volume 4 of *Kant's System of Perspectives*, is a serious misconstrual of Kant's intentions. A more defensible view of the role of political history for Kant is that human destiny is the key to understanding in what sense human nature is "good." A former student of mine, Cheng Kwan, pointed this out to me, adding that in this respect Kant and Confucius are very similar.

12. Yovel 1980, 21. Yovel goes on to opine "that Kant does not and cannot have a sufficient answer" to this question. By contrast, I shall argue in volume 4 of the *Kant's System of Perspectives* series that the principle of perspective is itself the bridge that enables us to recognize how rational history and empirical history fit together. I hope also to have an opportunity to compare and contrast Kant's philosophy of history with Hegel's—the two having "a close affinity" in spite of their notable differences (Yovel 1980, 11, 23–25). Whereas Kant moves from the transcendental to the empirical, Hegel's thought flows in the opposite direction, with concrete empirical facts serving to *reveal* the transcendental forms of experience. Webb (1926, 208) is therefore quite wrong to accuse Kant of being "profoundly *unhistorical* and *individualistic*." The fact that he also rejects the legitimacy of Kant's Copernican hypothesis as a whole (210f) explains why he finds the neglect of history in the *transcendental* wing of Kant's System so difficult to accept. Webb wants to see Kant taking socio–historical factors into consideration within his transcendental philosophy, but Kant's Copernican Perspective assumes that these two must be carefully distinguished in order for either to be understood properly.

13. Despland 1973, 246; see also *KCR* §VIII.2.B. Despland (1973, 246) earlier explains this point in more detail: "in the life of Jesus . . . a genuine existential breakthrough took place then and there. The hope in the growth of good on earth became a really live hope only in the Son of God. . . . Kant began to insist that in his person, through his work in history, Jesus Christ liberated us from an enslavement from which we could not liberate ourselves." Despland cites *CF* 7.43 and *RBBR* 6.82–83 as examples of passages where Kant develops such views.

14. In his study of primitive cultures, Hans Peter Duerr observes (1978, 122): "The 'dream place' is *in the centre*, and that centre is both everywhere and nowhere." We humans *must* "live an alienated life," he adds, because we stand between wilderness and civilization. Duerr's basic insight holds true for Kant's System as well, though Kant would have chosen other terms—perhaps "ignorance" and "knowledge"—to describe this fundamental existential dichotomy. The point of resonance here is that the Transcendental Perspective arises out of a dream-like center that provides the only reliable access to the speculations that lie at the circumference (see *KCR*, Figure III.8). This center is the *proper* "end of reason," as opposed to the attempt of some mystics, such as Swedenborg, to engage in "community with departed souls"—an experiment for which Kant thinks "there is no use of reason at all possible" (*LM* 28.448). That Kant's dream is fundamentally *theo*centric (see *KCR* §§I.1–3) is confirmed in *OP* 21.7, when Kant says that, because philosophy aims at wisdom, it is "directed toward something founded on God himself."

15. As I argued in *KSP* §VIII.3.B, the highest good is one of the key concepts in Kant's System. I have not emphasized its significance here, because it relates more to the idea of immortality (and so, to the political history of the human race) than to the idea of God (and religion). For our purposes it is enough to recall that Kant describes a world ruled by the highest good as "a *corpus mysticum*" (A807/B836); see Introduction, note 11.

Conclusion

Kantian Mysticism for the Twenty-First Century

The foregoing study bears witness to Kant's struggle to come to terms with the birth and death of reason, as it manifests itself in our immediate (though in itself unknowable, and therefore always mysterious) experience of the Oneness of all that is. We saw in Part I that Kant's Critical System was born (at least in part) out of the self-searching prompted by his intense, rational struggle to come to terms with the metaphysical claims that Swedenborg put forward on the basis of his mystical visions. In Part II we noted various mystical tendencies exhibited in Kant's personal life and explored a wide range of evidence for a positive interest in mysticism that crops up throughout his writings, despite his openly negative views on the "delirious" mental state that mysticism tends to induce and his persistent warnings against the danger of the delusory beliefs that are likely to arise out of an inappropriate interpretation of such experiences. Part III then offered an interpretation of Kant's elusive final work, the notes for which remained incomplete at his death: on the assumption that his so-called *Opus Postumum* was meant to be a Grand Synthesis of his entire philosophical System (see *KSP* §§III.3–4), I showed how it grounds theoretical and practical reason in a metaphysical Oneness that exhibits itself in our immediate experience yet cannot be reduced to the level of empirical cognition. I shall now conclude by providing a concise outline of how four of the main texts in Kant's philosophical System (see *KSP* §III.4), his three *Critiques* and *RBBR*, develop different facets of a Critical mysticism that can serve as a guide for our understanding of religious experience even at our present stage of history. Kant's Critical mysticism turns out to be highly relevant to some key debates in the philosophical discussion of mysticism over the past half century.[1]

Kant's *Critique of Pure Reason* is the first substantive step in the fulfillment of his lifelong goal of constructing a theoretical system that would provide the architectonic basis for both the metaphysician's *understanding* of the nature of reality and the mystic's immediate *experience* of that reality. While it is widely recognized that *CPR* puts forth a *metaphysics of experience*,[2] few have noted that the central role Kant gives to experience throughout the book, as the epistemological grounding for our metaphysical understanding of the nature of reality, also signals his concurrent desire to delineate a way of assessing claims regarding mystical experience, and so also to carve out a proper place for a refined form of mysticism. At the core of his theoretical system is a distinction between what our rational capacity *receives from* the world, through a mechanism he calls *sensible intuition* (whereby the mind limits all empirical cognition to objects that appear to us in *space* and *time*), and what we spontaneously *contribute to* the world, through the mechanism of *intelligible conception* (whereby the mind ensures that all legitimate cognitions conform to a set of basic organizational precepts (*Grundsätzen*), the most important of which is the law of the necessary connection of *cause and effect*). Empirical cognition—i.e., the process of obtaining the kind of determinate knowledge that, when organized systematically, constitutes *science*—can arise only when we apply our categorized concepts to content we have received from our five senses, through which we "intuit" objects in space and time. Because empirical cognition is limited to objects that *appear* (or at least *can* appear) to us, we must remain forever ignorant of the way things are *in themselves* (i.e., apart from our knowledge of how they appear to us), and this in turn means that the traditional claims of metaphysics—most notably, that God exists, that human beings are free to act in ways that are not necessarily determined by the law of causality, and that the human soul is immortal—can never become items of determinate knowledge for human beings. This much is standard fare for any Kant 101 course, so I have not focused on it in the main chapters of this book.

What the foregoing study demonstrates is that, in addition to defending the explicitly *metaphysical* ramifications of his transcendental epistemology, Kant also consistently showed a concern (at least implicitly) for its *experiential* significance—most notably, its implications for *mysticism*. Those who explore this connection between Kant's metaphysics of experience and mysticism almost always focus on its negative application—namely, Kant's insistence that any claim to have experienced an object of non-sensible intuition must be rejected as delusional. This is due, in large part, to the fact that Kant himself tends to reserve the word "mysticism" for positions such as the one Kant read Plato as defending, whereby human beings are believed to gain knowledge through direct experiences of noumenal objects; Plato's "mystical system," according to Kant, "asserted an *intuition* through pure understanding not accompanied by any senses" (A854/B882)—i.e., an *intel-*

lectual intuition of things in themselves.³ According to the basic principles of *CPR*, any such experience is impossible for human beings, "intellectual intuition" being reserved for the kind of creation–through–the–mere–act–of–thinking that God alone (presumably) has.

As Maharaj (2017, 321) points out, Kant calls this false type of intuition by a variety of different names, including "'intellectual intuition' (28:207), 'intuitive understanding' (5:406), 'supersensible intuition' (29:950–51), 'mystical intuition' (28/2.2:1325), 'mystical intellect' (29:761), and 'mystical understanding' (28:241)." In addition to Plato and Swedenborg, others whom Kant accuses of being mystical include Berkeley (*PFM* 4.293), pantheists such as Spinoza and "the Tibetans," and certain Chinese (probably Daoist) philosophers who, "sitting in dark rooms with their eyes closed, exert themselves to think and sense their own nothingness."⁴ Kant gives a (rather loaded) *definition* of "mystical intuition" in *LPDR* 28.1325: "Mystical intuition is the faculty to see things which are not objects of experience; e.g., the notion of spirits that are in community with us. . . . The mystic thinks that a higher reason should make the use of empirical reason superfluous." Kant thinks all such claims are fraudulent, because if the mystic were *really* able to obtain secret knowledge, then he or she should be able to know things that science later discovers, before their discovery. Thus, Kant's criticisms of Swedenborg in *DSS* are typically directed against Swedenborg's tendency to believe "that spirits are physically present to his senses" (Maharaj 2017, 318n).

What, then, is happening when someone believes that he or she has (for example) communicated with a departed spirit or heard the voice of God? The typical interpretation of Kant's view of mysticism nearly always neglects the fact that, by excluding the possibility of any *direct* experience of noumenal entities, Kant is not thereby rejecting *in*direct experiences of things in themselves. Quite to the contrary, one of the main purposes of his distinction between the phenomenal and the noumenal is to preserve the possibility of two other options: first, a mystic might experience some sensible object(s) but take it or them as a symbolic representation of a noumenal reality to which it points only indirectly;⁵ second, a mystical experience may have conceptual content that defies instantiation at the level of sensation, or perceptual content that defies linguistic explication, as is the case when someone claims to have experienced the world's underlying Oneness. These two options correspond directly to the traditional distinction between the "way of affirmation" and the "way of negation," defended by mystics from Pseudo-Dionysius to modern times.

Following the first option, Kant's System leaves ample room for the possibility that a person might have a sense-based experience which in some way points indirectly to a supersensible source (such as God). In this case, "God's voice" might be mediated through some *physical* object, such as the church bells ringing on a Sunday morning, the waves crashing against a nearby cliff, or an inspiring piece of music performed to perfection. Nothing in Kant's position prevents a religious person from interpreting such events as having their ultimate cause in God; it only requires everyone (both those who believe in the supersensible source of such experiences and those who do not) to admit that we do not know for sure what their ultimate cause may be. Kant's advice, from *DSS* onwards, is to stick as closely as possible to what we *do* know, which is that the immediate cause of such experiences is sensible *and* that morality commands us to act in certain ways; those who have such mystical experiences are free to interpret them in various *other* (e.g., religious) ways as well, as long as they do not regard these interpretations as releasing them from the universal human duties to be good and to seek reliable knowledge of the empirical world (see e.g., A651/B679). Just as Kant can be said to have replaced the traditional scholastic tradition of theoretical metaphysics with a *moral* metaphysics, so also his epistemology replaces an overly literal and thereby delirious interpretation of mystical experience not with the absence of any possible mystical experience but with an interpretation of it as necessarily enhancing our moral nature.[6]

What is almost always neglected in the secondary literature, even by those who recognize the important role Kant gave to symbolism, is that Kant's attempt to transform our understanding of mysticism also includes a new way to conceive of the so-called "negative path." That Kant (perhaps due to his obsession with Swedenborg) seems unaware that mystics themselves often refer to the mystical encounter as arising out of this very *breakdown* of our normal cognitive faculties, rather than as an application of them to a transcendent realm, does explain why Kant has a tendency to dismiss mysticism in general as irrelevant. Indeed, his claim that objects of experience can be *known* by us only if they appear to us through sensible intuition in a form that we can cognize through the formative agency of the categories leaves open the possibility that *some* of our experiences might involve intuitions that *cannot* come under any categorial concept, or concepts of wholeness that cannot ever be instantiated through intuition. In such cases, our experiences will never rise to the level of becoming "knowledge"; yet they are not for this reason any less legitimately regarded as part of our immediate experience.

The three ideas of reason that occupy so much of Kant's attention—namely, God, freedom in the world, and immortality of the soul—are themselves prime examples of ideas of *wholeness* that have a distinctively mystical character yet cannot be instantiated in the empirical world and are therefore not to be regarded as playing any constitutive role in scientific knowledge, even though they are far from being rejected by Kant for this reason. Indeed, they are the most important of all concepts, when it comes to living a meaningful life. As I pointed out in the Introduction, Kant's infamously opaque concepts of the "thing in itself" and the "transcendental object" share this same fate: they are concepts of something that we cannot intuit, because they signify a wholeness that goes beyond the level of what we can know empirically; yet presupposing their reality is absolutely necessary, in Kant's view, if we are to understand how knowledge itself arises. While Kant gives far less attention in *CPR* to the status of intuitions that we have but which cannot be conceptualized, he does focus on this option in *CJ*, as we shall see shortly. The main point here is that the mystic's way of negation forms the very starting point of Kant's epistemology, for he argues that all our knowledge arises out of a *fundamental encounter* between the transcendental subject and the transcendental object, yet he insists that the nature of this original encounter must remain forever obscured in what mystics have rightly called a "cloud of unknowing." An important aspect of Kant's mystical way of negation is that each *Critique* portrays God in terms of the negation of a human faculty's limit: whereas *CPR* limits human intuition to what is sensible, it depicts God as having *intellectual intuition*; while *CPrR* argues that we can never be more than virtuous (i.e., imperfectly good), it views God as *holy*; and whereas *CJ* examines various implications of human understanding being discursive, it suggests that God has *non-discursive* or *intuitive* understanding. Kant's Critical mysticism explores ways of interpreting non-standard human experiences *without* attributing to us what is properly reserved for God.

Because Kant's moral philosophy is so deeply concerned with establishing the *formal structure* of correct (Critical) reasoning, many commentators have overlooked the experiential thrust of Kant's System in this area as well. Kant's ultimate concern is consistently existential (in a moral/pedagogical sense): to motivate his readers to *become better human beings*. Even by the time he wrote *DSS* Kant had already (at least implicitly) formulated his Critical doctrine of the primacy of practical reason over theoretical (see *CPrR* 5.119–21); thus, as we saw in Chapter 2, when he considered the issue of whether or not Swedenborg's alleged visions might serve as evidence for an afterlife, Kant argued that any (theoretical) inference would be "superfluous" if "the heart of man" does not "contain within itself immediate moral prescriptions" (*DSS* 2.372). Moreover, key features of his argument in *GMM* and *CPrR* depend on an underlying assumption that we human beings have *direct access* to a *moral fact* that we can each encounter in our own experience of practical reasoning: namely, the fact that the moral law constrains our individual choices. What *is* this "moral law," other than the experienced awareness, via the one human instinct (i.e., conscience), that *all human beings* deserve equal respect? Surely Kant's moral philosophy is grounded in what might well be called a mystical intuition of the unity of human personhood—though Kant prefers to call it a commitment of moral faith. As we have seen, he shied away from using labels such as "mystical intuition" because (and herein lies the core of his criticism of any mystic who assumes otherwise than that) this moral mandate does nothing to extend our *theoretical knowledge* of the world.

A recent article by Lucas Thorpe explores in considerable detail the extent to which Swedenborg exercised a formative influence on Kant's moral theory. In particular (Thorpe 2010, 1), "Kant's conception of a realm of ends is modeled on Swedenborg's conception of heaven as a community of spirits governed by moral laws." While Kant's reading of Swedenborg appears to be what first gave him the idea that moral relationships can be defined in entirely spiritual terms, Thorpe claims that he modified Swedenborg's position in two crucial respects. First, Kant portrays the members of this moral–spiritual community as being autonomous persons who give themselves the law, rather than being merely passive recipients of a divine law (10–12). Second, Thorpe claims that "the mature Kant" (1–2) rejects Swedenborg's religious conception of the realm of ends in favor of "a political community, or ideal state, governed by juridical laws." As I demonstrated in SP–94 (and further elaborated in *KCR* and *CCKR*), however, Kant sees the juridical state as a step on the path *toward* an ethical community, not vice versa. Thorpe is therefore correct to point out that Kant's appropriation of Swedenborg's mysticism imposed the Critical requirement that we avoid making knowledge claims about a realm that we cannot possibly know;[7] but he is mistaken to think that the resulting Critical mysticism is political *rather than* religious.

A contemporary account of the moral core of mysticism that shares many features of Kant's vision of (what I call) Critical mysticism can be found in Ernst Tugendhat's *Egocentricity and Mysticism* (2016). Taking Kant's fourth philosophical question ("What is humanity?") as a guideline, he argues that human beings are essentially "I-sayers" and that our ability to think and communicate in first-person, propositional terms is what sets us apart from other higher animals, whose thought processes and communicative abilities are limited to what they can express in signs that refer directly to what they experience immediately. But the linguistic reality that we construct out of our I-saying ability also ironically alienates us from ourselves and calls for a therapeutic response that can offer us "peace of mind" (*Seelenfriede*). What the translators call his "rational mysticism" (Procyshyn and Wenning 2016, xix) offers a "decentering potential" that "provides relief from suffering" caused by the inevitable egocentricity of our linguistic nature; it tames desire (just as I am arguing with regard to Kant's implicit mysticism) without giving up a firm "commitment to intellectual honesty" (xx). A key difference between Tugendhat's mysticism and Kant's is that Tugendhat focuses almost entirely on appropriating Eastern forms of mysticism (especially Daoist and Buddhist), while Kant constructs his Critical mysticism on the basis of a Critique of his own, Christian/monotheistic religious tradition. Nevertheless, Kant's Critical mysticism affirms the core tenet of Tugendhat's mysticism (xxiii, quoting Tugendhat 2016), that "mystical experience involves a specific act of 'self-relativization' [*Selbstrelativierung*] in which one comes to see one's place 'in the whole.'"

The third *Critique* explores a range of issues whose diversity often baffles interpreters. What seems fairly clear, however, is that they all share two features: first, they concern types of human experience where the normal functioning of our cognitive faculties (i.e., of understanding, judgment, and reason in their function of determining empirical cognition, as argued in *CPR*) *breaks down*; and second, they all relate to some aspect of the all-important "space" that opens up *between* the theoretical and practical standpoints, as established in the first two *Critiques*—a space wherein reflective human beings are capable of *discerning* ways of synthesizing aspects of the practical and theoretical standpoints, through judgments that do not constitute empirical cognition yet nevertheless deserve to be part of a broader understanding of meaningful human experience.[8] The "reflective discernment" (*reflektierende Urteilskraft*) that generates such judgments reveals that our experiences of beauty arise when an object stimulates a subject's mind in a way that causes the person's imagination to exercise control over his or her understanding, whereas in ordinary, determinative (*bestimmten*) judgments the imagination plays a subordinate role, as servant of the understanding. Such experiences, Kant maintains, have a *moral* aspect insofar as they put us in touch with something "supersensible": when we discern beauty in an object, we think of it *as if* all others who perceive the object *ought* to agree with us, since our delight in the object is disinterested yet *necessary*. Likewise, we discern the sublime when we experience an intuition of such overwhelmingly great magnitude that it overpowers our understanding, yet in such a way that reason can remain aloof and mitigate the disconcerting feeling we experience when facing the sublime. These two examples, like Kant's third main example—our experience of organisms and other purposive objects in nature that give rise to the need to presuppose some kind of teleological substructure to the world—all have a mystical flavor: they describe situations wherein we encounter a mystery that lies beyond human comprehension yet, when we experience it, offers us the best possible justification for believing in an ultimate wholeness that confers meaning on the otherwise despair-inducing contingencies of the world.

Of the various texts where Kant explores types of experience that many people would regard as "mystical," none contains more substantive material than *RBBR*. As *CCKR* already provides a detailed discussion of this material, I will here only briefly mention two of the most significant examples. First, Kant's theory of religious conversion or "change of heart" involves the experience of a mysterious empowerment to moral improvement that Kant portrays as coming or seeming to come (at least potentially) from an external, divine source. Kant repeatedly insists that the question of whether or not there is really a God who *causes* such a change lies beyond the bounds of what reason can discover; what Kantian philosophers of religion *can* insist upon is that anyone who believes in such an external source must at least admit that the human person must choose to *take hold* of that divine assistance, otherwise we could not benefit from whatever goodness God has to offer.[9] Against the religious skeptic, he also insists that nobody can say for certain that it is *not* God who is ultimately behind such radical transformations of character that religious people sometimes experience. As Kant puts it in a subsequent discussion of religious education, the key is not to identify which theory is correct to teach, but to find ways of instilling in church members a respect for mystery: "Now the real solution to the problem (of the new man) consists in putting to use the idea of this power [of character transformation], which dwells in us in a way we cannot understand" (*CF* 7.59).

One of the best examples of Kant's treatment of religious experience in *RBBR* is his account of the "effects of grace," one of his four examples of "parerga" or by-products of religion within the bounds of bare reason that transcend yet press up against its bounds, therefore demanding some attention from philosophers (*RBBR* 6.52–53). The first parergon refers to "the supposed inward experience" of (presumably) God's assistance, whereby a person is *made good* without having to do anything other than receive the gift. Concerning this possibility Kant warns that "to expect an effect of grace means . . . that the good (the moral type) will be not our deed, but that of another being, [and] therefore that we can *acquire* the effect of grace by just *doing nothing*, which is contradictory." Kant is not rejecting this notion outright, as has often been assumed, but is merely pointing out its inherently paradoxical nature, for he goes on to *affirm* the mystery: "Therefore we can concede the effect of grace as something ungraspable, but cannot take it up into our maxim either for theoretical or for practical use." Similarly, when he returns to this topic at the end of the book, in the fourth and final General Comment, he explicitly presents his position as two-sided: he concedes the possibility that "in the mind there sometimes occur movements working toward what is moral, movements that we cannot figure out and about which we are compelled to admit our ignorance"; yet when we encounter the presence of such a mystery, we cannot "be aware of a supersensible object in the experience of any effects, still less [can we] have influence on it to draw it down to us" (174). In other words, Critical mysticism allows for the *possibility* of an immediate experience of divine grace, but bars us from claiming to *understand* the encounter in a way that can produce either theoretical cognition or practical rules for behavior. Here Kant is explicitly leaving open the possibility that God might be the ultimate cause of such effects; his point is only that we cannot have any *philosophical* justification for making such a religious claim.

Kant is even more explicit in affirming a moderately mystical position on religious experience in *CF* 7.54–59, where he compares and assesses two opposing "mystical" interpretations of the role of divine grace in conversion: those of the Pietists and the Moravians. Kant attributes to the Pietists (55–56) the belief that "a heavenly spirit" initiates the conversion experience by producing "a breaking and crushing of the heart in *repentance*, a grief . . . bordering on despair" that nevertheless ends in a "moral metamorphosis," which thus empowers the converted person to do good. The Moravians, by contrast, locate divine intervention on the other end of the encounter: they portray human beings as using reason to recognize their own guilt before the moral law, but once we have resolved to act on the basis of this newfound "moral conviction to the good" (56, alt.), "a *miracle*" is needed in order to prevent us from relapsing into evil. In analyzing the philosophical justification for these opposing claims, Kant does not deny them outright, but exercises the caution appropriate to a Critical mystic (58): "To claim that we *feel* as such the immediate influence of God is self-contradictory, because the idea of God lies only in reason." Yet this initial skeptical response is only the first step of his Critical resolution of the problem, for he goes on to claim that a principle that can be found even within the Bible provides a middle path between the Pietist and Moravian extremes. The *ought implies can* principle, he argues (58–59), rests on the observation that we *do* find in ourselves an

> *ability* so to sacrifice our sensuous nature to morality that we *can* do what we quite readily and clearly conceive we *ought* to do. This ascendancy of the *supersensible* human being in us over the *sensible* . . . is an object of the greatest *wonder*; and our wonder at this moral predisposition in us, inseparable from our humanity, only increases the longer we contemplate this true (not fabricated) ideal.

Here Kant is explicitly acknowledging that *something real* is happening in the conversion experience, and that this something has a wondrous, supersensible grounding, even though reason by itself gives us no further guidance on how to understand it. Indeed, he interprets the Bible itself as having "nothing else in view," given that "the spirit of Christ" is "manifested in teachings and examples," not in "supernatural experiences and delirious feelings which should take reason's place" (59, alt.).

With this sketch of Kant's multifaceted Critical mysticism in mind, let us now briefly examine how a Kantian approach might deal with some of the controversies and issues that have been raised by scholars writing on the topic of mysticism and religious experience in the past half century. We can, for example, take Part III as a demonstration that *OP* functions as confirmation of my suggestion in *KSP* (98) that *OP* can be regarded as a "Metaphysics of Religious Experience." As such, Kant's philosophical System can be understood as confirming Smith's claim (1968, 11) "that there is a religious dimension to human existence and that this dimension is unintelligible without reference to God or transcendent Being." Copleston (1974, 12) also expounds such a position at some length, arguing that "metaphysics has as its basis an experience which I should not hesitate to characterise as religious," inasmuch as it requires an "initial belief" in the dependence of "finite things" on a transcendent "One which is not itself seen." Echoing Kant's Critical mysticism (though without calling it such), he adds that such an experience may have no "cognitive value" [13, 59], because "if talk about God is basically a way of referring to and speaking of what a man regards as that which discloses itself in certain types of experience, we cannot adequately understand the language apart from the basic experience or types of experiences." Copleston (75) describes this type of experience as a subjective awareness "of being acted upon, of an intimate uniting and one-ing with a Being immeasurably greater than himself and which is felt to be in some sense the . . . ultimate reality." This is precisely Kant's point, when he argues that we may interpret our awareness of immediacy as profoundly religious, even though our immediate experience cannot produce empirical cognition without attaching itself to concepts, which in turn deprives it of its status as immediate.

Flew (1966, §6.7), by contrast, famously argues *against* the meaningfulness of religious experience: "The mere fact of the occurrence of subjective religious experience does not by itself warrant the conclusion that there are any objective religious truths to be represented." While this is technically correct (as Copleston 1974, 80, admits), it reveals more than anything else Flew's own bias for the objective (see *KCR*, Appendix IV.4). Unlike Kant, whose System of Perspectives allows truth to come in a variety of forms (e.g., as subjective certainty or as objective certainty), Flew requires anything called "true" to be based on objective fact. Kant, like most mystics, is fully aware of the subjective character of religious/mystical experience but does not think this necessarily makes it objectively false or illusory. The inadequacy of Flew's approach is further illustrated by the fact that he finds it problematic that the objective content of religious experiences differs widely between people in different religious traditions (Flew 1966, §6.6); this is not a significant problem for anyone who, with Kant, openly identifies the truth-bearing quality of such experiences with their *subjective form*. Thus, when Kant qualifies his standard definition of religion (in terms of "the cognition of all our duties as divine commands") by inserting the qualification "regarded subjectively" (*RBBR* 6.153), he is explicitly ruling out the relevance of such objective differences between different people's religious experiences—i.e., of what Kant also calls "historical faith"—to the ultimate determination of the *religious* truth of even these objective experiences. When Flew claims that such disagreements in the way different people experience religion stem from each culture's differing set of religious "categories," he uses the latter term in a thoroughly un-Kantian way; for Kant's categories refer to the universal *logical form* of all thinking (or, as applied to the organization of the "true church" in the form of universality, integrity, freedom, and unchangeableness [see *RBBR* 6.101–2], to the *existential form* of all authentic religious community), not to the *cultural content* of some people's objective experience.

The fault, as becomes evident in Flew 1966, §§6.16–18, is not entirely Flew's, for the conservative theologians against whom he was chiefly arguing tended to ignore Kant's Copernican hypothesis by assuming that the veracity of a religious experience requires God to be portrayed as an empirically objectifiable being rather than as a transcendentally subjective reality living within each individual's heart. Only by adopting the latter (Kantian) view as one's starting point, together with Kant's further claim that the legitimacy of religious cognitions is best assessed in terms of their moral–practical usefulness (see e.g., Copleston 1974, 80–82), can the theist respond effectively to Flew's most decisive argument, that a religious experience's "built in elusiveness to observation makes it impossible to falsify claims about the presence of God simply by indicating that there is in fact nothing there to be observed" (Flew 1966, §6.27). For Kant there *is* something to be encountered—but it is transcendental (not empirical) in form and practical (not theoretical) in content.

McCarthy 1986 similarly argues against the kind of mystically oriented and religiously affirmative interpretation of Kant that I have defended here, though at one point (99) he comes close to acknowledging the nuances that constitute Kant's Critical mysticism:

> The most that one may conclude . . . is that . . . the moral law is the nearest one comes to encountering the divine. But it is certainly not to be construed as a direct experience of God. To be sure, Kant took pains to deny any kind of such experience, particularly emphasizing the lack of any faculty for direct perception of God.

If McCarthy is referring *solely* to Kant's theory of intellectual intuition as a tool for distinguishing God's way of experiencing from the human way, which requires *sensible* intuition, then he is technically correct. However, such summary dismissals risk conflating *encountering God*, which can be quite properly rooted (as a matter of *faith*) in the universal human experience of immediacy, with the imagined *Godlike experience* of intellectual intuition, which Kant regards as impossible for us humans. (For evidence that McCarthy himself sometimes commits such a conflation, see note 9 of this Conclusion.) McCarthy continues (99): "Kant's understanding of religion . . . emphatically excludes . . . religious experience . . . [as] not practical." But this is simply false: claims to have such experiences are excluded only if they have a morally negative influence on a person.

The foregoing account of Kant's Critical mysticism, especially when considered together with its implications for more ordinary forms of *religious* experience (see *KCR*, Chapters VII and VIII, and *CCKR*), explains how an encounter with God is possible on Kantian grounds without presupposing any intellectual intuition whatsoever. To recap, Kant never denies the possibility of encountering God, provided that any claim to a mystical (or other religious) experience meets two conditions: first, the perceptions or feelings of encountering or being related to God must not be regarded as capable of producing objectively verifiable knowledge of God; and second, they must serve as motivations for the person to live a morally better life. McCarthy goes so far as to claim [99n] that "Kant's God could not appear . . . , for there would be no way to recognize him." But Kant would never dogmatically declare that *God cannot appear*; he would only warn that we can never know for *certain* if an appearance is of God.

In defending the possibility of a Kantian Critical mysticism, my point has been to emphasize that we can abide by the limits Kant places on mysticism playing any *constitutive* role in our theoretical or practical cognition and yet still affirm that religious experience plays a *regulative* role at various points throughout the Kant System. Indeed, in *CCKR* (see especially Appendix III) I demonstrate that Kant is careful to leave room even for the possibility that God might initiate the "change of heart" that plays such a major role in the argument of *RBBR*; however, he emphatically insists, over and over, that *if* God were to assist in this way, we could never *know* that the change was initiated by God, so it is wiser to assume that human beings are themselves responsible to effect such a change. In other words, the boundary conditions that Kant's System places on our theoretical knowledge and moral action also prevent us from knowing for certain that God does *not* initiate such changes, while at the same time providing good practical reasons for believing in a transcendent source who does serve in this role. As such, the Critical path emerges as one that leads us into a twofold appreciation of mystical experience: while encouraging us to be aware that linguistic structures arise out of the original oneness of immediate experience, it beckons us to move beyond language, to an encounter that may impart moral wholeness. As Kant's Critical mysticism has taught us, in other words, only the person who silently bares *all* human pretentions—the skeptical ones as well as the dogmatic—to reason's light, as Wittgenstein (1922, 6.5.4) famously put it, "sees the world rightly."

NOTES

1. *JL* 9.25; *C* 11.249. Due to limitations of space I have provided only a few key examples in what follows. Maharaj 2017 ends with a similar discussion of how Kant's qualified affirmation of mysticism relates to various recent debates. A potential application of Kant's Critical

mysticism that neither I nor Maharaj explicitly discuss is its relevance to debates, mainly among various analytic philosophers, regarding the status of unitive mystical experiences, where a person allegedly transcends the subject–object distinction itself. See e.g., Stace 1960 and Wainwright 1981. Nevertheless, the attentive reader will observe numerous hints of such an application in what follows. As Philip Rossi rightly observes, also (in part) with Kant's philosophy in mind, the outcome of such discussions of the difficult notion of "religious experience" depends, perhaps more than anything else, on "what counts as experience" (2008, 269, 281–3).

2. For the classical account of this way of reading the first *Critique*, see Paton 1936.

3. See also A314/B371, where Kant comments on what he takes to be Plato's "mystical deduction" of transcendent ideas.

4. *EAT* 8.335; cf. note 6.3. See also many of the pages of *LM* cited in note 4.2, above.

5. As I explained near the end of Chapter 4, Maharaj 2017 argues in detail for precisely this position with regard to "indirect"—or what I would call "symbolic"—mystical experiences.

6. To illustrate his position, Kant refers on several occasions (e.g., *RBBR* 6.87, 187, and *CF* 7.62–66) to the biblical example of Abraham hearing the voice of God and deciding on that basis to kill his son, Isaac, as a sacrifice to God. Kant argues that, although we can never know for certain that a "voice" is *really* God speaking to us, we *can* know when a voice is *not* from God: namely, when it tells us to do something immoral. For more on the issue of Kant's appeal to Abraham, see SP–09 and Maharaj 2017, 22–23.

7. Thorpe also argues (2010, 12–15) that Kant drew much of his mature view of life after death (as a transformation in our mode of perception) from Swedenborg's view of death.

8. Kant's technical term, *Urteilskraft*, typically translated as "power of judgment" (or often simply "judgment," thus making the term indistinguishable from its root, *Urteils*), is best translated as "discrimination" or "discernment." For a defense of the latter translation, see *CCKR* 525.

9. McCarthy (1986, 100), in his account of this theory, states that "Kant never entertains the possibility of religious experience . . . that might . . . play some role in the restoration of the right order of the moral incentives." In *KCR* 362n I conceded that McCarthy was "quite right" to make this point, adding only "that there is nothing in [Kant's] System that *prevents* us from supplementing his theories with such an emphasis." In the wake of *CCKR* (see also SP-2010c), however, I would now be less accommodating to McCarthy's position, for Kant never *denies* the possibility that God might do something to *cause* the change of heart; quite to the contrary, his whole argument presupposes this possibility. What he never entertains is the possibility that God could do this *without* the human being also playing some key role in the choice that leads to the change, such that the mere "feeling" of having such an experience of moral regeneration would by itself be sufficient evidence that a real change had taken place.

Works Cited

ABBREVIATIONS USED FOR KANT'S WORKS

Following the abbreviation, each entry gives the work's title, as found in the Cambridge Edition of the Works of Immanuel Kant (except *AA* and *RBBR*; the latter title is based on my translation in *CCKR*), followed by the year(s) of publication (or for works not published by Kant, the year of composition) and the volume number(s) in *AA* (except *IS*).

AA – *Kants gesammelte Schriften*, Preußischen Akademie der Wissenschaften (eds.), 29 vols. (Berlin: Walter de Gruyter, 1902–). The number immediately after "*AA*" (*Akademie Ausgabe*) stands for the volume number(s); the "*AA*" abbreviation is omitted wherever page numbers are given after the volume number.

APP – *Anthropology from a Pragmatic Point of View*, 1798 (7.117–333)
C – *Correspondence*, various dates (*AA* 10–13)
CBHH – *Conjectural Beginning of Human History*, 1786 (8.109–23)
CF – *The Conflict of the Faculties*, 1798 (7.1–116)
CJ – *Critique of the Power of Judgment*, 1790 (5.167–484)
CPR – *Critique of Pure Reason*, 1781/87 (*AA* 3, and 4.1–252); references cite the standard A/B pagination of the first and/or second German editions
CPrR – *Critique of Practical Reason*, 1788 (5.1–163)
DSS – *Dreams of a Spirit-Seer Elucidated by Dreams of Metaphysics*, 1766 (2.315–73)
EAT – *The End of All Things*, 1794 (8.325–39)
ENPM – *The Employment in Natural Philosophy of Metaphysics Combined with Geometry, of Which Sample I Contains the Physical Monadology*, 1756 (1.473–87)

GMM – Groundwork of The Metaphysics of Morals, 1785 (4.385–463)
HPE – History and Natural Description of the Most Noteworthy Occurrences of the Earthquake that Struck a Large Part of the Earth at the End of the Year 1755, 1756 (1.429–61)
ICNM – Attempt to Introduce the Concept of Negative Magnitudes into Philosophy, 1763 (2.165–204)
ID – On the Form and Principles of the Sensible and the Intelligible World [Inaugural Dissertation], 1770 (2.385–419)
IS – On Inner Sense, not in *AA* (see Robinson 1989, 252–61)
IUH – Idea for a Universal History with a Cosmopolitan Aim, 1784 (9.15–31)
JL – Jäsche Logic, 1800 (9.1–150)
LE – Lectures on Ethics, 1775–81 (*AA* 27)
LM – Lectures on Metaphysics, 1762–95 (*AA* 28–29)
LPDR – Lectures on the Philosophical Doctrine of Religion, 1783–84? (28.993–1121)
LPed – Lectures on Pedagogy, 1776–87 (9.437–99)
MFSN – Metaphysical Foundations of Natural Science, 1786 (4.465–565)
MH – Essay on the Maladies of the Head, 1764 (2.257–71)
MM – The Metaphysics of Morals, 1797 (6.203–493)
MPT – On the Miscarriage of All Philosophical Trials in Theodicy, 1791 (8.255–71)
OFBS – Observations on the Feeling of the Beautiful and Sublime, 1764 (2.205–56)
OP – Opus Postumum, 1796–1803 (*AA* 21–22)
OPA – The Only Possible Argument in Support of a Demonstration of the Existence of God, 1763 (2.63–163)
PFM – Prolegomena to Any Future Metaphysics that Will Be Able To Come Forward as Science, 1783 (4.253–383)
PJE – Preface to Reinhold Bernhard Jachmann's Examination of the Kantian Philosophy of Religion, 1800 (8.441)
PM – What Real Progress Has Metaphysics Made in Germany Since the Time of Leibniz and Wolff?, 1793 (20.253–311)
PP – Toward Perpetual Peace, 1795 (8.341–86)
R – Reflexionen, various years (*AA* 14–20)
RBBR – Religion within the Bounds of Bare Reason, 1793/94 (6.3–202)
RPTS – On a Recently Prominent Tone of Superiority in Philosophy, 1796 (8.387–406)
SEMF – Succinct Exposition of Some Meditations on Fire, 1755 (1.369–84)
TELF – Thoughts on the True Estimation of Living Forces and Assessment of the Demonstrations that Leibniz and Other Scholars of Mechanics Have Made Use of in This Controversial Subject, together

with Some Prefatory Considerations Pertaining to the Force of Bodies in General, 1747 (1.1–181)

UNH – *Universal Natural History and Theory of the Heavens*, 1755 (1.215–368)

ABBREVIATIONS USED FOR CITATIONS TO THE AUTHOR'S PUBLICATIONS

CCKR – *Comprehensive Commentary on Kant's Religion within the Bounds of Bare Reason* (Chichester, U.K.: Wiley, 2016).

KCR – *Kant's Critical Religion: Volume Two of Kant's System of Perspectives* (Aldershot: Ashgate, 2000).

KSP – *Kant's System of Perspectives: An Architectonic Interpretation of the Critical Philosophy* (Lanham, MD: University Press of America, 1993).

SP–87a: *Complete Index to Kemp Smith's Translation of Kant's Critique of Pure Reason* (Oxford and Hong Kong: distributed privately, 1987).

SP–87b: "Kant's Cosmogony Re-Evaluated", *Studies in History and Philosophy of Science* 18.3 (1987), 255–69.

SP–87c: "A Priori Knowledge in Perspective: (II) Naming, Necessity and the Analytic A Posteriori", *Review of Metaphysics* 41.2 (1987), 255–82.

SP–87d: "A Priori Knowledge in Perspective: (I) Mathematics, Method and Pure Intuition", *Review of Metaphysics* 41.1 (1987), 1–22.

SP–94: "'The Kingdom of God is at Hand!' (Did *Kant* Really Say That?)", *History of Philosophy Quarterly* 11.4 (1994), 421–37.

SP–00: *The Tree of Philosophy*[4] (Hong Kong: Philopsychy Press, 2000 [1992]).

SP–02: "Kant's Criticism of Swedenborg: Parapsychology and the Origin of the Copernican Hypothesis", in Fiona Steinkamp (ed.), *Parapsychology, Philosophy and the Mind: Essays Honoring John Beloff* (Jefferson, NC, and London: McFarland, Inc., 2002), 146–78.

SP–07: "Emergence, Evolution, and the Geometry of Logic: Causal Leaps and the Myth of Historical Development", *Foundations of Science* 12.1 (2007), 9–37.

SP–08: "Kant's Moral Panentheism", *Philosophia* 36.1 (2008), 17–28.

SP–09: "Three Perspectives on Abraham's Defense Against Kant's Charge of Immoral Conduct" (co-authored with Philip Rudisill), *Journal of Religion* 89.4 (2009), 467–97.

SP–10a: *Cultivating Personhood: Kant and Asian Philosophy* (Berlin: Walter de Gruyter, 2010).

SP–10b: "The Kantian Grounding of Einstein's Worldview: (I) The Early Influence of Kant's System of Perspectives", *Polish Journal of Philosophy* IV.1 (2010), 45–64.

SP–10c: "Kant's Ethics of Grace: Perspectival Solutions to the Moral Difficulties with Divine Assistance", *Journal of Religion* 90.4 (October 2010), 530–53.

SP–11: "The Kantian Grounding of Einstein's Worldview: (II) Simultaneity, the Synthetic A Priori and God", *Polish Journal of Philosophy* V.1 (2011), 97–116.

SP–12: "Analytic Aposteriority and its Relevance to Twentieth Century Philosophy", *Studia Humana* 1.3/4 (2012), 3–16.

SP–13: "Kantian Causality and Quantum Quarks: The Compatibility between Quantum Mechanics and Kant's Phenomenal World", *THEORIA: International Journal for Theory, History and Foundations of Science* 28.2 (2013), 283–302.

SP–15a: "What is Kantian *Gesinnung*? On the Priority of Volition over Metaphysics and Psychology in Kant's *Religion*", *Kantian Review* 20.2 (2015), 235–64.

SP–15b: "Bohm's Quantum Causality and its Parallels in Kant's Ideas of Reason", in *Death And Anti-Death, Volume 13: Sixty Years After Albert Einstein (1879–1955)*, ed. Charles Tandy (Palo Alto: Ria University Press, 2015), 99–128.

SP–16a: "Synthetic Logic as the Philosophical Underpinning for Apophatic Theology: Commentary on [William Franke's] *A Philosophy of the Unsayable*", in *Syndicate* (April 6, 2016); online at: syndicatetheology.com/symposium/a-philosophy-of-the-unsayable/.

SP–16b: "Kant's Perspectival Solution to the Mind–Body Problem: Or, Why Eliminative Materialists Must Be Kantians", *Culture and Dialogue* 4.1 (2016), 194–213.

OTHER WORKS CITED

Adickes, Erich (ed.), *Kants Opus Postumum* (Berlin: Rather & Reichard, 1920).

Akhutin, A.V., "Sophia and the Devil: Kant in the Face of Russian Religious Metaphysics", *Soviet Studies in Philosophy* 29 (1991), 59–89.

Alberg, Jeremiah, "What Dreams May Come: Kant's *Träume eines Geistersehers* Elucidated by the Dreams of a Coquette", *Kant-Studien* 106.2 (2015), 169–200.

Baelz, Peter, *Christian Theology and Metaphysics* (London: Epworth Press, 1968).

Baillie, John, *Our Knowledge of God* (London: Oxford University Press, 1939).

Barth, Karl, *Die Protestantische Theologie im 19. Jahrhundert*, 1952. Trans. B. Cozens and J. Bowden as *Protestant Theology in the Nineteenth Century* (London: SCM Press, 1972).

Bax, Ernest Belfort, "Preface", "A Biography of Kant", and "Kant's Position in Philosophy", in E.B. Bax (ed. and trans.), *Kant's Prolegomena and Metaphysical Foundations of Natural Science* (London: G. Bell & Sons, 1883; revised 1891), i–vi, xi–lxxi, and lxxii–cix.

Beck, Lewis White, review of G. Gawlick and L. Kreimendahl's *Hume in der deutschen Aufklärung*, in *Eighteenth-Century Studies* 21.3 (1988), 405–8.

———, *Kant's Latin Writings* (New York: Peter Lang, 1986).
———, *Early German Philosophy* (Cambridge, Mass.: Harvard University Press, 1969).
———, *A Commentary on Kant's Critique of Practical Reason* (London: University of Chicago Press, 1960).
———, Introduction and translator's notes to his revised edition of Immanuel Kant, *Prolegomena to Any Future Metaphysics*, trans. Paul Carus (New York: Bobbs-Merrill, 1950).
Beiser, Frederick C., "Kant's Intellectual Development: 1746–1781", in Guyer, *The Cambridge Companion to Kant* (Cambridge: Cambridge University Press, 1992), 26–61.
Broad, C.D., *Religion, Philosophy and Psychical Research* (London: Routledge & Kegan Paul, 1953).
Buchdahl, Gerd, "Reduction–Realization: A Key to the Structure of Kant's Thought", *Philosophical Topics* 12.2 (1982), 39–98.
Butts, Robert E., *Kant and the Double Government Methodology: Supersensibility and Method in Kant's Philosophy of Science* (Dordrecht: D. Reidel, 1984).
Byrne, Peter, *Kant on God* (Aldershot: Ashgate, 2007).
Cassirer, Ernst, *Kants Leben und Lehre*, 1921 (1918). Trans. J. Haden as *Kant's Life and Thought* (New Haven: Yale University Press, 1981).
Chapman, Mark D., "Apologetics and the Religious *A Priori*: The Use and Abuse of Kant in German Theology: 1900–20", *Journal of Theological Studies* 43.2 (1992), 470–510.
Clewis, Robert R., *The Kantian Sublime and the Revelation of Freedom* (Cambridge: Cambridge University Press, 2009).
Cohen, Alix, "The Ultimate Kantian Experience: Kant on Dinner Parties", *History of Philosophy Quarterly* 25.4 (2008), 315–36.
Collins, James, *God in Modern Philosophy* (London: Routledge & Kegan Paul, 1960).
———, *The Emergence of Philosophy of Religion* (London & New Haven: Yale University Press, 1967).
Comenius, John Amos, *The Orbis Pictus* (Syracuse, NY: C.W. Bardeen, 1887[1658]).
Cooke, Vincent M., "Kant's Godlike Self", *International Philosophical Quarterly* 28 (1988), 313–23.
Copleston, Fredrick C., *Religion and Philosophy* (Dublin: Gill and Macmillan, 1974).
———, *A History of Philosophy*, vol. VI, *Wolff to Kant* (London: Burns and Oates, 1960).
Crosby, Donald A., "Kant's Ideas about Ultimate Reality and Meaning in Relation to His Moral Theory: Critique of an Enlightenment Ideal", *Ultimate Reality and Meaning* 17.2 (1994), 117–36.
Davidovich, Adina, "Kant's Notion of Reflective Faith", in Edward Franklin Buchner and Hans Schwarz (eds.), *Papers of the Nineteenth Century Theology Working Group*, vol. 19 (Colorado Springs: Colorado College, 1993a), 20–40.
———, *Religion as a Province of Meaning: The Kantian Foundations of Modern Theology* (Minneapolis, MN: Fortress Press, 1993b).
Dell'Oro, Regina O.M., *From Existence to the Ideal: Continuity and Development in Kant's Theology* (New York: Peter Lang, 1994).
Despland, Michel, *Kant on History and Religion* (London and Montreal: McGill–Queen's University Press, 1973).
Di Giovanni, George, "On Chris L. Firestone and Nathan Jacobs's *In Defense of Kant's Religion*: A Comment", *Faith and Philosophy* 29.2 (2012), 163–69.
DiCenso, James, "The Concept of *Urbild* in Kant's Philosophy of Religion", *Kant-Studien* 104.1 (2013), 100–132.
Dister, John E., "Kant's Regulative Ideas and the 'Objectivity' of Reason", in Lewis White Beck (ed.), *Proceedings of the Third International Kant Congress* (Dordrecht, Holland: D. Reidel, 1972), 262–69.
Du Prel, Carl, *Die Philosophie der Mystik*, 1885. Trans. C.C. Massey as *The Philosophy of Mysticism*, 2 vols. (London: George Redway, 1889; reprinted New York: Arno Press, 1976).
Duerr, Hans Peter, *Traumzeit: Über die Grenze zwischen Wildnis und Zivilisation*, 1978. Trans. Felicitas Goodman as *Dreamtime: Concerning the Boundary between Wilderness and Civilization* (Oxford: Basil Blackwell, 1985).
England, F.E., *Kant's Conception of God* (London: Allen & Unwin, 1929).

Fang, J., *Kant-Interpretationen* (Münster: Verlag Regensberg, 1967).
Fendt, Gene, *For What May I Hope?* (New York: Peter Lang, 1990).
Firestone, Chris L. and Nathan Jacobs, *In Defense of Kant's Religion* (Indianapolis: Indiana University Press, 2008).
Fischer, Norbert, "Kants Idee »*est Deus in nobis*« und ihr Verhältnis zu Meister Eckhart. Zur Beziehung von Gott und Mensch in Kants kritisher Philosophie und bei Eckhart", in Wolfgang Erb and Norbert Fischer (eds.), *Meister Eckhart als Denker* (Stuttgart: Kohlhammer, 2017), 367–406.
Flew, Antony, *God & Philosophy* (London: Hutchinson, 1966). References are to chapter and paragraph numbers.
Florschütz, Gottlieb, *Swedenborgs verborgene Wirkung auf Kant*, 1992. Trans. J.D. Odhner and K. Nemitz as *Swedenborg's Hidden Influence on Kant*, in a series of installments published in *New Philosophy* 96–98 (1993–95): vol. 96 (1993), 171–225, 277–307; vol. 97 (1994), 347–96, 461–98; vol. 98 (1995), 99–108; etc. References are to the chapter and section numbers of the original version.
Forgie, J. William, "The Cosmological and Ontological Arguments: How Saint Thomas Solved the Kantian Problem", *Religious Studies* 31.1 (1995), 89–100.
Forman, Robert K.C., "A Construction of Mystical Experience", *Faith and Philosophy* 5.3 (1988), 254–67.
Förster, Eckart, "Introduction" (xv–lvii) and "Factual Notes" (257–88) to his translation of Immanuel Kant, *OP*.
———, "Kant's Notion of Philosophy", *Monist* 72.2 (1989), 285–304.
———, "Is There 'A Gap' in Kant's Critical System?", *Journal of the History of Philosophy* XXV.4 (1987), 533–55.
Friedman, R.Z., "Hypocrisy and the Highest Good: Hegel on Kant's Transition from Morality to Religion", *Journal of the History of Philosophy* 24 (1986), 503–22.
Friedrich, Carl J., "Preface" and "Introduction", *The Philosophy of Kant* (New York: Random House, 1949).
Galbraith, Elizabeth Cameron, *Kant and Theology: Was Kant a Closet Theologian?* (London: International Scholars Publications, 1996).
Gerding, Johan L.F., "Was Kant a Sceptic?", *Proceedings of the Parapsychological Association's 37th Annual Convention*, ed. Dick J. Bierman (Utrecht: Parapsychological Association, 1994).
Gilson, Étienne, *The Unity of Philosophical Experience* (New York: Charles Scribner's Sons, 1937).
Goldmann, Lucien, *Introduction à la philosophie de Kant*, 1967. Trans. Robert Black as *Immanuel Kant* (London: NLB, 1971).
Green, Ronald M., "The Leap of Faith: Kierkegaard's Debt to Kant", *Philosophy and Theology* 3 (1989), 385–411.
———, *Religious Reason: The Rational and Moral Basis of Religious Belief* (New York: Oxford University Press, 1978).
Greene, Theodore M., "The Historical Context and Religious Significance of Kant's *Religion*", in Immanuel Kant, *Religion within the Limits of Reason Alone*, trans. T.M. Greene and H.H. Hudson (New York: Harper & Row, 1960 [1934]), ix–lxxviii.
Grier, Michelle, "Swedenborg and Kant on Spiritual Intuition", in Stephen McNeilly (ed.), *On the True Philosopher and the True Philosophy—Essays on Swedenborg* (London: Swedenborg Society, 2002), 1–20.
Gulick, Walter B., "The Creativity of the Intellect: From Ontology to Meaning. The Transmutation of the Sensible and Intelligible Worlds in Kant's Critical Thought", *Ultimate Reality and Meaning* 17.2 (1994), 99–108.
Gulyga, Arsenij, *Kant*, 1985. Trans. Marijan Despalatovic as *Immanuel Kant: His Life and Thought* (Boston: Birkhäuser, 1987).
Guyer, Paul (ed.), *The Cambridge Companion to Kant* (Cambridge: Cambridge University Press, 1992).
Hare, John E., *The Moral Gap: Kantian Ethics, Human Limits, and God's Assistance* (Oxford: Clarendon Press, 1996).

Works Cited

Hedge, Frederic H., *Prose Writers of Germany* (Philadelphia: Carey and Hart, 1849[1847]).
Heidegger, Martin, *Kant und das Problem der Metaphysik*, 1929. Trans. J.S. Churchill as *Kant and the Problem of Metaphysics* (London: Indiana University Press, 1962).
Heine, Heinrich, *Zur Geschichte der Religion und Philosophie in Deutschland*, 1834. Trans. J. Snodgrass as *Religion and Philosophy in Germany* (Boston: Beacon Press, 1959).
Hicks, Joe H., "Old Lampe's Consolation: Ruminations on Kantian Piety", in Gerhard Funke (ed.), *Akten des 4. Internationalen Kant-Kongresses: Mainz 6.–12. April 1974*, vol. II (Berlin: Walter de Gruyter, 1974), 381–87.
Hund, William B., "The Sublime and God in Kant's *Critique of Judgement*", *New Scholasticism* 57 (1983), 42–70.
Insole, Christopher J., *Kant and the Creation of Freedom: A Theological Problem* (Oxford: Oxford University Press, 2013).
Jachmann, Reinhold Bernhard, *Immanuel Kant geschildert in Briefen an einen Freund* (Königsberg: Nicolovius, 1804).
Jaki, Stanley L., "Introduction" and "Notes", in Immanuel Kant, *Universal Natural History and Theory of the Heavens*, trans. S.L. Jaki (Edinburgh: Scottish Academic Press, 1981), 1–76 and 209–97.
Johnson, Gregory R., (ed.), *Kant on Swedenborg: Dreams of a Spirit-Seer and Other Writings*, trans. Gregory R. Johnson and Glenn A. Magee (West Chester, PA: Swedenborg Foundation, 2003).
———, "Swedenborg's *Positive* Influence on the Development of Kant's Mature Moral Philosophy", in Stephen McNeilly (ed.), *On the True Philosopher and the True Philosophy—Essays on Swedenborg* (London: Swedenborg Society, 2002), 21–38.
———, "Kant on Swedenborg in the *Lectures on Metaphysics*: Part 2", *Studia Swedenborgiana* 10.2 (May 1997), 11–39.
Jonsson, Inge, "Swedenborg, Emanuel", *The Encyclopedia of Philosophy*, ed. Paul Edwards, vol.8 (London: Collier Macmillan, 1967), 47.
Josephson, Jason Ānanda, "Specters of Reason: Kantian Things and the Fragile Terrors of Philosophy", *J19: Journal of Nineteenth-Century Americanists* 13.1 (Spring 2015), 204–11.
Kemp Smith, Norman, *A Commentary to Kant's "Critique of Pure Reason"* (London: Macmillan, 1923 [1918]).
Kiblinger, W.P., "Brooding and Healthy Reason: Kant's Regimen for the Religious Imagination" in *International Journal of Philosophy and Theology* 76.3 (2015), 200–17.
Kim, Chin-Tai, "A Critique of Kant's Defense of Theistic Faith", *Philosophy Research Archives* 14 (1988–89), 359–69.
Klinke, Willibald, *Kant für Jedermann*, 1949. Trans. M. Bullock as *Kant for Everyman* (London: Routledge & Kegan Paul, 1952).
Kroner, Richard, *Kants Weltanschauung*, 1914. Trans. John E. Smith as *Kant's Weltanschauung* (Chicago: University of Chicago Press, 1956).
Kuehn, Manfred, *Kant: A Biography* (Cambridge: Cambridge University Press, 2001).
———, "Kant's Transcendental Deduction of God's Existence as a Postulate of Pure Practical Reason", *Kant-Studien* 76.2 (1985), 152–69.
———, "Kant's Conception of 'Hume's Problem'", *Journal of the History of Philosophy* 21.2 (1983), 175–93.
Kvist, Hans-Olof, "Immanuel Kants über die Mystik und die Deutung von ihm als Mystiker", in Martin Tamcke (ed.), *Mystik—Metapher—Bild: Beiträge des VII. Makarios—Symposiums, Göttingen 2007* (Göttingen: Universitätsverlag Göttingen, 2008), 101–20.
Kwan, Tze-wan, "The Idea of God in Kant's Moral Theology", *Tunghai Journal* 25 (1984), 261–86.
Lawrence, Joseph P., "Moral Mysticism in Kant's Religion of Practical Reason", in Predrag Cicovacki (ed.), *Kant's Legacy: Essays in Honor of Lewis White Beck* (Rochester, NY: University of Rochester Press, 2001), 311–31.
Laywine, Alison, *Kant's Early Metaphysics and the Origins of the Critical Philosophy* (Atascadero, Ca.: Ridgeview Publishing Company, 1993).
Lind, P. von, *Kants mystische Weltanschauung, ein Wahn der modernen Mystik* (Munich: Poessl., 1892).

Loades, Ann, "Immanuel Kant's Humanism", in Keith Robbins (ed.), *Religion and Humanism* (Oxford: Basil Blackwell, 1981), 297–310.

MacKinnon, Donald M., "Some Epistemological Reflections on Mystical Experience", in Steven Katz (ed.), *Mysticism and Philosophical Analysis* (New York: Oxford University Press, 1978).

Macquarrie, John, *Jesus Christ in Modern Thought* (London: SCM Press, 1990).

Maharaj, Ayon, "Kant on the Epistemology of Indirect Mystical Experience", *Sophia* 56.2 (2017), 311–36.

Manolesco, John, "Translator's Preface", "Introduction", and "Commentary on the Dreams of a Spirit Seer", in Immanuel Kant, *Dreams of a Spirit-Seer*, trans. J. Manolesco (New York: Vantage Press, 1969), 5–8, 13–28, 99–146.

McCarthy, Vincent A., *Quest for a Philosophical Jesus: Christianity and Philosophy in Rousseau, Kant, Hegel, and Schelling* (Macon, Ga.: Mercer University Press, 1986).

———, "Christus as Chrestus in Rousseau and Kant", *Kant-Studien* 73 (1982), 191–207.

McQuillan, J. Colin, "Reading and Misreading Kant's *Dreams of a Spirit-Seer*", *Kant-Studies Online* (2015), 178–203.

Moskopp, Werner, "The Ubiquity of Transcendental Apperception", chapter 14 in Stephen R. Palmquist (ed.), *Kant on Intuition: Western and Eastern Perspectives on Transcendental Idealism* (New York: Routledge, 2019), 192–99.

Norburn, Greville, "Kant's Philosophy of Religion: A Preface to Christology?", *Scottish Journal of Theology* 26 (1973), 431–48.

Oakes, Robert A., "Noumena, Phenomena, and God", *International Journal for Philosophy of Religion* 4 (1973), 30–38.

Otto, Rudolph, *Das Heilige*, 1917. Trans. J.W. Harvey as *The Idea of the Holy: An Inquiry into the Non-rational Factor in the Idea of the Divine and its Relation to the Rational* (London: Oxford University Press, 1950[1923]).

Paton, Herbert James, *Kant's Metaphysic of Experience: A Commentary on the First Half of the Kritik Der Reinen Vernunft*, 2 vols. (London: George Allen & Unwin, 1936).

Paulsen, Friedrich, *Immanuel Kant: Sein Leben und seine Lehre*, 1898. Trans. J.E. Creighton and Albert Lefèbvre as *Immanuel Kant: His Life and Doctrine* (New York: Frederick Ungar, 1902).

Peccorini, Francisco L., "Transcendental Apperception and Genesis of Kant's Theological Conviction", *Giornale di Metafisica* 27 (1972), 43–65.

Peters, Curtis H., *Kant's Philosophy of Hope* (New York: Peter Lang, 1993).

Procyshyn, Alexci, and Mario Wenning, "Translator's Introduction", in Tugendhat 2016, vii–xxiv.

Rabel, Gabriele (ed.), *Kant* (Oxford: Clarendon Press, 1963).

Raschke, Carl A., *Moral Action, God, and History in the Thought of Immanuel Kant* (Missoula, Montana: Scholars Press and American Academy of Religion, 1975).

Robinson, Hoke, "A New Fragment of Immanuel Kant: 'On Inner Sense'", *International Philosophical Quarterly* 29.3 (1989), 249–61.

Rossi, Philip J., "The Authority of Experience: What Counts as Experience", in L. Boeve, Y. de Maeseneer, and S. van den Bossche (eds), *Religious Experience and Contemporary Theological Epistemology* (Leuven: Leuven University Press, 2008), 269–84.

Schleiermacher, Friedrich Daniel Ernst, *Über die Religion*, 1799. Trans. J. Oman as *On Religion: Speeches to Its Cultured Despisers*, abridged by E.G. Waring (New York: Frederick Ungar, 1955).

Schrader, George, "Kant's Presumed Repudiation of the 'Moral Argument' in the *Opus Postumum*: An Examination of Adickes' Interpretation", *Philosophy* 26 (1951), 228–41.

Schweitzer, Albert, *Die Mystik des Apostels Paulus*, 1930. Trans. W. Montgomery as *The Mysticism of Paul the Apostle* (London: A. & C. Black, 1931).

———, *Die Weltanschauung der Indischen Denken: Mystik und Ethik*, 1935. Trans. C.E.B. Russell as *Indian Thought and Its Development* (London: A. & C. Black, 1951).

Sewall, Frank, "Preface" (vii–xi), "Introduction" (1–33), and "Appendices" (123–62), in Immanuel Kant, *Dreams of a Spirit Seer Illustrated by Dreams of Metaphysics*, trans. E.F. Goerwitz (London: Swan Sonnenschein, 1900).

Shell, Susan Meld, *The Embodiment of Reason: Kant on Spirit, Generation, and Community* (Chicago: University of Chicago Press, 1996).
Silber, John R., "The Ethical Significance of Kant's *Religion*" and "Preface to the Second Edition of This Translation", in T.M. Greene and H.H. Hudson, *Religion within the Limits of Reason Alone* (New York: Harper & Row, 1960 [1934]), lxxix–cxxxiv,cxxxix–cxlii.
Smart, Ninian, *Philosophers and Religious Truth*² (London: SCM Press, 1969[1964]). References are to chapter and paragraph numbers.
Smith, John E., *Experience and God* (Oxford: Oxford University Press, 1968).
Stace, W.T., *Mysticism and Philosophy* (London: Macmillan, 1960).
Sullivan, William J., "Kant on the Existence of God in the *Opus Postumum*", *Modern Schoolman* 48.2 (1971), 117–33.
Swedenborg, Emanuel, *Vera Christiana Religio, continens Universam Theologiam Novae Ecclesiae* (Amsterdam, 1771). Trans. John Clowes, *The True Christian Religion containing the Universal Theology of the New Church* (1781); trans. Jonathan S. Rose, *True Christianity*, 2 vols. (West Chester, Penn.: Swedenborg Foundation, 2010–11). References cite Swedenborg's numbered sections.
———, *Sapientia angelica de divino amore et de divino sapientia* (London, 1763). Trans. John C. Ager, *Angelic Wisdom concerning Divine Love and Wisdom* (West Chester, Penn.: Swedenborg Foundation, 2009). References cite Swedenborg's numbered sections.
———, *De Fide Athanasiana* (1760), in *Apocalypsis Explicata Secundum Spiritualem Sensum, ubi Revelantur Arcana quæ ubi Prædicta et Hactenus Ignota Fuerunt* (London: 1789). Trans. anonymously as *On the Athanasian Creed and Subjects Connected with It* (New York: General Convention of the New Jerusalem, 1867). References cite the numbered sections added in the posthumous publication.
———, *De Caelo et Eius Mirabilibus et de inferno, ex Auditus et Visis* (London, 1758). Trans. John C. Ager, *Heaven and Its Wonders and Hell: From Things Heard and Seen* (West Chester, Penn.: Swedenborg Foundation, 2009). References cite Swedenborg's numbered sections.
———, *Arcana Coelestia* (London, 1746–56). Trans. John Clowes, *The heavenly arcana contained in the Holy Scripture or Word of the Lord unfolded, beginning with the book of Genesis*; revised and edited John Faulkner Potts (West Chester, Penn.: Swedenborg Foundation, 2009). References cite Swedenborg's numbered sections.
Temple, Denis, "Kant's Vision of the Moral Hero and the 'Laws of Arithmetic'", *Ultimate Reality and Meaning* 17.2 (1994), 108–17.
Thomas, S.B., "Jesus and Kant: A Problem in Reconciling Two Different Points of View", *Mind* 79 (1970), 188–99.
Thorpe, Lucas, "The Realm of Ends as a Community of Spirits: Kant and Swedenborg on the Kingdom of Heaven and the Cleansing of the Doors of Perception", *Heythrop Journal* 48 (2010), 1–24.
Tsang, Lap-Chuen, *The Sublime: Groundwork towards a Theory* (Rochester: University of Rochester Press, 1998).
Tugendhat, Ernst, *Egozentrizität und Mystik. Eine anthropologische Studie*, 2003. Trans. Alexei Procyshyn and Mario Wenning as *Egocentricity and Mysticism: An Anthropological Study* (New York: Columbia University Press, 2016).
Vaihinger, Hans, "Bericht über die Kantiana für die Jahre 1862 bis 1894", *Archiv für Geschichte der Philosophie* 8.4 (1895), 513–64. Excerpt trans. in Sewell 1900, 24–25.
———, *Kommentar zu Kants Kritik der reinen Vernunft*, vol. II (Stuttgart, Berlin, and Leipzig: Union Deutsche Verlagsgesellschaft, 1892).
Velkley, Richard L., "On Kant's Socratism", *The Philosophy of Immanuel Kant*, ed. Richard Kennington (Washington, D.C.: Catholic University of America Press, 1985).
Vlachos, George, *La Pensée politique de Kant* (Paris: PUF, 1962).
Vleeschauwer, Herman-J. de, *L'evolution de la pensee Kantienne*, 1939. Trans. A.R.C. Duncan as *The Development of Kantian Thought* (London: Thomas Nelson and Sons, 1962).
Völker, Jan, "Kant and the 'Spirit as an Enlivening Principle'", *Filozofski vestnik* 30.2 (2009), 69–80.

Vries, Hent de, *Religion and Violence: Philosophical Perspectives from Kant to Derrida* (Baltimore: Johns Hopkins University Press, 2002).
Wainwright, William J., *Mysticism: A Study of Its Nature, Cognitive Value, and Moral Implications* (Madison: University of Wisconsin Press, 1981).
Wallace, William, *Kant* (London: William Blackwood and Sons, 1901).
Walsh, W.H., "Kant, Immanuel", *The Encyclopedia of Philosophy*, ed. Paul Edwards (London: Collier Macmillan, 1967), vol.4, 305–24.
———, "Kant's Moral Theology", *Proceedings of the British Academy* 49 (1963), 263–89.
Walshe, M. O'C., *Meister Eckhart, Sermons and Tractates*, Vol. 1 (London: Watkins, 1982).
Ward, Keith, *The Development of Kant's View of Ethics* (Oxford: Basil Blackwell, 1972).
Webb, Clement C.J., *Kant's Philosophy of Religion* (Oxford: Clarendon Press, 1926).
Weber, Alfred, *Histoire de la philosophie européenne*,[5] 1892. Trans. Frank Thilly as *History of Philosophy* (New York: Charles Scribner's Sons, 1896).
Werkmeister, W.H., *Kant: The Architectonic and Development of His Philosophy* (London: Open Court, 1980).
White, Roger M., "'Ought' Implies 'Can': Kant and Luther, A Contrast", in George MacDonald Ross and Tony McWalter (eds.), *Kant and His Influence* (Bristol: Thoemmes Antiquarian Books, 1990), 1–72.
Wiebe, Don, "The Ambiguous Revolution: Kant on the Nature of Faith", *Scottish Journal of Theology* 33 (1980), 515–32.
Wilmans, C.A., *De similitudine inter Mysticismum purum et Kantianam religionis doctrinam* [*On the Similarity between Pure Mysticism and the Kantian Religious Doctrine*] (Halle, 1797).
Wisnefske, Ned, *Our Natural Knowledge of God: A Prospect for Natural Theology after Kant and Barth* (New York: Peter Lang, 1990).
Wittgenstein, Ludwig, *Tractatus Logico-Philosophicus*, trans. C.K. Ogden (New York: Harcourt, Brace, 1922).
Wolff, R.P., "Kant's Debt to Hume Via Beattie", *Journal of the History of Ideas* 21 (1960), 117–23.
Wood, Allen W., *Kantian Ethics* (Cambridge: Cambridge University Press, 2008).
———, "Translator's Introduction" to Kant's *Preface to Reinhold Bernhard Jachmann's Examination of the Kantian Philosophy of Religion*, in *Religion and Rational Theology* (Cambridge: Cambridge University Press, 1996), 331.
———, "Rational Theology, Moral Faith, and Religion", in Guyer, *The Cambridge Companion to Kant* (Cambridge: Cambridge University Press, 1992), 394–416.
———, "Kant's Deism", in Philip J. Rossi and Michael Wreen (eds.), *Kant's Philosophy of Religion Reconsidered* (Bloomington and Indianapolis: Indiana University Press, 1991), 1–21.
———, *Kant's Moral Religion* (London: Cornell University Press, 1970).
Yovel, Yirmiyahu, *Kant and the Philosophy of History* (Princeton: Princeton University Press, 1980).
Zweig, Arnulf, *Kant: Philosophical Correspondence 1759–99*, trans. and ed. (Chicago: University of Chicago Press, 1967).

Index

Abraham, 147n6, 151
a priori, 13, 27, 32, 36–37, 40n1, 54, 59, 71, 94, 99n15, 104, 108, 110, 112n15, 116–118, 120n9, 151, 153. *See also* synthetic *a priori*
Adickes, Erich, 90–91, 97n5, 98n9, 99n15, 107–108, 111n2, 111n5, 112n11, 112n12, 115, 152, 156
aesthetics, 40n4, 69, 73
Akhutin, A.V., 110, 112n17, 121, 152
Alberg, Jeremiah, 41n8, 152
Allais, Lucy, 97n5
Allison, Henry, 7n1, 97n5
American Transcendentalists, 4, 7n10
analytic *a posteriori*, 61n4, 96–97, 99n16, 110, 116–119, 120n7, 120n9, 129, 151
antinomy/ies, 38–40, 85n12
apparition(s), 18–19, 22–23, 27, 56, 64–65
appearance(s), 14, 17, 34–35, 91, 114, 146
apperception, 72, 83, 92; transcendental, 71–72, 156; unity of, 28n6, 71
archetype (*Urbild*), 111n9, 123–125, 131n2
architectonic, 11, 32, 41n5, 73, 82, 89, 116, 118, 120n10, 130, 136, 151, 158
Aristotle, 42n12
atheism/-ist, 14, 78–79, 84n5

Baelz, Peter, 53, 152
Baillie, John, 54, 152
Barth, Karl, 98n10, 152, 158

Bax, Ernst Belfort, 76n10, 76n11, 84n2, 84n4, 84n7, 115, 152
Beattie, James, 16n1, 158
beauty/-iful, 4, 58, 69, 73, 81, 83, 85n11, 104–105, 141, 150; as the symbol of morality, 72
Beck, J.S., 90, 97n4, 98n10
Beck, Lewis White, 12, 16n1, 16n2, 82, 85n12, 112n11, 152, 153, 155
Beiser, Frederick C., 16n4, 153
belief, 7n8, 17, 21, 23, 28n3, 31, 38–39, 44, 46n1, 50–51, 53, 56, 63, 66, 78, 81, 84, 103, 106–107, 123, 129, 143–144. *See also* faith
Beloff, John, xiii, 151
Berkeley, George, 137
Bible/-ical, 58, 60, 104, 125, 127, 143, 147n6
Bird, Graham, 97n5
bare/-ing (*bloß*-), xi–xii, 2, 4, 33, 46, 54, 72, 105, 111, 123, 131, 142, 146
Boerhaave, Hermann, 29n10
Borowski, Ludwig Ernst von, 28n6
bounds/-ary/-aries, 14–15, 19, 27–28, 41n9, 82, 85n12, 116, 126, 130, 142
boundary conditions, 2, 36, 146
Broad, C.D., 28n4, 153
Bubbio, Diego, xi, xiv
Buchdahl, Gerd, 95, 153
Buddhist, 140
Butts, Robert E., 16n3, 132n5, 153

Byrne, Peter, 61n9, 153

Caloric. *See* ether
Cartesian, 20
Carus, Paul, 12, 153
Cassirer, Ernst, 41n9, 61n6, 84n4, 153
categorical imperative, 75n6, 89, 92, 101, 103–108; as voice of God, 101, 103, 105
category/-ies, 5, 11, 71, 99n15, 117, 138, 144–145; religious, 109, 144
causality, 16n1, 16n2, 34–35, 37, 110, 136, 152; noumenal, 27, 35, 40n1, 46
cause(s), 5, 23, 27, 34, 36, 84, 136, 138, 147n9; highest, 102; ultimate, 138, 142; uncaused, 124
Chapman, Mark D., 76n8, 108, 153
Christ, 50, 123–125, 127, 130, 131n2, 133n13, 143; mystical body of, 7n11, 125. *See also* Jesus
Christian/-ity, 53, 60, 61n7, 66, 69, 75n2, 123, 125, 131n2, 140
Clarke, Samuel, 33, 38, 42n12
Clewis, Robert R., 76n12, 153
cognition, 5, 14, 17, 27, 35, 37, 40, 54–56, 59, 61n2, 66, 68, 71–72, 76n8, 80, 91, 93, 95, 108, 110, 116, 129–130, 135–136, 141–142, 144–146
Cohen, Alix, 84n6, 153
Coleridge, Samuel Taylor, 7n10
Collins, James, 98n12, 111n3, 123, 129, 131n1, 153
Comenius, John Amos, 119n4, 153
common sense, 26–27, 83–84, 119n4
community, 6, 17, 21–22, 29n12, 44, 133n14, 137, 140; religious, 145
Confucius, 133n11
conscience, 6, 32, 64–66, 69–70, 72, 74, 75n2, 75n6, 77, 81–82, 84, 102, 111n9, 139
contemplation, 79–81
conviction (*Gesinnung*), 34, 51, 52n1, 60–61, 63, 66–67, 74, 75n2, 143
Cooke, Vincent M., 124, 153
Copernican hypothesis, xiii, 11, 13, 15, 16n2, 25, 32–33, 35, 37–38, 40, 41n8, 42n12, 54, 78, 80, 98n13, 106, 133n12, 145, 151

Copernican insight, 13, 36, 38, 40, 41n9, 49
Copernican Perspective, 37, 50, 54, 111n9, 133n12
Copernican revolution, 3, 11, 13
Copernicus, Nicolaus, 105
Copleston, Frederick C., 33, 40n1, 40n4, 58, 98n10, 98n11, 98n12, 99n15, 106, 108, 112n11, 112n15, 132n5, 144–145, 153
corpus mysticum, 6, 7n11, 44, 65, 70, 74, 75n6, 125, 133n15
cosmotheology, 96, 114
Critical method, 13–15, 19, 25–26, 31, 36–37, 39–40, 41n9, 41n10, 49, 58
Critical System, 2, 15, 36, 43–44, 49, 51, 60, 95, 97n7, 120n10, 127, 132n4, 135
Critique, xiii, 3–5, 13–14, 18, 23, 36, 38–39, 46, 47, 61, 67, 75, 81–82, 93, 98n13, 105, 107, 110–111, 123, 128, 140; Kantian, xii, 21, 44, 53–54, 67
Crosby, Donald A., 78, 153

Dao/-ism/-ist, 37, 125, 137, 140
Davidovich, Adina, 81, 109, 153
Davies, James Keith, xiv
delirium/-ious, 3, 5, 13–14, 16n5, 18, 23, 33, 44, 49, 53, 57–58, 60–61, 64, 75n4, 82, 103, 130, 135, 138, 143
Dell'Oro, Regina O.M., 16n4, 61n4, 153
delusion, 5, 14, 16n5, 19, 22–23, 58, 64, 75n4, 103
Democritus, 26
Descartes, René, 42n12
Despland, Michel, 70, 95–96, 98n10, 98n12, 103–105, 127–128, 130, 132n10, 133n13, 153
devotion, 66
Di Giovanni, George, 84n5, 153
DiCenso, James, 125, 153
direct mystical experience ("DME"), 46, 136–137. *See also* indirect mystical experience ("IME")
discernment (*Urtheilskraft*), 6, 65, 96, 141, 147n8
Dister, John E., 95, 153
divine, 56, 58, 60, 61n2, 63, 66–67, 70–71, 75n2, 77, 80–81, 101–103, 106–107, 111n1, 111n2, 115, 125, 132n9,

132n10, 140–145, 152
dogmatic slumber, 11, 16n5, 16n9, 38–39; awakening from, 12, 38–39
dogmatic/-ism/-ist, 5, 12, 14, 20, 26, 28n3, 31, 34, 36–40, 40n2, 41n9, 84, 132n5, 146
double affection, 7n1, 90, 97n5
dream(s), 18, 24, 28n6, 29n11, 40, 45, 69, 83, 85n12; Critical, xiii; metaphysical, 17, 24
dreamer, 23, 69
dreaming, 16n5, 16n9, 33, 38–39
Du Prel, Carl, 29n11, 43–46, 46n2, 54, 153
Duerr, Hans Peter, 133n14, 153
duty, 14, 22, 64

Eckhart, Meister, 71, 154, 158
Einstein, Albert, 41n9, 120n6, 152
embodiment, xi, 123
Emerson, Ralph Waldo, 7n10
empiricism/-ist, 18, 61, 121, 126; Hume's, 12; skeptical, 26
encounter, xii, 2, 4–5, 24, 43–45, 50–51, 53–55, 57, 64–67, 69–74, 76n8, 78, 81, 84, 91, 93, 101, 103, 105, 107–108, 110, 111n5, 119n5, 121, 124–126, 128–129, 131, 138–139, 141–143, 145–146. *See also* experience
England, F.E., 102, 153
enthusiasm, 3
ether, 89, 113–114, 117–119, 119n1, 120n8, 120n9
evil, 34, 51, 66, 70, 81, 143
experience, xii, 5, 11, 20, 27, 34, 40n1, 43–44, 53–56, 58, 68, 71, 73–74, 78, 82, 84, 90, 94–95, 99n16, 109–110, 114–118, 119n2, 120n8, 124, 126, 133n12, 136, 138, 141, 144–145; boundaries of, 14–15; immediate, xii, 3–4, 16n6, 21, 24, 27, 30n15, 32, 45, 54–58, 63, 68, 70, 72, 79, 82, 85n11, 89–95, 98n10, 104–105, 107–108, 113, 119n5, 120n7, 125–126, 128–131, 135–136, 138, 142, 144; limitations of, 19; mystical, 1, 3–6, 7n5, 12, 15, 18–19, 32, 40, 43, 45–46, 49–51, 56, 58, 64, 68, 72, 74, 80, 120n7, 123, 126, 128, 136–138, 141, 144, 146, 146n1, 147n5; reflective forms of, 30n15;

religious, xii, 3, 6, 50–51, 69, 74, 75n4, 79, 98n10, 103, 105, 111n8, 135, 142–146, 146n1, 147n9. *See also* encounter
Extra Sensory Perception (ESP), 45

faith, 53–54, 58, 67, 78, 103, 105, 108, 132n3, 145; historical, 67, 123, 125, 131, 144; moral, 27, 82, 139; practical, 25, 67, 111; rational, 25, 92, 113, 116; reflective, 81; religious, xii, 112n12, 131. *See also* belief
Fang, J., 41n9, 154
fasting, 66, 84n7
fatalism, 14
feeling, 21, 46, 56, 61n2, 72, 75n4, 78, 80, 85n11, 91, 101, 109, 141, 146, 147n9; aesthetic, 79; delirious, 143; inner, 64; moral, 22, 56–57, 64; mystical, 56, 129; philosophy of, 57; principles of, 40n4; religious, 73–74, 128, 132n10
Fendt, Gene, 69, 154
Fichte, J.G., 90, 93, 95, 98n9, 98n10
Firestone, Chris L., xiv, 84n5, 154
Fischer, Norbert, 5, 71, 154
Flew, Antony, 111n8, 144–145, 154
Florschütz, Gottlieb, 28n1, 154
focus imaginarius, 23
Forgie, J. William, 120n9, 154
Forman, Robert K.C., 71, 154
Förster, Eckart, 89, 93, 97n1, 97n3, 99n14, 99n15, 121, 154
freedom, 6, 14, 31, 35, 51, 82, 93–94, 96, 98n9, 101, 104, 108, 110, 125, 130, 132n5, 138, 145; practical, 21
Friedman, R.Z., 93, 126–127, 154
Friedrich, Carl J., 130, 154
Fries, Hans, 108

Galbraith, Elizabeth Cameron, 123, 127, 131n2, 154
Garve, Christian, 38, 120n9
Gegenstand, 4, 7n9, 97n4; transcendental, 4. *See also Objekt*
Gerding, Johan L.F., 45, 154
Gilson, Étienne, 98n10, 154
God, 1–2, 5, 28n3, 31, 47, 50–51, 53–55, 57, 59–60, 61n1, 61n4, 63–71, 73–74, 75n2, 75n3, 75n5, 76n8, 77, 80–82, 84,

85n10, 85n11, 89–96, 97n3, 97n7, 97n8, 98n9, 98n12, 101–111, 111n1, 111n2, 111n3, 111n4, 111n6, 111n7, 111n9, 112n11, 112n14, 114–116, 119, 119n5, 121, 123–126, 128–130, 132n5, 132n8, 132n10, 133n11, 133n13, 133n14, 133n15, 137–139, 142–146, 147n6, 147n9; as creator, 18, 80–81; existence of, 67, 75n1, 78–79, 81, 104, 106–107, 111n3, 111n9, 112n16, 113, 119, 128, 136; fear of, 70, 74; as highest being, 92, 111n6; as judge, 65–66, 74, 111n1, 123; as knower of hearts, 77; presence of, 18, 55, 66, 69, 78, 81–82, 102, 105, 107–108, 111n9, 114, 119n5, 145; as prime mover, 115; as supreme being, 63, 128; as sustainer, 18; voice of, 59, 64–65, 69–70, 81–82, 101, 103–104, 106, 111n4, 137, 147n6
God–man, 121–124, 128, 131
Goldmann, Lucien, 95, 127, 132n8, 154
grace, 30n16, 51, 81, 142–143, 152
Green, Joseph, 76n10, 80, 84n7
Green, Ronald M., 132n5, 132n7, 154
Greene, Theodore M., 102, 111n3, 111n5, 111n9, 112n11, 129, 132n5, 154
Grier, Michelle, 28n6, 154
Ground of Being, 59
Gulick, Walter B., 13, 154
Gulyga, Arsenij, 16n3, 154

Hamann, Johann Georg, 16n1, 115, 129
Hare, John E., 61n9, 154
Hedge, Frederic H., 69, 76n9, 155
Hegel, Georg Wilhelm Friedrich, 126–127, 133n12
Heidegger, Martin, 71, 97n5, 97n6, 155
Heidelberg School, 90
Heine, Heinrich, 69, 155
Herz, Marcus, 16n1, 40n4
heuristic fiction, 19
Hicks, Joe H., 68, 155
highest good, 65, 109, 127, 131, 133n15
Hodges-Kluck, Jana, xiv
holy, 65, 67–68, 98n9, 111n1, 139
Holy Spirit, 65, 102
hope, 24, 28, 32, 73, 104, 121, 130, 133n13
Hume, David, 12–13, 16n1, 18, 33, 35–40, 40n2, 41n9, 41n10

Hund, William B., 73–74, 81, 155

idealism, 14, 90, 93, 98n11; German, 98n9; Kant's, 28n5; mystical, 7n5; objective, 28n5; Platonic, 53–54; Refutation of, 2; spiritual, 34; transcendental, 34
ignorance, 24, 26, 32, 50, 59, 93, 111, 112n17, 126–127, 132n6, 133n14, 142
imagination, 20, 22–23, 25, 71, 97n6, 141; metaphysical, 31
immortality, 31, 51, 74, 93–94, 98n9, 130, 132n8, 133n15, 138
indirect mystical experience ("IME"), 46. *See* direct mystical experience ("DME")
infinite, 18, 47, 64, 73–74
Insole, Christopher J., 93, 155
intuition, 5, 37, 40, 56, 67–68, 80, 97n2, 97n6, 110, 116–117, 136–139, 141; forms of, 11, 32; inner, 91; intellectual, 1, 46n2, 129, 136–137, 139, 145–146; mystical, 57, 91, 129, 137, 139; non-sensible, 46, 136; pure, 59, 61n8, 94, 97n7, 151; sensible, 5, 68, 136, 138–139, 145; supersensible, 61, 137
inward(ness), 34–35, 56, 60, 64, 67, 78, 113–114, 119n4, 123, 126, 142
Isaac, 147n6

Jachmann, Reinhold Bernhard, 61n9, 78, 80, 84n7, 85n11, 155
Jacobi, Friedrich Heinrich, 115
Jacobs, Nathan, 84n5, 154
Jaki, Stanley L., 85n9, 119n5, 155
Jesus, 29n7, 66, 76n7, 123, 125, 128, 133n13. *See also* Christ
Johnson, Gregory R., 19, 41n6, 132n5, 155
Johnson, Jonathan, xiv
Jonsson, Inge, 42n12, 155
Josephson, Jason Ānanda, 7n10, 155
Jung, Carl, 29n11
Jung–Stilling, Johann Heinrich, 43

Kant–Laplace theory, 79
Kemp Smith, Norman, 85n12, 91, 97n4, 97n5, 97n7, 98n11, 99n15, 107, 111n3, 151, 155
Kierkegaard, Søren, 110, 127, 132n7
Kim, Chin-Tai, 109–110, 155

Klinke, Willibald, 16n3, 69, 78–79, 84n3, 84n7, 85n8, 85n11, 155
Knoblock, Charlotte von, 18
knowledge, 1–2, 4–5, 7n1, 7n2, 18, 26–27, 30n15, 36, 41n9, 53, 55–56, 68, 71–72, 75, 76n8, 87, 90–91, 97n7, 98n10, 98n12, 103–104, 106–107, 109–110, 113, 115–116, 118, 120n7, 121, 126, 128–129, 133n14, 136, 138–139, 146; determinate, 54, 136; hypothetical, 125; immediate, 126; judicial, 83; limits of, 32; lust for, 13; moral, 74; mystical, 126; objective, 55; practical, 82; reflective, 16n6, 32; secret, 5, 137; speculative, 25; theoretical, 55, 57, 68, 82, 112n11, 140, 146; thirst for, 26
Kraus, Christian Jakob, 115
Kroner, Richard, 76n13, 155
Kiblinger, W.P., 28n6, 155
Kuehn, Manfred, 12, 76n10, 83, 84n3, 155
Kwan, Cheng, 133n11
Kwan, Tze-wan, 132n8, 155

Labèrge, Pierre, 61n4
Lambert, Johann Heinrich, 40n4, 98n13
Langton, Rae, 97n5
Lawrence, Joseph P., 8n12, 155
Laywine, Alison, 28n1, 28n5, 28n6, 29n8, 41n8, 80, 155
Leibniz, Gottfried Wilhelm, 11–12, 33, 38, 42n12
life, 1, 3, 17, 21–22, 28n3, 29n10, 35, 50, 69, 71, 120n7, 128, 130; alienated, 133n14; meaningful, 138; moral, 58, 74, 106, 112n16, 132n8, 146; principle of, 21, 24; religious, 127; respect for, 129; spiritual, 17, 21; vision of, 84; waking, 39; way of, 3
light, xii, 22, 37, 39, 73, 75, 105
Lind, P. von, 33, 155
Liu, Lynn, xiv
Loades, Ann, 70, 156
Love, Brandon, xiv, 7n9
Lown, Guy, 7n9

MacKinnon, Donald M., 120n7, 156
Macquarrie, John, 132n5, 156
magic(al), 13, 16n5, 50, 57. See also magical mysticism

Maharaj, Ayon, xiv, 45–46, 137, 146n1, 147n5, 147n6, 156
Maharishi, Mahesh Yogi, 7n10
Maimon, Salomon, 90
Manolesco, John, 7n5, 12, 16n3, 28n5, 28n6, 46n1, 70, 78, 156
Marburg School, 90
materialism, 14; eliminative, 29n9, 152
mathematics, 59, 61n8, 151
McCarthy, Vincent A., 29n7, 78, 131n2, 145–146, 147n9, 156
McQuillan, J. Colin, xiv, 41n8, 156
meditation/-ive, 7n10, 21, 25, 49, 66, 72, 77–78, 85n8; Critical, 72–73; transcendental, 4, 7n10
Mendelssohn, Moses, 18–19
Merchant, John, 30n14
metaphysics, 2, 4–5, 13–15, 16n3, 18–19, 23, 25–26, 28n3, 31–32, 40, 40n4, 45–46, 49, 59, 93, 95–96, 98n13, 101, 107–108, 124, 127–128, 132n3, 136, 143–144; Critical, 34, 82, 85n14; moral, 6, 138; problems of, 13–14; speculative, 13, 18, 26, 130; theocentric, 129; theoretical, 138
miracle, 143
moral calling, 4
moral law, 53, 56, 59, 61, 63–65, 70–74, 77, 82, 85n11, 91, 95, 101–103, 105–107, 109–110, 111n9, 112n11, 132n10, 139–140, 143, 145
morality, xi, 14, 21, 31, 34, 40n1, 40n4, 58, 61, 67–68, 72–74, 77–78, 95, 98n10, 105, 108, 111n9, 112n11, 132n8, 138, 143
Moravians, 143
Moskopp, Werner, 71, 156
mystery/-ies, 23, 56, 67, 70–72, 75, 111n1, 121, 129, 131, 141–142
mysticism, xi, 2–3, 5–6, 7n5, 8n12, 16n5, 18, 40, 43–44, 46, 46n2, 49–51, 53–54, 57–61, 61n9, 67, 76n8, 79, 82–83, 112n11, 135–138, 140, 143, 146, 146n1; Critical, xi–xiii, 3–4, 6, 7n4, 15, 24, 31, 44, 49–52, 58, 60, 61n4, 67, 69–70, 75, 75n6, 76n8, 77, 81–84, 87, 89–90, 93, 111, 112n11, 113–114, 121, 126, 131, 132n6, 135, 139–140, 142–146, 146n1; critique of, xiii, 3, 44,

47, 57, 67; delirious, 49, 53, 58, 82, 130; ethical, 50; intellectual, 50; Kant's, 50, 58, 61n4, 70, 75, 75n6, 76n8, 77, 83, 90, 93, 111, 132n6, 135, 139–140, 144–146, 146n1; Kantian, 50, 61n9, 135, 146; magical, 50, 57; moral, 5–6, 8n12, 22, 32, 59, 61n6, 72, 138–140; of Swedenborg, 17, 44, 140; primitive, 50; pure, 60; rational, 140
myth(s), xi, 41n9, 126–127

nature, 7n10, 21, 34–35, 43, 56, 61n4, 64, 70–74, 77–82, 84, 85n10, 85n11, 85n12, 90, 95–96, 98n12, 98n13, 101, 103–104, 108–109, 111n6, 113–115, 124–125, 128–129, 141; immaterial, 21, 29n10; moral, xi, 7n7, 138; purposiveness in, 4, 72–73, 81, 95, 98n12, 141; spiritual, 6, 17, 27, 44; substratum of, 34, 73, 78
negation, 44; way of, 137, 139
Newton, Isaac, 11, 120n6
Newtonian, 117
Norburn, Greville, 63, 106, 111, 156
noumenon/-a, 28n6, 35, 93; negative, 30n13; positive, 30n13

Oakes, Robert A., 68, 156
object-overall, 4
Objekt, 4, 7n9, 97n4; transcendental, 4; *See Gegenstand*
organism(s), 115, 118, 119n3, 141
Otto, Rudolph, 68, 74, 76n8, 77, 108–110, 112n15, 156

panentheism, 115, 119n5, 121, 124, 151
pantheism, 57, 119n5, 124, 137
paradox, 61n4, 96, 110, 116, 130; logic of, 91
parapsychology/-ical ("psi"), 45
Paton, Herbert James, 147n2, 156
Paul (the Apostle), 50
Paulsen, Friedrich, 12, 16n2, 28n5, 119n5, 156
Peccorini, Francisco, 75n1, 127, 156
Person(ality), 95, 98n12, 101–104, 111n2, 115, 139
perspective(s), 1–2, 22, 26, 44, 68, 70, 81–83, 90–91, 93, 102, 105, 128–129;

Critical, 57; empirical, 2, 90; hypothetical, 2, 31, 40n1, 120n10; logical, 2; mystical, 34; principle of, 2, 26, 54, 107–108, 119n5, 133n12; spiritual, 34; System of, 15, 25, 54, 82, 84, 91, 105, 108, 129, 144; transcendental, 2, 34, 72, 74, 90, 127, 130, 133n14. *See* Copernican
Peters, Curtis H., 7n11, 112n13, 156
philosophy, 11–14, 22, 26–27, 29n10, 51, 57, 59, 65, 89–90, 93, 95, 98n10, 111, 116, 121, 125–129, 131, 133n14; Chinese, 61n3; Critical, xii, 2–4, 7n5, 8n12, 13, 15, 18, 28n6, 32–34, 43, 46, 47, 49, 51, 54, 59–60, 63, 78, 81, 119n2, 127, 129; Enlightenment, 41n9; Hume's, 12; Kant's, 2–6, 8n12, 28n6, 29n7, 29n11, 32, 34, 41n9, 41n10, 44, 47, 49, 51, 54, 61n9, 63, 66, 69, 73–74, 78, 81, 83, 104, 108, 119n5, 120n6, 124, 127, 130, 133n11, 133n12, 139, 146n1; Kantian, 7n10, 45, 59; moral, 40n4, 139; natural, 15, 79, 114; occult, 21; practical, 66; pure, 59; speculative, 12; theoretical, 2, 74, 84; transcendental, 32, 36, 45, 87, 93, 95–96, 101, 122, 133n12
physics, 96, 97n3, 99n15, 113, 115–116, 118
Pietism/-ist(s), 59, 78–79, 143
Plato/-nic/-nism, 17, 28n5, 46n2, 53, 58, 125–126, 136–137, 147n3
Pluhar, Werner, 3, 52n1
Poncelet, S.J., 106
prayer, 66–67, 69, 80
providence, 70, 85n10, 95, 98n12, 127
Pseudo-Dionysius, 137

Rabel, Gabriele, 28n4, 28n5, 70, 76n11, 156
Raschke, Carl A., 133n11, 156
rational, 6, 20, 26, 46, 51, 53, 55, 59, 61n7, 66, 69, 74, 78, 81, 91–92, 104–105, 107, 109–110, 112n16, 117–118, 121, 124, 131, 133n12, 135–136. *See also* faith, mysticism, and religion
rationalism, 121; dogmatic, 26
reality, 1–2, 17, 54, 68–69, 73, 75n6, 83, 90–91, 93, 97n2, 102–103, 105–106,

110, 111n5, 112n14, 136, 139, 145; highest, 128; mystical, 82; noumenal, 137; objective, 17, 93, 106; spiritual, 1, 25, 43, 111n3; ultimate, 144

reason, xii, 13–14, 18, 20, 22–27, 28n6, 32, 36, 38, 40, 43, 53, 57–58, 69–70, 73–75, 84, 90, 102–103, 105, 117, 126, 129, 141, 143; death of, 49, 58, 104, 109, 126–128, 130, 132n4, 132n7, 135; human, 2, 9, 14, 19, 26, 74, 81, 93, 97n8, 101, 103–105, 115, 126–127; ideas of, 2, 31, 93, 105, 138; light of, xii, 23, 33, 46, 57, 72, 105, 111, 123, 146; limits of, 19, 26, 126; need of, 49, 107; powers of, 4–5; practical, 14–15, 56, 58, 63–65, 67, 73, 81, 87, 90, 97n8, 103–104, 108, 111n7, 111n9, 115, 135, 139; pure, 34, 38, 43, 59, 69, 71, 73, 98n9, 116; scales of, 24, 32; speculative, 14, 81; theoretical, 14, 55, 69

religion, 14, 50–51, 63, 69, 78, 109, 112n11, 142, 144–145; bare, 33; Critical, 50; genuine, xi, 67; historical, xii, 33; Kant's theory of, xi–xii, 61n7; Kantian, xii, 7n4, 61n9; moral, 61n9, 67; organized, 50–51, 131; philosophy of, 40n4, 69, 73; rational, 67, 131; standpoint of, 103; true, 115, 132n3

ritual(s), xi, 50
Robinson, Hoke, 150, 156
Rosen, Michael, 97n3
Rousseau, Jean-Jacques, 41n8

Schelling, Friedrich Wilhelm Joseph, 95
Schiller, Friedrich, 85n10
Schleiermacher, Friedrich Daniel Ernst, 98n10, 108, 156
Schrader, George, 57, 103, 107–108, 111n4, 112n12, 112n14, 156
Schulze, J., 90
Schweitzer, Albert, 50, 58, 81, 156
sensibility, 14, 21, 92
Sewall, Frank, 13, 18, 28n4, 28n5, 33–34, 38, 41n6, 41n7, 43–44, 46n1, 132n5, 156
Shell, Susan Meld, 28n2, 157
Silber, John R., 112n12, 157

skepticism, 5, 12, 14, 16n1, 18, 28n3, 31, 36–37, 39, 40n2, 41n10
Smart, Ninian, 53, 157
Smith, John E., 128, 143, 155, 157
Socrates, 126–127, 130
soul, 2, 20–21, 23, 27–28, 28n6, 29n8, 29n11, 40, 58, 71, 75n2, 77, 92–93, 103, 108, 113, 130, 133n14, 136, 138
space, 5, 7n2, 11, 32, 36–37, 114–115, 117, 120n6, 136; empty, 26, 117; transcendental ideality of, 13
space–time, 1–2, 7n2, 61n1, 116
Spinoza, Baruch, 80, 91, 97n7, 115–116, 137
spirit(s), 17, 19–20, 22, 28n2, 31, 35, 43, 51, 80, 84, 92, 103, 132n4, 137; communion of, 21–22, 50, 137, 140; evil, 66; heavenly, 143; human, 17, 103, 111n2, 111n3; Kant's belief in, 21
spirit–seer, 18, 24, 29n12
spirit–world, 17, 21–22, 24–25, 33, 35, 46n1
spiritualism, 29n9, 105
spirituality, 51
Stace, W.T., 146n1, 157
standpoint, 1–2, 15, 20, 24, 35, 54–55, 81, 91–96, 98n10, 102–103, 107–108, 110, 111n9, 112n11, 112n13, 114, 125–126, 128; hypothetical, 91; judicial, 2, 24, 34, 51, 72, 81, 96, 108–110, 112n12, 124–125, 132n3; practical, 2, 14, 31, 34–35, 40n1, 54, 56, 74, 112n12, 141; speculative, 14; theoretical, 2, 14, 31, 35, 54–55, 64, 72, 92, 141
Steinkamp, Fiona, xiii, 151
Strawson, P.F., 97n5
subject–object distinction, 4–6, 146n1
sublime, 47, 64, 73–74, 76n12, 81, 141; dynamically, 74; mathematically, 74
substance, 34, 89, 91, 101–102, 106, 108, 113, 115–116, 118–119, 123, 127
Sullivan, William J., 97n8, 104, 106–107, 112n10, 112n16, 115, 157
supersensible, 46, 55–56, 58, 61, 73–74, 94, 104, 137–138, 141–143
superstition, 14, 44
Swedenborg, Emanuel, 3–5, 7n5, 7n6, 9, 13, 17–19, 25, 27, 28n1, 28n5, 28n6, 29n8, 30n14, 33–38, 40, 41n6, 41n10,

42n12, 43–44, 46, 49–51, 57, 59, 132n4, 133n14, 135, 137–140, 147n7
symbol(s), xi, 22, 29n11, 33, 35, 57, 68, 72, 74, 98n10, 104
synthesis, 14, 98n12, 102, 116, 119, 121, 124–125, 132n6, 135; mystical, 119; original, 89, 94; threefold, 89
synthetic *a priori*, 95, 110, 116–118, 152. See also *a priori*

Tantalus, 120n9, 127
teleology, 73
Temple, Denis, 53, 157
theology, 7n5, 59, 69, 76n11, 109; Christian, 123; Kant's, 7n4, 73, 123; philosophical, 114
thing in itself, 1, 4, 7n1, 7n8, 55, 90, 92–93, 97n4, 98n9, 105, 109–110, 114, 116, 124–126, 139
Thomas, S.B., 66, 157
Thorpe, Lucas, 16n3, 140, 147n7, 157
time, 5, 7n2, 11, 22, 32, 34, 36–38, 61n1, 110, 115, 120n6, 124, 136; transcendental ideality of, 13
Thoreau, Henry David, 7n10
totality, 4, 21, 24, 95, 113–114
transcendent, 45, 53, 55, 57–59, 61, 63, 65, 68–70, 74, 89, 92, 94, 102, 105, 108–111, 111n5, 112n17, 121, 124, 126–127, 129–130, 138, 144, 146, 147n3
transcendental object, 4, 7n9, 90, 97n4, 109, 139
transcendental reflection, 4–5, 92
transcendental subject/ivity, 33, 38, 92, 139
Trinity, 65, 111n1, 131n2
Tsang, Lap-Chuen, 76n12, 157
Tugendhat, Ernst, 140–141, 157

understanding, 21, 23, 57, 64–65, 141; human, 2, 23, 26, 40, 71, 83–84, 139; intuitive, 137, 139; limits of, 24; mystical, 137
unknown "x", 5

Vaihinger, Hans, 33, 43–44, 90, 157
Velkley, Richard L., 84, 126, 157
virtue, 30n16, 128

visions, 12, 18–19, 28n5, 35, 42n12, 46, 64, 139; mystical, 17–18, 45, 55, 135
Vlachos, George, 96, 157
Vleeschauwer, Herman-J. de, 93, 95, 157
Völker, Jan, 28n2, 157
Vries, Hent de, 61n9, 158

Wainwright, William J., 146n1, 158
Wallace, William, 16n3, 54, 76n11, 79, 84n2, 84n3, 84n6, 85n8, 85n9, 158
Walsh, W.H., 72, 85n11, 98n9, 158
Walshe, M.O'C., 71, 158
Ward, Keith, 12, 53, 57, 63, 67, 91, 101, 107, 111n9, 112n11, 129, 158
Webb, Clement C.J., 51, 53, 65, 67–69, 77, 85n11, 98n9, 101–102, 109, 111n2, 111n4, 112n11, 115, 133n12, 158
Weber, Alfred, 105, 158
Werkmeister, W.H., 28n3, 28n6, 41n10, 158
White, Roger M., 59, 158
whole(ness), 1–2, 6, 64, 70, 74, 94, 96, 118, 123, 128, 138–139, 141; idea of, 2, 89, 96, 97n2, 98n10, 121, 138; light of, 75; moral, 146; mystical, 124; vision of, 4, 70; ultimate, 1, 141
Wiebe, Don, 54, 158
Wilmans, Carl A., 59–61, 61n9, 158
Wisnefske, Ned, 76n11, 76n13, 158
wisdom, 26–27, 65–66, 80, 87, 96, 126–129, 133n14, 146
Wittgenstein, Ludwig, 20, 146, 158
Wolff, Christian, 12, 40n1, 42n12
Wolff, R.P., 16n1, 158
wonder, 56, 125, 143
Wong, Simon, xiv
Wood, Allen W., 24, 61n9, 84n5, 107, 109, 112n11, 132n5, 158
world–soul, 115
worship, 70, 80, 128

Yovel, Yirmiyahu, 130, 133n12, 158

Zoroaster, 90
Zweig, Arnulf, 98n10, 158

About the Author

Stephen R. Palmquist is professor of Religion and Philosophy at Hong Kong Baptist University, where he has taught since earning his doctorate from Oxford University (St. Peter's College) in 1987. His 200 publications, which have been translated into at least thirteen different languages, include about 110 refereed articles and book chapters. The following fourteen journals have each published two or more of his articles: *Aretè: International Journal of Philosophy*; *Ethics and Bioethics* (in Central Europe); *Faith and Philosophy*; *Journal of Chinese Philosophy*; *Kantian Review*; *Kant-Studien*; *Philosophia Christi*; *Philosophia Mathematica*; *Philosophy & Theology*; *Polish Journal of Philosophy*; *Sogang Journal of Philosophy*; *The Heythrop Journal*; *The Journal of Religion*; and *The Review of Metaphysics*. Among his twelve books are *The Tree of Philosophy: A Course of Introductory Lectures for Beginning Students of Philosophy* (1992/2000), *Kant's System of Perspectives: An Architectonic Interpretation of the Critical Philosophy* (1993), *Kant's Critical Religion: Volume Two of Kant's System of Perspectives* (2000), *Kant and the New Philosophy of Religion* (co-edited with Chris L. Firestone, 2006), *Cultivating Personhood: Kant and Asian Philosophy* (edited anthology, 2010), *Comprehensive Commentary on Kant's Religion within the Bounds of Bare Reason* (2016), and *Kant on Intuition: Western and Asian Perspectives on Transcendental Idealism* (edited anthology: 2019). In 1999 he founded the Hong Kong Philosophy Café, which now has several branches and over 800 members.

www.ingramcontent.com/pod-product-compliance
Lightning Source LLC
Chambersburg PA
CBHW032150010526
44111CB00035B/1427